THE GASTRONOMICAL TOURIST

THE GASTRONOMICAL TOURIST

MEMORIES AND RECIPES OF A BISTRO CRAWLER AT HOME AND ABROAD

Arthur Bloomfield

CREATIVE ARTS BOOK COMPANY
Berkeley ~ California

for Cecily

Copyright © 2002 by Arthur Bloomfield

No part of this book may be reproduced in any manner
without the written permission of the publisher,
except in brief quotations used in articles or reviews.

For information contact:
Creative Arts Book Company
833 Bancroft Way
Berkeley, California 94710
www.creativeartsbooks.com

ISBN 088739-442-6

Library of Congress Catalog Number 2002115025

BOOK DESIGN BY STEVEN ZAHAVI SCHWARTZ
Printed in the United States of America

ACKNOWLEDGEMENTS

This book would not have seen the light without the love, patience and efficiency of my wife Anne who guided me through the mysteries of using an almost animate and frequently temperamental (or was it simply miscued?) word processor. My friend Don Frediani read every word with devotion and care, issuing critiques almost daily: without his helpful bulletins I would have lost the anchovies here, left the bacon uncooked there, given you a hopelessly over-sugared chutney on another page.

If Don concentrated especially on the recipes, my sister Anne Saltonstall applied her literary expertise to the anecdotal material, blocking several unhappy metaphors without insisting I change them. My daughter Cecily, often in residence at our house during this book's gestation, is responsible for a number of the desserts set before you and was an excellent advisor on numerous cooking matters. To Helen Gustafson, a million thanks for serving so vibrantly and well as my mother confessor/guardian angel: without her, this book would not be in your hands. As for Jean Galeazzi, she is not only a spirited writer and a world class belly dancer but a most simpatico copyreader, with an X-ray vision for spotting typos.

I would also like to thank Julia Bloomfield, Alison Bloomfield, Marcus Colombano, Lucy Bloomfield, Mary Kelley, Emily Warner and Kevin Johnson for recipes as well as support, and the list of marvelous encouragers would be incomplete without John Bloomfield, Gus Gustafson, Jane Ivory, Dan Duncan, Bob "Kebob," Sally O'Toole, Cathy Furniss, "Freitag," Connie Crawford and Mark Gottlieb, Kate Jones, Susan Pearman, Don and Joyce Tayer, Gail Moore, Renata Gasperi, Alice Waters, Carlo and Lisa Middione, Marion Cunningham, Fred Martin and Sandy Mullin and all the gang at Browser Books, Jackie Montgomery, Alan Luks, Victoria Shoemaker, Bill Eddelman, Mary Keil, Swift Barnes, an enviable number of Kanner, Frisch and Zeisler cousins, Ben Kinmont and Naomi, Douglas Scott, Phil Saltonstall and MaryAnn Caperna, Becky Saltonstall and Neal Goldstein, Richard Hilkert, Beverly Duncan, Aviva Shane, Pam Lee, Dan Warner, the Wiley family, Michel Lipman, Ray O'Brien, Stanley Eichelbaum, Mary Miles Ryan, Wayne and Lorelei Kennedy, Ernie and Maria Levinger, Ellen Brown, Dick and Tina Wahlberg, Robert Finigan, Leland Burstein, the Breezes, Patti Unterman, Jason Epstein, Ruth Reichl, Joyce Goldstein, Nadia Derkach, Dorothea Douglas, Sasha the painter, Carol, Serge, Olga, Matthias, Thea, Henry, Kathleen, Marvin, Ivy and Alexis Blumenfeld (the surname of the last to be pronounced the French way), Gerald Adams, Bob Danley, Tom Holmes, Beth Crossman, Fran McCullough, Tom Rubbert, David Hunter, Carl Bryant, all the gang at Rose's, William Corbett Jones, Michele Ferrier, Susan Kelley, Jean Hyson, Larry Campbell, Aaron Peskin, Nancy Shanahan, Lise Ostwald, Ray and Frieda Reider, Joan and Joe Sutton and Kirke and Doe Mechem, not to mention Juliana Duncan and Oliver Iberien, my faithful companions in the Egg Twist Society, and Penny Summers, Elizabeth King and

John Peterson, members of the *Lakeshore Limited* "Jeeps." Then, at Creative Arts Book Company, I've been delighted by the enthusiasm of publisher Don Ellis and my editor, Paul Samuelson.

Also, I've doodled first drafts onto more than my fair share of paper napkins at that inimitable think tank, the Royal Ground coffee house at the corner of Fillmore and California in San Francisco. It was there, an itinerant afternoon guitarist twanging nicely in the background, I realized a book-in-progress is like a haystack where the gaffes, and the inspirations, are buried — along, I suppose, with the proverbial needle.

INTRODUCTION

One point of this book is to provide you with enough recipes to keep a home bistro bubbling along indefinitely with comforting stews, salads, pastas and the occasional timbale — I like the idea that you *present* food to family and friends as a good restaurant would, the food you've found through reading, touring, experimenting in the kitchen, seizing on serendipitous gastronomic connections.

The book is also, in fact rather more about the associations many of its recipes have for a veteran inn crawler and saucepan addict. Often for him the eating of a dish is inextricably bound with the memory of an acrobatic waiter, a heavenly view, a missed train, a near-escape from kitchen disaster, a moment of joy or longing. Spice, in short, in the life of a gastronomical tourist.

The dishes offered range from traditional to trendy, accent on the former. For fun and taste adventure I've picked up on devices of "contemporary" cuisine — layering of ingredients, for instance, which I suspect is not an everyday procedure in most amateur kitchens, many of them having been deeply influenced as mine was by Mom — but a lot of the recipes are Old French or Italian, or, for that matter Old American, not to speak of the occasional venerable Greek or Moroccan. The majority of preparations are not complicated, their spokesman being neither a chemist nor the most patient of cooks.

Your home bistro *Menu* follows, serving as table of contents.

NOTE: Recipes in this book are for two generous or three light servings, unless otherwise noted.

NOTE: Much attention is paid to cooking without fat whenever possible, without compromising taste value. And very few of the recipes add salt.

MENU

SALADS

Rice, Shrimp and Bacon — two arrangements	1
Avocado and Shrimp Balsamico	2
Shrimp, Leek and Egg	2
Niçoise grand or simple and a Niçoise Rice Salad	3
Blue Caesar Maison	4
Little Caesar	5
Leek, Beet and Egg with Walnut Oil Dressing Ardèche	5
Hotel Salad Périgourdine, souvenir of Brantôme	5
Lo Coco with Currants, Pecans and Blue Cheese	6
Pear, Mortadella, Pinoli Nouvelle	7
Cracked Crab Remoulade	7
Salad of Warm Chicken Livers, Frisée and Corn with Raspberry Vinaigrette	8
Wurstsalat and its first cousin	9
Frisée with Bacon, Croutons and Poached Egg Balsamico	9
Vegetable Salad Traviata, a salute to Zef	10
Ricotta and Tomato with Hunan Onion Cakes Mexicano	11
La Salade Aveyronnaise, saluting Sam Chamberlain	11
Chef's Salad with a Cumin, Coriander and Tomato Vinaigrette	12
Sardines, Cress, Tomato and Avocado on a Potato Cake, Vinaigrette	13
Balzar Salad: sardines, etc., old brasserie style	13
White Bean, Bacon and Tomato with Caper Vinaigrette	14
Warm Cabbage Slaw with Goat Cheese and Pecans	15
Zucchini Slaw and Avocado Belle Donne	16
Two Bean Salad	23
Smoked Trout, Basil Mayonnaise	35
Lightly Vinaigretted Artichoke Bottoms and Potato, Basil Mayonnaise	35
Tomatoes stuffed with a Sardine, Egg, Pinoli Mayonnaise	35
Raw Mushroom Salad with Olive Oil, Lemon and Shaved Parmesan Cheese	35
Marcus' Potato Salad Garni	48
Raie in a warm salad with Currant Vinaigrette, souvenir of Beaulieu-sur-Dordogne	89
Chicken Salads: Cooled Chicken en Cocotte with Greens	96
Cold Chicken Elizabeth David	115
Five Spice Chicken with Crispy Things Balsamico	121

SIMPLER VEGETABLES
(but main course!)

Asparagus alla Parmigiana	*17*
Asparagus, Egg Vinaigrette	*18*
String Beans and Pinoli, Vinaigrette	*18*
Broccoli Lupo Vinaigrette, souvenir of old North Beach	*18*
Italian Beans Lupo Vinaigrette	*18*
Chard Sauté with Garlic and Lemon	*19*
Brussels Sprouts, Pinoli and Bacon, Marjoram Butter	*20*
Baked Potatoes (white or sweet) with a Garlic Herb Butter	*20*
Corn on the Cob, in season, à la Jimmy	*21*
Baked Vegetables Julie with assorted toppings	*22*
Roasted Japanese Eggplant Vinaigrette (or with Vegetable Cassoulet)	*22*
Fava Bean and Pancetta Ragoût	*23*
Steamed Cabbage and Chard with Scallion	*24*
Warm Cabbage, Bacon Vinaigrette	*86*

and see:

Baked Crumbed Brussels Sprouts with Capers	*20*
Hummus	*35*
Quick Potato Gratin	*87*
Creamed Spinach	*92*
"Broasted" Potatoes	*103*
Chestnut Purée	*122*
Gigi's Sweet Potato Croquettes	*122*
Squash Fritters Gigi	*166*
Baked Kale	*170*

PLATS DU JOUR
(main courses, but in some cases excellent accompaniments as well)

Trouffade Auvergnate, a bacon-cheese potato cake	*25*
Bûcheron Potatoes and a circle of vinaigrette	*26*
Prosciutto-wrapped Asparagus with Two Sauces	*27*
Stuffed Giant Zucchini Egyptian	*28*
Sausage-stuffed Tomatoes à la Dumas	*28*
Four Onion Gratin Garni	*29*
Grilled Leeks (or Asparagus) with Bacon and Caper Cream	*30*
Tortillas stuffed with Pipérade	*31*
Caponata — four treatments	*32*
Eggplant Anchovy Terrine	*32*
Eggplant Parmigiana old trattoria style	*33*
Antipasto Misto: Roasted Sweet Peppers and Green Goddess Eggs, et al.	*34*
Corn Fritters à l'Orange with Bacon	*36*
Corn Soufflé Pudding Peter Pan	*36*
Cheese Soufflé; Spinach or Pesto Soufflé	*37*
Torta del Pastore Trentina	*28*
Tarte à l'Oignon Place Pereire	*39*
Crêpes Cauchoises, souvenir of Rouen	*40*
Falafel de luxe	*41*
Red Bean Chili Maison	*41*
Vegetable Pudding XXIV December, Sauce Mousseline	*42*
Torta di Ricotta with Tomatoes and Pesto	*43*
Beefsteak Tomatoes Pomiane	*44*
Timbale of Corn, Bacon, Figs and Goat Cheese	*44*
Sautéed Portobello Mushrooms on Toast	*75*
Oeufs au Vin Bonne Femme	*114*
Marrow Marchand de Vin	*150*

SOUPS

Purée Mongole with Yellow Split Peas and Curry Cream	47
Black Bean	48
Southwest Pinto Bean with Sausage	49
Black-Eyed Pea and Scallion Etc. Minestrone	49
Onion Garlic Chez Nous	50
Corsican Soup Maxim, also known as Aïgo Ménagère (finished with poached egg or mussels)	51
Avgolemono	52
Zuppa Maritata	52
Peruvian Shrimp Chowder Francesca	53
Turkish Red Lentil and Tomato Soup (Kirmizi Mercimek Çorbasi)	54
Curried Lentils with Yogurt	54
Gazpacho Thanksgiving-style	55
Leek and Potato XXIV December	56
Gigi's Alsatian Soup with Cabbage, Garlic Sausages and Honey	57
Chicken Saffron Minestrone with Toasts	58
Red Pepper and Corn with Sour Cream and Jack Cheese	59
Quasi-Hungarian Mushroom and Asparagus	59
Ciuppin Genovese, a puréed fish soup anchovy-flavored	61
Purée of Cauliflower and Watercress	62
Leonida's Farinata (and next day Polenta Cassoulet)	62
Zanzibar Chicken Soup with Avocado and Capers	63
Caponata Soup (eggplant, zucchini and olive purée)	32
Lamb and Red Lentils, a half-soup	54
Ragoût of Pasta Le Nord, souvenir of Lyon	81
Waterzooi de Bruxelles, souvenir of Taverne du Passage	106
Mulligatawney Menlo Park, a half-soup	107
Bouillabaisse de Poulet with Saffron Mayonnaise Toasts	118

RISOTTOS

Risotto	with Dried Fruits and Pine Nuts	65
	with Baby Grapes and Basil	65
	with Salami and Nectarines (or Mangoes)	66
	al Limone	66
	with Portobello Mushroom Sauté	66
	with Shrimp and Bacon (or Juniper Berries)	66

Risotto Verde 66
Risotto Meneghina, from a Milan trattoria 66
Risotto del Cambio, from a Turin ristorante 66
Sun-dried Tomato Risotto 67
Risotto with Pancetta and Chestnuts 67
Risotto with Brussels Sprouts, Pine Nuts and Bacon 20
Risotto with Chicken, Olives, Anchovies and Vinegar 120
Risotto with Sautéed Chicken Livers, Mushrooms & Parsley à la Nick 192

Paella "Home Bistro" and demi-Paella 111
Pilaf Anna served with Mary Kelley's Chutney 129

PASTAS

al Pomodoro, house tomato sauce	69
alla Busseto, souvenir of Carlo Bergonzi's albergo — two versions	69
al Agrodolce: tomatoes, pinoli, yellow raisins and chocolate chips	70
al Pesto (pinoli, walnut or pistachio nuts)	70
al Pesto Trapanese	71
al Gorgonzola	71
Aglio e Olio or "Quasi Bagna Calda"	72
alla Carbonara della Casa	73
"Trasimeno" — egg, coppa, peas and lemon zest	74
Portobello: mushroom garlic sauté, sausage and cream	75
Niçoise — tomatoes and anchovies	75
With Bacon, Sautéed Leeks and Tomato Vinaigrette	76
With Beurre Noir and Balsamic Vinegar	76
With Three Onions and Almonds	77
Prawn Saffron Pasta	77
Vermouth Zucchini Pasta	78

(In principle, all with fettuccine except the Niçoise and Vermouth Zucchini with shells; but penne, rigatoni, the various tubular pastas, are excellent options too — certainly in up-to-date restaurants this is the Age of the Tube . . . my current favorite is bucatini, the garden hose of the pasta pantry)

Prosciutto-stuffed Tortellini three ways	78
Mock Cannelloni	79
Lasagne Bolognese alla nostra maniera	80
Ravioli Stuffed with Squash, Macaroons and Mostarda	81
Ragoût of Pasta Le Nord, souvenir of Lyon	81

Pasta with Japanese Eggplant and Watercress Pesto	23
Pasta with Prawns, Leeks and Bacon Cream Rio	30
Pasta with Caponata and Sausage	32
Pasta with Pistachio Nut Sauce	85
Pasta with Chicken and "Many" Cloves of Garlic	100
Pasta with Saffron Lamb Shanks and Eggplant	125
Aushak (Afghan Ravioli)	134
Afghan Pasta with Two Sauces (Yogurt and Meat)	135
Guacamole Almond Pasta	148
Pasta with Daube Provençale	156

FISH

Corsican Soup with Mussels — *51*
Peruvian Shrimp Chowder Francesca — *53*
Ciuppin Genovese — *61*

Various, pan-fried, with:

- Tomato Basil Vinaigrette — *84*
- Diced Avocado Vinaigrette — *84*
- Ravigote de Luxe — *84*
- Sicilian Salsa — *84*
- Brown Butter with Lemon, Garlic and Parsley — *85*
    (and optional capers) — *85*
- Brown Butter and Sage — *85*
- Cilantro Pesto (with or without poached egg) — *85*
- Red Pepper Purée Santa Fe — *85*
- Pistachio Sauce — *85*
- Rhubarb Cream Broth — *85*
- Orange Sauce Catalonia (kumquats optional) — *86*
- Succotash Nouvelle — *86*
- Bacon Vinaigrette and Steamed Cabbage — *86*

Cracked Crab or Petrale Sole with Remoulade — *8*
Salmon with Bean, Bacon and Tomato Salad, Caper Vinaigrette and Aioli — *14*
Fish of the day over a Corn-Fig-Bacon Timbale — *44*
Poached Salmon with Pesto Trapanese — *71*
Baked Salmon and Three Sauces — *85*
Baked Butterfish Green Herbs and Mustard (or Wasabi) Gratiné — *87*
Baked Filet of Red Snapper in a Tomato Olive Sauce or with Indian Spices — *87*
Baked Salmon with a Shrimp Mushroom Yogurt Stuffing — *88*
Raie Beurre Noir or with Sauce Moutarde, or with a Currant Vinaigrette — *89*
Halibut Mousse with Cucumber Vinaigrette — *90*
Calamari Fritti on Greens, Saffron Mayonnaise — *91*
Salmon Auberge St-Jacques — *91*

CHICKEN

Pollo alla Crema	94
Baked Chicken with Portobello Mushroom and Cream	95
Chicken en Cocotte	96
Chicken Sauté with Garlic Butter Pasta Onslow-Ford	97
Chicken Sauté with Balsamic Vinegar, Garlic and Tomato	97
Poulet à l'Indienne with Cucumber Sauté	99
Marcus' Red Thai Curry	99
Chicken with Many Cloves of Garlic	100
Chicken with Leeks, Dried Fruits and Cream	101
Lemon Milk Chicken Frediani	101
Pancetta Roast Chicken in Parchment with Oil-Roasted Potatoes	102
Chicken with Basil, Ginger and Orange	103
Chicken, White Beans and Leek-Feta-Sour Cream Salsa with Tortillas	103
Boiled Chicken with Saffron Mayonnaise	104
Milanese Boil à la Crispi, otherwise known as Bottaggio	105
Waterzooi de Bruxelles, souvenir of Taverne du Passage	106
Mulligatawney Menlo Park, a half-soup	107
Poulet Diable	108
Poulet Madame, souvenir of the thirteenth arrondissement	108
Fricassée de Poulet à l'Auvergnate	109
Chicken with Roquefort and Raisin Stuffing	110
Paella "Home Bistro" and demi-Paella	111
Pollo Trentina	112
Coq au Vin	113
. . . and Oeufs au Vin Bonne Femme	114
Virtually Vin-less Coq au Vin (Chicken en Cocotte II)	115
Cold Chicken Elizabeth David with Rice Vinaigrette	115
Chicken Catelli, variation on a Geyserville theme	116
Old School Chicken with Prosciutto, Fontina and Sage	117
Pollo Cisterna, a salute to San Gimignano	117
Bouillabaisse de Poulet with Saffron Mayonnaise Toasts	118
Chicken and Polenta à la Chester	119
Chicken Sauté with Green Olives, Anchovies and Red Wine Vinegar	120
Five Spice Chicken with Crispy Things Balsamico	121
Poulet Basquaise Rue Webster	121
Fricasée de Poulet Normande	138
and	
Chestnut Purée for Turkey Nights	122
. . . or Gigi's Sweet Potato Croquettes	122

MEATS

Lamb Shanks Chez Nous I and II	*125*
Lamb St-Paul-de-Vence (five items)	*126*
Sonoma Lamb Parfait	*127*
Tenerumi d'Agnello Samuele	*127*
Lamb Cacciatora, an anchovy-flavored stew	*128*
Pilaf Anna served with Mary Kelley's Chutney	*129*
Ali's Asian Chops with Rice or Black Bean Purée	*130*
Moroccan Lamb Stew with Olives and Saffron	*131*
Yugoslavian Baked Lamb Garni	*132*
Moussaka Chez Nous	*133*
. . . and Aushak (Afghan Ravioli)	*134*
Osso Buco della Casa	*135*
Escalope Milanese	*136*
Côte de Veau à la Crème two ways	*137*
Mustard-coated Roast Veal with Plum Catsup Kelley	*138*
Vitello Tonnato à la Don	*139*
Veal Chops Poitou, with Squashes	*140*
Veal Sauté with Sausage and Artichokes	*140*
Calf's Liver à l'Orange with Toasted Almonds	*141*
Veal and Eggplant Napoleon	*142*
Bollito Misto with White Beans, Mostarda di Frutta,	*143*
Salsa Verde and Mustard Tomato Sauce . . . also Olive Sauce	*144*
Second Day Bollito after Tante Marie	*144*
Round Steak "Mariniers du Rhône" with Caper Vinaigrette	*145*
Polpette I and II — Lombardian and Neapolitan	*146*
Lentil Stew Frediani, a demi-chili	*147*
Hamburger with Guacamole, Remoulade or Orange Mayonnaise	*148*
Hamburger Marchand de Vin on a bed of Chard Sauté	*149*
Tartare: plain, or in Eggplant Sandwich Val Sassina	*150*
Terrine Ardèche, souvenir of Lo Podello	*151*
Anne's Meat Loaf with Tomato Sauce	*152*
Goulash 88 with Polenta or Sour Cream Cornbread	*153*
Korean Beef Ribs	*155*
Daube Provençale Chez Nous	*156*
Bistecca alla Fiorentina	*157*
Pepper Steak and Tossed Leeks	*158*
Manzo Donaldo with Vegetables Rondalla	*158*
Carbonnades Flammandes	*159*
Pastel de Choclo: a Chilean casserole of beef, corn and black olives	*160*
Chicken Apple Sausages	*161*
with Black Bean Purée, Avocado Vinaigrette and Sour Cream	
Italian Sausage with White Beans and Salsa Verde or Poached Apples	*161*

Mini-Cassoulet	*162*
Choucroute Garnie	*163*
Red Cabbage with Garlic Sausages Landais	*164*
Carmel Ham and Peaches Anna with Sweet Potato Biscuits	*165*
Pork Chops Courlandaise and Squash Fritters Gigi	*166*
Pork Chops with Mustard Sauce	*167*
Pork Chops al Latte with Grapes	*167*
Roast Pork or Duck with Glazed Dried Fruits	*168*
Retro Pork Shoulder Pot Roast with Cider	*168*
Confit de Canard and Dordognian trimmings	*169*
Wurst with Warm Potato Salad and Simple Greens or Baked Kale	*170*
Oxtail Stew with Turnips and Fennel	*171*
Savoie Supper	*171*
Dinner at Alex's: a ranch style meal from Middle California	*172*
Lamb Chops with Cheese, Spinach or Pesto Soufflé	*37*

DESSERTS

Mini Macédoine	*176*
Cottage Pudding with Chocolate Sauce . . . or upside down with marmalade	*176*
Pear Bread Pudding with an Apricot Jam Sauce	*177*
Chocolate Bread Pudding with Chocolate Sauce	*178*
Oranges Terrazza, souvenir of London's Soho	*179*
Hot Fruit Salad Costa-Lacy	*180*
Raspberry Tortoni "Pickwick"	*180*
with a Chocolate Cookie Crumb base	*181*
Soufflé in disguise: Warm Chocolate Tarts	*181*
Chocolate Soufflé Caruso, souvenir of Ravello	*182*
Prune Whip Cincinnati with Crème Anglaise	*183*
Crêpes Balkan Grill, souvenir of Vienna	*184*
Blitz Torte Old St. Paul with assorted additions	*185*
Seven-Layer Cake (or higher) à la Gigi	*186*
Lemon Pie Charleston	*188*
Gâteau Basque Le Trinquet	*188*
Lucy's Celebration Cake, souvenir of a christening	*189*
Cecily's Mango Cake	*190*
Alison's High Altitude Cake	*190*
Our Breton "Sundae": vanilla ice cream	*191*
with crème de marrons and chocolate sauce	
Nicholas Roosevelt's Raspberry Ice Cream	*191*
Chocolate-dipped Hazelnut Cookies Maison	*192*
Sweet Ravioli Old North Beach	*194*
Our Fruit Crisp	*195*
Brunch Dessert: Cecily's Veritable Kouign-Amann from Brittany	*195*
Summer Dessert in Old Verona: Gorgonzola and Peaches	*196*

Postscripts

Postscript at the Drake	*16*
Portrait of a Hotel	*24*
A Considerable Postscript (lunch with M.F.K. Fisher)	*45*
Remembrance of Things Lost	*64*
Sartorial Note	*67*
Postscript Hollandaise	*82*
Postscript in D flat	*92*
Interlude: Mozart by Moonlight	*115*
Manhattan Postscripts	*123*
Interlude on Track Ten	*142*
Train Spotter's Interlude	*154*
Postscript by the Sea	*173*
Sidewalk Postscript	*174*
Envoi	*197*

THE GASTRONOMICAL TOURIST

"We are alive, and now.
When else live, and how more pleasantly
than supping with sweet comrades?"
—M.F.K. Fisher, *Serve It Forth*.

—SALADS—

RICE, SHRIMP AND BACON SALAD
—two arrangements, one with tomato—

The salad a heap of travel couldn't quite put together. Risottos are popular as steak in the U.S. now, at least in the gourmet ghettos that dot the land, but rice salads remain the culinary business of Provence, Italy, Spain; they're rare even in California Cuisine restaurants up to their ears in a Mediterranean aesthetic. And they tend to bump against roadblocks philosophical-gastronomical: some ingredients just "won't do."

Now shrimp and bacon in one configuration or another you'd find at counters or tables in our smoke-happy country, and vinaigretted rice and a puffy tomato we've frequently enjoyed in Italy, in a neighborhood place, say, on Rome's majestic Piazza Navona, baroque fountains splashing as we dallied with our Orvieto, or in a seedy trattoria in Ascoli Piceno where the padrone wore a hat in the manner of a gangster out of Ben Hecht and we figured we might have to run for our lives, plate of rice salad or sausage and lentils in hand — and wasn't there a station restaurant in Bologna that filled the bill just before I rushed to the track and panicked because North and South had suddenly flip-flopped in my mind? But the addictive combinations suggested on this page are, apparently, foreign to either shore. Even in sushi, I think.

So it's with great pleasure we deliver this pantry puzzle with no pieces missing and border guards of the kitchen off duty.

PLAN I
Combine about 1/3 pound of **cooked shrimp** with 1 cup of boiled and cooled **long-grain rice** and perhaps 10 little oblongs per person of **thick cut or slab bacon** (the latter preferred), cooked quite dark on the first side, much less on the second and drained on paper towels and cooled.

Then work in 2/3 cup of roughly chopped **red and green sweet peppers** for added color and taste interest, and some soft **lettuce** torn into small pieces — not enough lettuce to obscure the dominant rice-shrimp-bacon-peppers.

Toss well with a dressing made by whisking **red wine vinegar** into a small 1/4 teaspoon of simple **Dijon mustard** (a fork will do the job), then **olive oil** along with a sprinkle of **dill weed** (**tarragon** is nice too), in a proportion of slightly more than 2 oil to 1 vinegar. I like my vinaigrette a little wetter than is fashionable in today's trendiest restaurants: you will have to suit yourself as to liquidity and have no fear of food police.

PLAN II

Reduce the **lettuce** content in this case to a minimum and arrange your **rice-shrimp-bacon-peppers** over and around large **tomato** halves in soup bowls.

NOTE: For most salads I use "pure" olive oil rather than the heavier, toasty "extra virgin" which tends to upstage vinaigrette-mates.

AVOCADO AND SHRIMP SALAD BALSAMICO

The great old glitzless grills of San Francisco's financial district with their waiters in rumpled tuxedoes — Jack's, for instance, an ancient hangout for Who's Who-ers as diverse as Lucius Beebe and Jascha Horenstein, not to mention a macho novelist from Key West and a cinema Casablancan or two — are where I learned to float this mellifluous salad across an enchanted palate. It's a California classic, given a timely twist with the balsamic vinaigrette that came into our lives with the gastronomically roaring 80s. For an artistic presentation you could cup the shrimp and avocado in large lettuce leaves half shell style. And you might want to pretend you're eating at one of those no-nonsense downtown grills 'neath a short mile of coat hooks, fat pats of butter at the ready for your sourdough, and a saucer of lemon wedges handy in case of need.

Combine about 1/3 pound of **cooked shrimp** with slices of a medium-sized **avocado** and a fairly generous amount of **butter lettuce**.

Toss gently with — or pour over individual servings at the table — a dressing made by whisking a little **lemon juice** and more **balsamic vinegar** into a dab of **Dijon mustard** and slowly adding **olive oil**, in a proportion of 2-1/2 or 3 oil to 1 vinegar/lemon.

SHRIMP, LEEK AND EGG SALAD

Another homogeneous salad, without sharp edges, but scarcely bland. The tomatoes here are optional: you want to use juicy, vine-ripened specimens, tomatoes with soul, not those stiff supermarket grenades that have as much taste as a gleaming shopping cart. Pray for a farmers' market near you, even if it's like a mad al fresco emporium I know where feisty aunties unresponsive to the niceties of waiting in line for one's beautiful produce must be tactfully ignored. Or make friends with zealots who grow their own.

In this recipe all the ingredients have more or less equal prominence: about 1/4 pound of **cooked shrimp**; 2 or 3 medium-sized **leeks**, steamed, cooled and sliced; slices of hard boiled **egg**, 1 egg per person; small **tomato** wedges; and the leaves of **soft lettuce** along with some **"boutique" lettuces**, those curly-coily combinations of arugula, radicchio, etc. found in most supermarkets and all outlets for "whole" or "real" food.

As for the leeks, I generally use the white parts and a little of the green. Vigorous washing before steaming goes without saying!

Dress this salad with the basic **mustard-dill vinaigrette** of our first recipe. A little chopped **scallion** is not amiss — if it's visible dotting the outer edges of your vinaigrette you win points in the display department.

SALADE NIÇOISE

What a Niçoise is, is a question, we've learned, not to be settled by any tribunal in black robe and white toque. When we had a salad of this title at Da Bouttau in Nice in '69 there was celery, radish and sliced onion in the mix along with the tomato, egg, anchovies and olives of the recipe on this page — and no tuna, string beans and potatoes. A tad austere, perhaps, but we were satisfied. A good French recipe we know adds green peppers to some Bouttau items as well as several favored by the Bloomfields. Radicals, meanwhile, insert . . . but we won't go into that. And there you are, viewing from the sidelines as many interpretations of Salade Niçoise as you'll find of Beethoven's Fifth in Mr. Schwann's catalog. And Nice itself doubles (triples?) as big city, resort and hill town: it's an enchanting place, full of flowers, benign in temperature, port of call for romantic ferry rides into the Mediterranean, yet a bit unsatisfying in its multiplexity-by-the-sea, one attribute nibbling at another. In former Nizza you have, of course, a chance of being served your salade by an arugula Romeo who uses French but seems to talk it in Italian, as if to give any visiting linguistics professors a challenge.

. . . Our *Baby Niçoise* is for days when you pine for the zip of a complex Provençale salad but don't want to muster *all* the ingredients. And the rice opus I've lifted from our daughter Alison's diary of her aromatic, sandy summer with a French family near Agde. I've always commanded the girls to keep good gastronomic records.

In a rather large salad bowl arrange a hub-and-circle of more or less equal opportunity components:

> 1/3 pound of steamed, cooled **Blue Lake string beans**, in half lengths
>
> 2 cooled hard boiled **eggs**, halved
>
> 2 boiled and cooled **red potatoes**, cut in two and sliced
>
> 2 **tomatoes**, quartered
>
> some **butter lettuce** leaves
>
> tinned **tuna** (3 to 6 ounces),
>   preferably "solid," packed in olive oil, and drained

several filets from a tin of **anchovies**, drained of course, and some baby **Niçoise olives**

Display your pretty-as-a-picture salad, then toss it gently with a dressing composed of **red wine vinegar** and after that **olive oil** whisked into a bit of **Dijon mustard**; pressed **garlic** to taste; and some **dill weed or tarragon**. The proportions of oil to vinegar would be 2 or 2-1/2 to 1. If you're of the school believing a garlic clove should be peeled before putting it in the press, just smash it with your fist: I don't think Jacques Pépin would berate you.

BABY NIÇOISE

Simply combine — with the dressing just above — 3 or 4 "Niçoise" items, for instance tuna, potatoes and string beans. Consider employing that wild card, broiled oil-brushed artichoke halves (previously boiled, of course). Onion rings might play a role as well.

NIÇOISE RICE SALAD

Combine the **tomatoes**, **eggs**, **anchovies** and **olives** of some Niçoises with boiled, cooled **rice**. Toss with the above dressing.

BLUE CAESAR SALAD MAISON

A book could be written on Caesar Salad variations — this one is as inauthentic as the next. Why all the serial tossing? Because the ingredients are so varied in texture they might fly about indiscriminately if not battened down relatively early in the game. Now why, I wonder, is there no Salade César in France? Our Gallic friends put croutons in Lyon salads and even Niçoise salads (great idea!); for the foodie of Toulon or Marseille anchovies are as mother's milk. And an egg — not something to be sneezed at. Probably the style, the tone of this rather aggressive and likely-to-be-creamed up confection with its barrage of grated cheese, extra-virgin ovoid element and sizeable quarry of fried bread isn't quite right when proper gastronomical values are under fire: culinary franglais could be dangerous.

Of course the French, love them as I do, can take a few centuries to be convinced. Remember how french horns in their orchestras used to sound like bassoons or saxophones? Well, the passion so easily found when eating on French soil remains beyond dispute. Anyone retreating from the ubiquitous schnitzels of Austria or homey spud rhapsodies of Switzerland can vouch for that. And now . . *Mon Dieu* . . fusion cuisine is creeping (don't look) into the sacred Gallic kitchen and lo, a Chinese bistro in Paris has gained a Michelin star. Will Césars be nibbled on every corner?

First, tear a head of **romaine lettuce** into bite-sized pieces, working from the crisp, more interesting inner leaves out, and drop them in a playing field-sized salad bowl. Then sprinkle the lettuce with a good cup at least of grated **dry jack or parmesan** and toss well.* Then add almost as much crumbled **blue cheese** of good quality (Castello, for instance) and toss your compounding salad again.

Now add 8 or 10 drained **anchovy** filets and toss.

And crack an **egg** into the salad and toss.

Next, pour over your salad a dressing made as follows: whisk **red wine vinegar** into 1/3 teaspoon of **Dijon mustard**, add **olive oil**, a good squeeze of **lemon**, and at least 1 pressed **garlic** clove, the proportion of oil to vinegar/lemon 2 or 2-1/2 to 1.

To top off your increasingly mountainous salad, add 15 or 20 medium-sized croutons made by slowly sautéing **French bread** cubes with a dab of **butter** in a non-stick pan, then toss well your fully orchestrated Caesar.

LITTLE CAESAR

Just a medium head of **romaine,** 2 or 3 halved **tomatoes,** lots of grated **dry jack or parmesan**, and the Caesar dressing above.

*We prefer the dry jack which is more robust and a little less sharp — and virtually unknown, we gather, in Manhattan! Historical note: dry jack was created during World War II when San Francisco Italians were deprived of their imported parmesan flow.

LEEK, BEET AND EGG SALAD WITH WALNUT OIL DRESSING ARDÈCHE

Souvenir of the Hôtel du Nord in tiny Thueyts (pronounce it 2-A, more or less) with its lovely patio, our room overlooking a lettuce patch, Granny in the parlor, muttering English at dinner, a sycamore-lined *rue* outside, no traffic but the occasional lorry passing through from Le Puy. Reality intruded only when an old gent in the road asked us for a précis of our new president, Monsieur Ray-Gun. Beets, I tend to think, are better with company on the plate than alone, and this shrubby salad solves the problem.

On each salad-eater's plate combine about 4 medium-sized **beets**, boiled, cooled, peeled and sliced; 3 well-washed **leeks**, trimmed, sliced, steamed and cooled; 2 hard boiled **eggs** cooled and halved, and some **soft lettuce**. Be sure to position the beets between the leeks and the lettuce to avoid clashing shades of green — this problem will be somewhat less acute if you elect a two-toned mix of "boutique" greens including radicchio. Dress red-white-and-green with a new vinaigrette combination:

> **Dijon mustard**, a good 1/4 teaspoon
> **red wine vinegar**, 1 part
> **canola oil**, 1 part
> **walnut oil**, 2 parts or more
> crumbled **walnuts** to taste

HOTEL SALAD PÉRIGOURDINE, FROM BRANTÔME

Brantôme is a "destination" in the northern hills of Périgord with its imposing fairy tale abbey squeezed pristinely between a balustraded river and an impatient cliff. Sunk in its non-tourist-trapping obscurity, the town rather resembles a stage set for some faithful old production of a classic, a bit frayed at the edges perhaps. The salad adjacent is a crisp memento of the Hôtel du Soir and its lone waiter, a "why worry?" type who might have invented the French shrug: with a drowsy precision he steered us toward a great Cahors ("like Beaujolais, but stronger!") and this salad with its artistically blackened bacon was a revelation.

We reached the Soir by antique regional bus, patronized mostly by babushkas with bundles, the pixilated driver addressing his urge for a short snort midway from Angoulême. And our slanting double cost us seven 1981 dollars. Could this be the "cheap, clean, elementary inn" Virginia Woolf stopped at fifty years earlier?

A cautionary note: since I began this chronicle, slab bacon as a Brantôme butcher knows it has slipped out of American shops and floated off into positively Jurassic status, nor do supermarket versions of packaged "thick cut" bacon tend to be the stuff of a bistro chef's dreams. But pancetta, thanks be, is quite readily available if your charcuturial quest threatens to be a flop. With its slightly tangy flavor pancetta is actually a shade more elegant — more, perhaps, a reedy tenor than a bellowing baritone — and can of course be cut to order.

> Combine **butter lettuce or fresh spinach** (well washed!) with 2 or 3 **tomatoes** halved or in wedges, 2 halved hard boiled **eggs**, some crumbled **walnuts** and a dozen small oblongs of (in principle) **slab or thick cut bacon** fried very dark on one side and minimally on the other, then drained on paper towels. Toss with the **dill Dijon vinaigrette** of our first salad recipe.

LO COCO SALAD WITH CURRANTS, PECANS AND BLUE CHEESE

To notice the good red brown of Lo Coco's meat sauce bubbling in the sunlight at a crowded street fair in San Francisco's North Beach is to experience a sudden al fresco epiphany. And scarcely less enchanting is the neighborhood cattedrale looming through the poplars from the bus stop where the paesani sit, a friendly Romanesque-cum-Disney. Italian bakeries nearby give way in an instant key change to pure Hong Kong, and down Columbus Avenue you can see the forever of Sausalito sliding to the Bay as if on a Japanese scroll — and when an antique street clock on the avenue was knocked unintentionally to smithereens by a backing delivery van you better believe such an affront to this emotionally-charged neighborhood made the front pages.

Now if it's summer, sun and fog will be locked in a filmy combat over Washington Square, an energetic wind breathing on these not unamorous atmospheric contestants. Whatever the season, the lattes will flow and the eggplants on focaccia satisfy. Behind the scenes, feisty politicos who swim the bay at dawn will be making sure no big-chain coffee house brings its conformity into the 'hood. Tai Chi'ers will levitate, almost, on the Washington Square lawn, and Mr. Ferlinghetti will lunch at the U.S. Restaurant as the padrone rolls his "Parma flowers" *con amore* and puts 'em in the oven. Restaurants in the area multiply as I write, Mediterranean, Asian, retro, nouvelle, one devoted to garlic as the tonic for all earthly angst. Lo Coco's inspired the luxuriantly crunchy salad on this page — from which I subtracted the teeth-assaulting little olives lying in wait.

In a mixing bowl combine — you will doubtless end up using your hands for the mixing — several tablespoons of crumbled **blue cheese** with similar amounts of **currants** and **pecans** in little bits.

Arrange in a salad bowl a bed of **butter lettuce or romaine** and a circle of quartered **tomatoes** (about 1 good-sized tomato per person). Spoon the mixture from the first paragraph over all and toss with our standard **mustard vinaigrette** (from the first recipe in this book) with the mustard element slightly lightened and the dill weed eliminated.

A NOUVELLE SALAD WITH PEARS, PINOLI AND MORTADELLA

And the textures of this salad, slippery, crunchy, *VERY* light, leaving extra room for a fairly decadent dessert, I picked up at a bistro around the corner from our house in San Francisco's Upper Fillmore. Well, one of the twenty-five bistros in the eight or nine blocks of Fillmore constituting "around the corner."

Arrange prettily on plates: leaves of **butter lettuce or spinach**, 1 cored, sliced **pear** and 2 rolled slices of **mortadella** per person, and a little minced **shallot**. Top with toasted **pine nuts** and a vinaigrette made with **olive oil**, **raspberry vinegar** and **lemon juice** in a 4 to 1 to 1 proportion. The nuts you should sauté in a small skillet over moderate heat until they turn dark — careful, if you use a lightweight skillet as I usually do they *will* burn while you're not looking.

CRACKED CRAB REMOULADE

Home on weekends from Stanford, I was habitually served by my doting mother a plate of cracked crab with homemade mayonnaise. Now I will not conceal my difficulties in concocting a really satisfactory flavor-smooth mayonnaise from scratch; whisking oil into other ingredients at one of Lennie Bernstein's "Pathétique" tempos is not my strong point. Luckily though, store-bought products if properly doctored so the usual sweetness is brought under control make a good takeoff point for quite a selection of respectably "gourmet" mayonnaise sauces. The remoulade on this page is Exhibit A, a slightly tamed version of our friend Emily Warner's killer remoulade with chopped dill pickle and anchovy paste as well.

Those collegiate Saturdays proceeded from midday crab-a-thons, complete with Baltimore beer, and accompanied by the Metropolitan Opera broadcast of the week ("There go the house lights," the delightfully unctuous Milton Cross would tell us, "and our conductor, Cesare Sodero, is making his way into the pit; in a few moments you'll hear those quiet opening measures . . ."), to dinners sparked by herb-rich marsala chickens, good coq au vins, formidable choucroutes garnies, not to mention appropriate bottles of Napa's Beaulieu or Livermore's Wente, with the occasional Pommard for kicks or perhaps the new-kid-on-the-block Orvieto, which that hushed emporium of fine comestibles Simon Bros. was featuring for the Pacific Heights matrons who'd telephone in their orders from their Arts and Crafts and Georgian Revival mansions.

Reared in the gastronomical realm of fine southern cooking at the knee of a Downstairs Julia Child vintage 1900, later an observant faculty wife on the Strasbourg sabbatical of a rising Johns Hopkins internist (who almost invented penicillin), my mother faithfully read her Louis Diat and the latest M.F.K. Fisher — by coincidence the Bloomfields as well as the young Fishers enjoyed the charms of the Pension Elisa in Strasbourg, a few years apart in their stays — and seemed to know automatically what good food and wine were all about. Only the rumblings of romance in senior year — and they were gastrically challenging, I must tell you — curtailed my headlong rushes to her weekend table.

Serve fresh **cracked Dungeness crab** with a sauce based on good-quality commercial **mayonnaise**, adding **Dijon mustard**, **lemon juice**, pressed **garlic**, chopped hard boiled **egg**, **large capers** and **dill weed** in the balance you desire. I recommend you start with the proportion 3 mayonnaise to 1 mustard to about 1/5 lemon and correct it if necessary. Don't stint on the dill, and note also that a fearless splash of **dry sherry** will guarantee your remoulade taking flight. A bit of minced **onion** will do no harm, either. Be sure to use a whisk to duplicate the velvety texture of authentic mayonnaises as dispensed by beloved bistros on streets with names like St-Jacques.

AND: This sauce — plus an extra squeeze of lemon! — is a classic accompaniment for luxuriant petrale sole which you flour, dip in lightly beaten egg and fry briefly in a moderately hot pan with a good tablespoon of olive oil. Spiffily titled Petrale Doré, this is a staple at San Francisco's "Joe's" restaurants, sassy open-kitchen brasseries where grizzled waiters in black tie conceal their utter efficiency behind smokescreens of absent-mindedness.

SALAD OF WARM CHICKEN LIVERS, FRISÉE AND CORN WITH RASPBERRY VINAIGRETTE

Numerous additions and subtractions are possible when one works with the old bistro marriage of livers and greens. In Lyon they'd add croutons and egg and find the corn absolutely bizarre. Nancy Oakes of San Francisco's Boulevard goes beyond the corn, wrapping spinach in pancetta and adding roasted peppers. I'm attracted to the simple trinity of our version, the impact of the rich, earthy livers softened by the austerity of the frisée and the sweetness of the corn without jostling from other elements.

But I do admire Ms. Oakes' ability to sculpt a scrumptious salad into a Trojan horse.

Steam an ear of fresh **corn** for about 10 minutes with a pinch of **sugar**, cool it a little and — holding the ear almost vertical — scrape the kernels off with a knife. Now sauté about 2/5 pound of **chicken livers** with a dab of **butter** in a moderately hot pan until they're brown on all sides but pink inside: they'll take no more than 5 minutes. Let them cool just a little.

Then fill dinner-size plates *almost* to the edge with a bed of **frisée lettuce**, spoon the corn onto the middle of the greens, the livers on top of all, and dress the lot with a vinaigrette combining **olive oil**, **raspberry vinegar** and **lemon juice** in a 4 to 1 to 1 balance.

And you know what? Fresh sliced peaches, as a matter of fact, would be a delightful summer addition to this salad: brown 'em slightly.

WURSTSALAT

Our only "Rathskeller" dish, calling up memories of eating in great basement mess halls in northern Europe. Hanseatic Luebeck's on a dismal February Sunday had us feeling we were at the end of the world, caught in some wintry aspic of culinary homeyness lapping up the local equivalent of corned beef hash. In Munich, no surprise, the vibes were more worldly — and we were off to the Prinz Regenten to bathe in a warming five hours of *Die Meistersinger*, genial Hans Knappertsbusch at the helm, brushing away applause at his entrance as was his habit with a "now-to-business" downbeat. The theater's epauletted head usher looked like an Emperor himself, bristles blazing, or at least the maitre d' of some mythical Mittel Europa Ritz. This was 1954: the city was still half in ruins, a panorama of pomp and rubble, but the whipped cream piled up in the cafés like so many Alpine avalanches. The cream Richard Strauss set to music.

Years passed, Munich spruced itself up, and we were back for more music: a *Magic Flute* with scenery all too suggestive of Emmentaler left much to be desired, but the experiencing, from the fourth row, of Rafael Kubelik throwing himself into a deeply moving performance of Brahms' Requiem in the Herkules Saal reached epiphanal heights. Forty-four years after that *Meistersinger* we were in Munich between trains, one bright spring evening; the brasserie we chose in the hauptbahnhof was forlorn, but the sausages as echt Muenchen as ever.

On a bed of **escarole** arrange warm rounds of boiled **red, white or gold potato** and **garlic or Polish sausage** (slicing the potatoes before boiling will, of course, save you some time). Dress these wheels-within-wheels with our **dill mustard vinaigrette** (first recipe), rather emphasizing the mustard element and adding lots of minced **parsley**.

NOTE: Rearrange these items as unsliced **sausage** with warm **potato** cubes and **greens** to the side with their dressing and you have a different dish.

FRISÉE WITH BACON, CROUTONS AND POACHED EGG BALSAMICO

This is our version of a rich bistro classic we were introduced to at Don and Renata Frediani's, one of the great "home" restaurants. Don is one of those lucky Americans of advancing age who was brought up on garlic — while the rest of us languished in damnable aioli-free zones, vaguely dissatisfied with our lives. In fact, his mother used it as a cold remedy. Well, at least my mother was into anchovies. Don reports that home Italo-American eating was regional: that's to say, only the Ligurians knew or cared about pesto, the folks from Naples didn't do risotto.

> Combine **frisée** (tickly lettuce as it's known in our family), a generous amount of dark-fried **slab or thick cut bacon** and a similarly untimid distribution of **croutons** (see page 5).
> Toss with a dressing made by stirring 1 pressed clove of **garlic**, a little **lemon juice** and some **balsamic vinegar** into a good 1/2 teaspoon of **Dijon mustard,** then slowly adding **olive oil** to arrive at a proportion of 2-1/2 or 3 to 1 oil to vinegar/lemon. That accomplished, top each serving with a poached **egg**.

VEGETABLE SALAD FROM THE TRAVIATA RESTAURANT

A bracing salad from La Traviata in San Francisco's Mission District, an opera-maniac's place run by a dour but exceedingly friendly Albanian and patronized by Plàcido Domingo on his nights off. One can't help playing Opera Quiz here, the background music averages fifteen to eighteen arias per meal: it's a veritable factory of Tenors. Fun, but I do tend to like my dinner accompanied by nothing more than good, not too charged conversation (has anyone proved that politics aids digestion?) or a contemplative stare at a poetic view across some Auvernian or Mendocinan meadow.

Well, I will own to a soft spot for the rare candlelit bistro where a suave host takes your order to the tune of a little Hotel Carlylese spilling gently from the Steinway in the corner, piloted by a pencil-mustached meister in Navy blue or a hip old Sophie Tucker of the keys — and the keyboard of course is in black tie! Pheasant in Madeira cream and Cole Porter, now that's an item.

And we musn't forget the *Third Man* zitherist twanging darkly in the bar of romantic old Vanessi's in North Beach. In my bones, of course, is my cousin Moriz Rosenthal's cascading *Blue Danube* waltz which is perhaps the most dazzling eight or nine minutes of "cocktail lounge piano" there ever was. Food for geneticists is the fact our daughter sings Gershwin and Porter with exactly the same teasing little pauses Moriz put in a Chopin etude.

Moriz, by the way, tells in his unpublished autobiography, penned on stationery of the old Great Northern Hotel next to Carnegie Hall ("more northern than great," wrote this compulsive quipper) of the "superb" chicken soup, chicken livers and "Polish delicacies" served at his childhood home in old Lvov, c. 1870. But when the future Jupiter of the Octaves and court pianist to the Queen of Rumania would approach the Pleyel, the family cook, evidently fearing the vibrations of genius, would scream, "Don't play, you'll ruin the keyboard!"

> Steam, chill, and combine **broccoli, asparagus, carrots, zucchini** etc. along with some thawed frozen **peas** in the shapes and proportions of your choice. Dress with a simple

vinaigrette of **olive oil** and **red wine vinegar** in a 2 to 1 balance, adding at least 1 pressed **garlic** clove.

NEXT COURSE? Since this is a non-protein salad we generally follow it with cheese, proceeding thence to fruit or a heavier dessert.

RICOTTA AND TOMATO SALAD

The definition of This Won't Kill You food, this is the salad for the day after a gastronomic binge. It's also a starting-off point for substitutions and additions taking you into deeper caloric waters, for instance you could cancel the vinaigrette and dribble pesto (see page 19) over the ricotta-and-tomatoes, you could retain the dressing and drape veg-and-ricotta over a handsome slab of French bread dipped in olive oil and fried, and we also recommend pairing this salad with the Hunan onion cakes one recipe down.

On rings of sliced **tomato** arrange several spoonsful of **ricotta**. Dress with **Lupo Vinaigrette** (page 19) topped with chopped **fresh basil**.

HUNAN ONION CAKES MEXICANO

If you serve these as a solo dish, dip them in melted plum jam: homemade would be ideal. There's no need to depend on "store bought" since I can bring you word of Juliana Duncan's Almost Instant Two Jars of House Produced Confiture: gently boil for a short hour a saucepan of washed, smooshed-down fruit-of-choice to which you've added half a cup of sugar; cool, let sit out overnight, then refrigerate. Rapture ensues.

Begin with small ready-made **flour tortillas**. Brush two of them with **sesame oil** (the clear variety, not the dark) followed by beaten **egg**, then sprinkle chopped **scallion** on cake No. 1 and cover with cake No. 2, coated side down, pressing firmly and aligning the "sandwich" neatly. Repeat the process at least once.

Heat a large pan until it's quite hot and coat it with **canola oil**, then slide in the double cakes, turning them every 15 seconds with tongs and cooking them until they're crispy. Remove the cakes and hold them over the pan vertically to let any unwanted oil drip off.

To serve, cut the cakes into wedges.

LA SALADE AVEYRONNAISE

This rib-sticker of a salad is a souvenir of the Sam Chamberlain travel/photo/cookery books we embraced in the 50s when you couldn't begin a year without the latest Chamberlain calendar proposing a recipe for each week along with a black-&-white of a forlorn riverbank, a storybook auberge, a cornucopian flower stall, washing hung out on a picturesque line, cattle and sheep on their rounds, hillside habitations of a medieval sort, some cliff, terrace or arcade, or a period Peugeot (wallflower of the road!) dozing by Madame Dupont's vegetable stand. And there were usually enough fishing boats and yachts bobbing about in assorted picturesque waters to mount a not inconsiderable armada, perhaps a Dunkerquean flotilla. And many ancient stone bridges primly eyeing their humpy reflections. Yes, what a talent he had for seeing moments of pastoral photographic truth. And lots of them: one's reminded of Roger Fry's comment to Vanessa Bell (he was writing, actually, about the south of France), "Every bit of old wall, every tiled roof seems as though it were exactly right and only needed to be painted."

Meanwhile Mr. Chamberlain in his courtly prose embraced an endearing passion for the adjective "aromatic." And disciples carried his heavy books to Europe for chefs to put their names in, next to their recipes for coq au vin, raie beurre noir and so on . . .

> Now this Aveyron salad, could it be France's answer to ranch dressing?
>
> First off, let me say you can save yourself several pockets of change by finding a good not-too-dry **Wisconsin blue cheese**. I've balanced my books by locating a buttery Mindoro at $5 a pound at our local cheese store, this in place of the prescribed and very pricey Roquefort for which $14 is not an unusual tab.
>
> Mash 6 tablespoons of the cheese of your choice and blend in a cup of **cream,** 1/3 cup of **light sour cream** and a good 1/8 cup of **lemon juice** (but the two creams could be replaced by a sexy crème fraîche, and consider also a little pressed garlic), adding **black pepper** with a free hand along with an equally liberal helping of chopped **fresh tarragon**. Lumps should be eliminated as assiduously as if you were making a milk shake, by whatever ruthless means. Combine this dressing with **romaine lettuce**, shredded or not, and **tomato** halves.

CHEF'S SALAD WITH A CUMIN, CORIANDER AND TOMATO VINAIGRETTE

This tangy quasi-Cobb of a salad with its little cheese boulders strikes me as half Manhattan and half Santa Fe. Or should I be thinking Fès? A Paul Bowles salad?

The dashing pink dressing looks a little like Thousand Island, and tastes, I think, much better. On second thought, Thousand Island is not such a bad concept. Call it a slightly gaudy and perhaps corruptible distant cousin to Green Goddess positioned around the bend on the color wheel. I had an excellent one once.

The problem must be an unfortunate plethora of overly sweet commerical mayonnaises — or too much ketchup, the condiment I plan to ban when I become president — worming their way unchecked into the vast majority of those pinky salads found especially on insanely cluttered Tex-Mex combo plates. Here's where the "Serve It In Solemn State" movement needs to get to work.

> Dress a combination of **romaine**, **tomato** wedges, **Swiss cheese** juliennes and a little chopped **scallion** (plus if you wish bacon bits and/or hard boiled egg) with a conservatively spicy vinaigrette made as follows:

In a blender or food processor blend until emulsified 1/4 cup of **red wine vinegar** and 1/2 cup of **olive oil** along with 1 pressed **garlic** clove, at least 1/4 teaspoon each of **cumin** and **turmeric**, a mini-fraction less of **lime juice** and a hint of **cayenne**. Add 2/3 cup of chopped **tomato** and a small handful of chopped **coriander** leaves — cilantro, that is — and blend until smooth.

SARDINES, CRESS, TOMATO AND AVOCADO ON A POTATO CAKE VINAIGRETTE

Now we propose a contest of the new and the old. First, a contemporary combo representing the 1990s/2000/etc. . .

Begin with the potato cake: grate several **red potatoes** using the largest holes on the grater, then squeeze out the accumulated liquid, lightly **flour** the shreds, flatten them and cook in a tablespoon or more of **butter** in an eight-inch skillet for about 11 or 12 minutes on one side, 3 or 4 on the other, over a lowish flame: you can use a spatula in each hand to pry the cake loose for flipping.

Place on each diner's plate half or a third of the potato cake and arrange decoratively thereon a centerpiece of **watercress** (washed and de-stemmed, of course), surrounded by a circle of **tomato** wedges and alternating spokes of drained **sardines** from the standard tin (which provides enough for two or three main course salads), plus chunks of **avocado** and **English cucumber** wherever they seem to fit in the scenic scheme. Dress this salad with our regulation **mustard vinaigrette** (first recipe).

BALZAR SALAD (SARDINES, ETC., OLD BRASSERIE STYLE)

. . . And here, a salad of a sort probably known in the 1890s. We've named it after a brisk and playful Paris brasserie where you'd have no trouble finding this kind of fare. Balzar is the sort of place, club-like but not exclusive, where the professor at the next table is likely to be telling her concert violinist companion her book on Goethe will be out next week.

Meanwhile, an inch to the right, a benignly crusty waiter in long white apron eases a dubious matron into the notion the beautiful-looking sole he's presently de-boning so artistically is, in point of fact, "très bon, madame, très bon" . . . and behind him a garçon rushes a gravy boat of Hollandaise to the cadaverous editor-type furrowing his brow in the corner . . . Ah, with the Sorbonne and other intellectual hotbeds just around the corner, the air at Balzar *is* thick with intelligence. Enough, it seems, to make the place blow some great fuse of Brilliance and stop the kitchen in its tracks.

But there's charm too. And stylish women as well as forbidding female professors of a certain age. Combine the ingredients of fascination at Balzar's address and is it any wonder this is Adam Gopnik's favorite Paris restaurant? And mine, too, as you can clearly see. Except that my favorite Paris restaurant often seems to be in San Francisco where the Euro-vibes are so strong, with a ribbon of fog over the bay for an added *je ne sais quoi*.

As you prepare this salad, fantasize in your apron of choice (mine are custom-made from a laundry bag Cecily stole, I believe, from a French Railroad's sleeping car) that your dining area has become a Balzarian place of many mirrors, brass rails, and hat stands — and I will sit in the No Smoking zone, thank you, a better one, I hope, than Balzar's contaminated corner for non-puffers.

In this context of petty theft, Anne and I must confess to a minor Bonnie and Clyde escapade, lifting a Rome Express signboard from the vestibule of a train crossing Picardie one gloomy February afternoon in 1971, the consist including an Art Nouveau diner when such a delightfully panelled relic was standard equipment, not just for the folks who pay a bundle for a luxury excursion complete with keyboard tinkler and superfluous red carpets.

Timing was everything as we waited, an invisible Alfred Hitchcock coaching us from the corridor, to see if the coast was clear of conductors, brakemen, food trolley pilots or anyone from mainstream society who might interrupt our crime. With not too mixed feelings I can report that our mission was accomplished, even with ease. Well, I would have gladly paid (the offer stands!) $20 for our trophy — if only the French Railroads would accept my offering.

> Combine **butter lettuce**, **sardines** — or the truer brasserie ingredient **canned smoked herring** — slices of boiled and cooled **potato** and hard boiled **egg,** plus some raw **onion** rings and, if your teeth will accept them, a few **juniper berrie**s. Dress with the same **mustard vinaigrette** as in the recipe immediately above.

WHITE BEAN, BACON AND TOMATO SALAD WITH CAPER VINAIGRETTE

A passion for those homely white beans beloved of the Tuscans can overtake you, and this is the first of several recipes calling them into play. It's recommended as an independent main course or a stalwart contributor to an antipasto plate. Stand reminded that white beans come in several denominations, including "Large Limas" at the heavyweight end of the shelf as well as bean-ettes that look as if they might shrink into lentils — so suit yourself. We're lucky in the Bay Area to have a bean emporium extraordinaire, Ratto's in old Oakland. I like to hop the 10 a.m. post-commute ferry (with the receding San Francisco skyline, Golden Gate Bridge, Alcatraz, Angel Island, Belvedere, Mount Tamalpais, the works, all to myself — I could be on some capsule freighter cruise to the Land of Spice, no passengers, no doctor, an almost phantom crew) and rendezvous with Ratto's burlap lineup, many bags-full of edible pearls.

Then, outside the beanery, it's fun to knock resolutely on the verticals of vintage buildings in ornamental iron — Oakland's Old Town is almost a Tribeca West — and listen to the response, a certain hollow *t-h-u-d* or *k-l-u-n-k* that "sings" to the inquiring fists of architectural historians, the one, for instance, that I've shared a Victorian with for many years.

After knocking about for a while it's home on the bow, dancing spray in the face, the scenery positively Mediterranean, as if those Marin hills looming over the fabled hot tubs were mimicking the Azure Coast where so many inspirations for California Cuisine were hatched. I am not in this rumination traveling on one of the grand old ferry boats of my San Francisco youth, miniature Mauretanias complete with at least a single funnel and lunch rooms serving if I remember right good pub food and beer, but the puny vessels of 2001 will do.

> Place 1-1/4 cups of **cannellini or Great Northern beans** in a saucepan, add water to cover, bring the beans to a boil, cook them 1 minute, remove them from the heat and soak for an hour, then drain them. Now gently boil the beans in fresh water, covered, for an hour or more (or you could use beans left over from a hot dish), then cool them.
> Combine your beans with 2 large diced **tomatoes** and 20 or 30 small cooked cubes of **slab or thick cut bacon or pancetta**. Toss with a dressing of 2 parts **olive oil** to 1 part **red wine vinegar** with perhaps a dozen **large capers** and some chopped **parsley,** and a little minced **onion** as well.
> ATTENTION SYBARITES! Lightly dressed, this salad may also be put to work as a bed for pan-fried salmon accompanied by dollops of mayonnaise happily invaded by a light squirt of garlic along with a drop or so of lemon juice. Ah, we're not in gastronomical Kansas anymore, the Franks & Beans of blue collared yesteryear have given way to a haricotal up-marketing scarcely imaginable in more innocent times.

WARM CABBAGE SLAW WITH GOAT CHEESE AND PECANS

Almost a red Caesar, this was one of Jeremiah Tower's famous concoctions in the swinging salad years of his flagship San Francisco restaurant, a slaw he admitted doing differently every time. The jury computing the legacy of this impossibly monarchical man-about-kitchens — melted butter running down a diner's wrists was his Henry the Eighthly notion of a blissful experience — is presently out. Me, I think he was the most interesting American chef of the 80s, cutting edge enough you might bleed almost on some of his ideas. Whenever I suggest bookending a fish or meat with salsa AND aioli, it's thanks to JT's influence. Recently I chanced to participate in a sybaritic summer evening barbecue high on Sonoma Mountain, that Cal-Provence nirvana, and lo, it felt like basking inside a mellow photo spread across a pair of handsome pages in a towering Tower cookbook, written of course by the inventor of Pleasure.

I suspect my mother with her pantry-full of cookbooks and crusading culinary spirit might have jumped on the Jeremiahan bandwagon for a while. She would, I know, have considered him a prima donna, but she enjoyed creative people practicing their profession on the edge of a limb with scant concern about doubters ready to saw it off.

> Halve, core and comprehensively chop a small **red cabbage** and toss the shreds in a bowl in 2-plus tablespoons of **red wine vinegar,** plus some **pepper**. Also fry little oblongs of **slab or thick cut bacon** (a dozen per person) in a large skillet and crumble 4 tablespoons of **walnuts.**
> Now in the remaining fat from frying the bacon toss the cabbage, bacon and walnuts for

at least 3 minutes. Serve your slaw surrounded by large **garlic**-topped **croutons** with a 2 oz. pillow of **goat cheese** in the center of each portion — to make the croutons, preferably prior to the above 3 minutes, slowly sauté **French bread** rectangles with a little **butter** in a non-stick pan; for the topping use pressed garlic.

ZUCCHINI SLAW WITH AVOCADO BELLE DONNE

And this velvety slaw is the latest thing from Florence, from a trattoria scarcely more than 10' by 10'.

Simply grate several trimmed **zucchini** and immediately before serving dress with a little **olive oil**, **lemon juice** and **pepper**; top with **avocado** slices. And our nomination for partner is thin slices of pistachio-dotted mortadella.

Postscript at the Drake:

Salads should always be served on plates large enough to gracefully accommodate the assembled ingredients. I remember poking nervously at a delicious salad in the Drake Hotel in Chicago because the plate was so tiny the feet of the lettuce leaves, so to speak, were dangling over the edge, creating on the diner's part a certain Sisyphean frustration while the traffic sloshed by on Upper Michigan Ave. Of course that was thirty years ago, these days margins are generally treated with respect, the great gods of trend-setting have shot us into the era of plates (or multi-purpose bowls for that matter, and usually large ones) as painter's canvas.

The chances are now exceedingly good your salad, stew or crisp will be counterpointed with micro-acres of "negative space" worthy of one of 57th Street's best: for every forest of food there will be a circling meadow of s-p-a-c-e to keep the gustatory attraction du jour in focus. Or, to change the image, there'll be room for tasty rubble tumbling from a nervous Vesuvius of an "architectural" plat du jour deconstructing under your fork: I'm reminded of a recently enjoyed timbale of fresh anchovies that unrolled upon contact with cutlery as if they were descending a Guggenheim Museum ramp. And this principle of centripetal styling may easily be applied at home where it's so much fun to play Restaurant, the grownup equivalent of the classic lemonade stand or lining up Mom's cans of tuna and Campbell's soup as we did at the age of six and charging for them too.

. . . I must also call your attention to Cousin Tom's "Anything Goes" Citrus Vinaigrette, excellent with a chef's, fruit or Périgourdine salad, which seemed tailor-made for a patio lunch "au bord d'un lagoon" at Newport Beach with power boats all about but should be exportable to less tropical venues: combine 1) olive oil, 2) a mix of balsamic, raspberry and red wine vinegars, 3) grapefruit juice, a little sugar and a good heap of Dijon mustard. Play with this one . . . AND: lately I've been adding a short teaspoon of "Asian tamarind sauce" to olive oil/red wine vinegar dressings — plus baby helpings of oregano and ginger. Makes them throb! A charmoula-type dressing is interesting too: olive oil, lemon, garlic, parsley, and almost enough paprika to immobilize a Hungarian.

—SIMPLER VEGETABLES—

(suggested as main course material, followed by salad or cheese
— whichever is appropriate — and dessert)

ASPARAGUS ALLA PARMIGIANA

Even with this classic quickie there are disagreements: do you, for instance, belong to the "browned butter" school or the "unbrowned"? I am a fervent member of the Browns. And while I break off the tough stalk ends only a raging masochist would leave on, I find all the trimming and peeling prescribed in many excellent Italian cookbooks a total waste of time. As for the prevalent notion of lining up your asparagus head to toe, that suggests the reclining inhabitants of an over-populated flophouse. I must also record here my preference for stalks of at least moderate girth. Thistley specimens need not apply, their taste is too elusive, unsavorable. My chief dining companion of the last forty-three years will tell you I like all my food "large" (toothsome Schwarzeneggerian strawberries, for instance), but that would be grossly unfair.

> Steam a good dozen **asparagus** stalks per person for main course eating. Place the stalks on an oval serving platter, hide them (almost) under a blanket of grated **dry jack or parmesan cheese** and pour over it enough browned **butter** to somewhat melt the cheese. Serve with a generous supply of **lemon** wedges.
>
> Cooking time? I recommend steaming your asparagus until the stalks are still an attractive green but no longer chewy. A delicate balance, of course, rather like that confronting airplane pilots who want to land on the last yard of bayside runway and not in the drink. That zealous advocate of grey food, Jane Austen's Mr. Woodhouse, obviously wouldn't get it. And fiction, I'm afraid, is full of characters so busy sleuthing, seducing, philosophizing, contemplating their psychic navels, they have scant time left for a really interesting plate of food.
>
> Flaubert, of course, could conjure a feast, a feast of comically hyperbolic proportions, and Dickens could wax interestingly on the subject of "apoplectic opulence"; elsewhere among the masters we're often left with literarily and gastronomically lo-fat crumbs. Meanwhile there's writing about bad food that's so vivid in its suggestiveness you even

enjoy the thought of that badness, as in the "meat loaf and mashed potatoes and brown Betty at the Faculty club" (lucky we don't have to eat it) in an Edmund White short story.

ASPARAGUS, EGG VINAIGRETTE

... And leftover saffron mayonnaise (page 59) will work very nicely with asparagus as well as the vinaigrette of the title above.

Steam **asparagus stalks** and cool; dress them with our standard mustard vinaigrette (page 1) combined with mashed hard boiled **egg** and minced **parsley** in rather liberal amounts: 1 egg would be sufficient for 2 servings. I would also tend to intensify the mustard element: in other words, more than 1/4 teaspoon is indicated. Remember, asparagus and mustard go in for heady assignations.
And note as well that the haunting combination of chopped cilantro and fresh tarragon is an impressive substitute for the parsley above.

STRING BEANS AND PINOLI, VINAIGRETTE

This is for nights when "I'm too tired to cook," "I'm too fat" or "I can't stand food any more," only it's much tastier than such deleted expletives suggest.

Steam about 1 pound of **Blue Lake or Kentucky Wonder string beans** and cool. Then toast 2 or maybe 3 tablespoons of **pine nuts** (this amounts to shaking them for a minute or more in a small skillet), mix with the beans and serve beans-and-nuts with our regulation **mustard vinaigrette** (page 1) dotted with minced **parsley** and perhaps a little minced onion.

BROCCOLI OR ITALIAN BEANS LUPO VINAIGRETTE

The adjacent dressing is a slight variation on a lemony lubricant I've been lapping up at Lupo's, now Tommaso's, a checkered-tablecloth trattoria in San Francisco's North Beach, for forty years at least. The near-anachronistic Lupo's, I mean Tommaso's, is the sort of restaurant — with Bay of Naples mural, candles in Chianti flasks, other presudo Campanian knicknackery — that belongs in an old Capra comedy with Jimmy Stewart stutttering over his spaghetti and maybe Mischa Auer a pirouetting waiter. Almost lost amidst a flock of distinctly un-Capran topless bars, Code-clueless, Tommaso's recently asserted its identity with handsome new signage in tune with the gastronomical revival sweeping a sleaze-troubled corner of the Beach. To think that two generations ago this was the only pizza-serving restaurant in a city of 700,000 bon vivants white- or blue-collared. Obviously a case of stunted culinary evolution. To think, also, that back in the 70s our teenage son was mastermind of the sound system at the disco across the street.

By the way, the flat Italian mega-beans perform well in a Niçoise salad. Their season, alas, is compressed and unpredictable, as if the god of Absolutely Unboring Vegetables were hoarding them for his or her own dining terrace in the sky. And prices vary like those for the techiest sort of stock.

> Now be advised that "Italian beans" are sometimes called Roma beans in this country — and in a market in Ferrara, Italy I recently saw them under the hat of "Spanish beans."
> So: trim **broccoli or Italian beans** of whatever "nationality" appropriately — I, for one, like to eat as much broccoli stem as possible (I favor laying out the stems in plain view, but my mother back in the Georgian 40s used to chop them up and bury 'em, more as sin than treasure, in the brush) — then steam your veg and cool. Dress them with our good friend Lupo Vinaigrette: add to 2-plus parts **olive oil** 1 part combined **red wine vinegar** and **lemon juice** in approximately equal amounts, plus a liberal squeeze of pressed **garlic** and a light sprinkle of **oregano** and **rosemary**.
> VARIATION: For a little added snap I sometimes subdivide the olive oil element in this vinaigrette, using, say, 1/3 "extra virgin" to 2/3 "pure."

CHARD SAUTÉ WITH GARLIC AND LEMON

Rather a downer at first. The washing is a chore, then in the pot the chard shrinks as if it would escape you altogether. But snatched in time and given the "aglio e olio" treatment it can please the soul, and the next day it makes a nice bit of cold antipasto. Chard sauté was always our starter at Little Italy, a soulful Noe Valley trattoria of the 80s and 90s where one achieved a kind of ecstasy crowded together in its smash of diagonally jousting tables, waitpersons retrieving dishes with the help of hands braced efficiently on enchanted diners' backs: this was the Room of the Great Reach.

And how I hate to write that in the past tense (even as the Little Italy space seems to be being turned into something simpatico). Obituaries of restaurants are frequently painful, the likelihood being you've lost a place where you *enjoy* life. Even changes in management can be highly traumatic. I was scarcely a teenager, I remember, when Pierre's, my parents' favorite San Francisco restaurant, evolved, if that's the word, into Camille's and no longer seemed as good; perhaps we were too sensitive to even the slightest deviation from the weekly norm. That was a relatively mild case. Once in Rome, wife and I returned to a much-prized trattoria only to find that, while the place was physically the same, with a fairly similar menu, spiritually it had curled up and died a thousand deaths. We made the mistake of asking the padrone, obviously a new one, if the management had changed. Never again, because such a question is exceedingly likely to result in protestations of Continuity unsubstantiated by the clear view of a door through which the soul of the original restaurant fled.

> Wash 1 to 1-1/2 bundles of **chard** per person and cut off the white stems (or cook them separately). Drain the leaves, chop them and cook 'em in a large pot without additional water until they're somewhat past raw, then transfer them to a skillet in

which you've lightly browned 10 or so thin discs of **garlic** per person in several tablespoons of **olive oil**. Toss the chard with the garlic for a minute or so, adding more olive oil if it's too dry, and a very healthy splash of **red wine vinegar** for pizazz — we call this stage "Little Joe-ing" because this is how they finish vegetables at that old faithful North Beach cheaperia.

Serve with a good supply of lemon wedges: I cannot italicize enough the fact this dish's life support system is based on the acidic element.

BRUSSELS SPROUTS, PINOLI AND BACON

Stepchildren, these. They don't appear at all in *The Greens Cookbook* and I can find no sprouts in the whole oeuvre of my dear Elizabeth David. Well, to a foodie Brit they would be the veg of infamy, messenger of the great dowdy kitchen GREY of yore. Mrs. David, who was, it seems, something of a femme fatale as well as a gastronomical pioneer storming through the enemy territory of her own country, was a woman of very strong opinions; I don't think it would have been politic to ask her what she thought of the vegetable under discussion here. Well, they do need a little help — else they might emerge as the "limp discolored pygmy cabbage" M.F.K. Fisher, a good friend of the lowly sprout, often encountered (and I seem to remember such from an ill-advised visit to the Nowhere of a Bloomsbury hash house a bit down from Russell Square). I think I can safely say that, adorned as here, they make quite good — that *quite* is very English! — entertainment for the palate.

An alternative: steam your sprouts, bisect them, roll 'em in olive oil and breadcrumbs, then bake for 30 minutes, turning them once and adding capers.

Trim the stems of 12 to 15 washed **Brussels sprouts** per person, cut an X in them so the sprouts cook evenly, then steam the veg until they're softish but still a lively color. Now toast several tablespoons of **pine nuts** (shake them for a minute or more in a small skillet) and fry about 10 little oblongs of **thick cut or slab bacon** per person. Combine the sprouts with the pine nuts, bacon, and **butter** accented with **marjoram**. AND: You could, of course, bury your sprouts-nuts-bacon in a well-cheesed risotto (see our risotto chapter); in that case you'd want to chop the veg — and sprouto-phobes wouldn't know what hit them, the combination is so harmonious and pleasant.

BAKED POTATOES (WHITE OR SWEET) WITH A GARLIC HERB BUTTER

I remember, many years ago in Paris, being startled but delighted that the little Alsatian restaurant we were lunching in near the Opéra Comique served mashed potatoes as a separate course, after our cold roast and mayonnaise. In the same spirit, but without carnivoral overture, we offer a vegetarian solo by the adjacent butter-bathed potatoes taking a well-deserved place in the sun.

Scrub and skewer 1 large **potato** per person and bake at 400° for about an hour, at which point I usually squeeze them a little to see if they "give."

Open each potato and squeeze thereon pressed **garlic** to taste (but more is better than less), then sprinkle them with **dill weed** and **tarragon** and pour some browned **butter** over the garlic-and-herb mix, spreading the combined ingredients over the full opened surface.

Serve your potatoes "in solemn state" as my mother used to say, on rather large plates.

CORN ON THE COB, IN SEASON, À LA JIMMY

The idea of corn on the cob as a solo course we got from a poolside lunch at our friend Jimmy Schwabacher's under that up-market Carmel Valley sky. That was some time back, but not as long ago as the 30s when I remember traveling "up the valley" with my parents (could I have been in the rumble seat of the green '37 Chevy?) to buy corn at thirty cents a dozen, the price from outer space. Jimmy served us three ears each and I would say two are the minimum — with nothing else on a big plate. He was right, of course: corn on the cob does need one's undivided attention. Wasn't there an old cartoon showing a diligent canine gastronome working his way across the kernel keyboard until the bell rings?

And as for that expression to serve a vegetable "in state," I can trace it back another generation. My Zeisler Bloomfield grandmother, an expert, by the way, in the art of seven layer cakes — and she had a diploma in piano from the Vienna Conservatoire, signed by Hellmesberger himself — was writing home from Algiers in 1905 where she'd accompanied her Sanskritologist husband to a conference of "Orientalists," and the dinner she reports on from the garden-surrounded Beau Séjour Hotel positioned a nice helping of spinach exactly thus. But one didn't dine on spinach alone in old Algiers, there was soup, fish, chicken and artichokes, mutton and lettuce salad, hot baked apples, figs, nuts and raisins.

Back at 861 Park in Baltimore, my father and aunt read that this meal was "rather well cooked."

My grandmother, perhaps for her sanity, only played her Steinway at holiday parties on Park Avenue. Concertizing she left to her assorted cousins including the one who was known as the Jupiter of the Octaves and scared the cook with his budding keyboard genius — I'm sure he was a little stuck up as well.

Her letters from the field were a little bossy when my teenage father with his head in the clouds needed to be reminded about some prosaic duty, probably monetary, but the warmth in them is unmistakeable. They unroll a Time Machine tapestry of travel in the age before airborne cattle cars came into vogue; the inconveniences in 1905, except for what one sea captain called "that confused ocean," were simply different.

Read here about the market in Gibraltar with its profusion of flowers and fruits along with "live chickens and doubtful looking eggs," potato races and three-legged races on board the Dominion liner crossing the Mediterranean (I don't think this was a "Love Boat"), "noise and fleas" in Bologna (bad luck, I suspect) and only delight in Venice . . .

> Steam your allotment of ears of **corn** with a pinch of **sugar** for about 10 minutes and serve with a crock of **butter** and no frills.

BAKED VEGETABLES JULIE
—with assorted toppings—

The verduran building blocks of this misto cry out for interesting placement on your diners' plates. The architectural challenge will be a little greater if you borrow some Japanese eggplant, sans vinaigrette, from the recipe after this one . . .

Vegetables, excellent ones, gorgeous ones, prima donnas of the boutique farms, we investigate them every Saturday in San Francisco at the Embarcadero farmers' market, the "yuppie market" as it's called to distinguish it from the Wednesday do favored by the babushka set over behind the Orpheum, on the border of Civic Center's Beaux Arts splendor and the land of the Homeless. Theatrical rainbows of peppers, exquisite string beans, tomatoes good enough to eat rather than use for some sort of target practice, this is the lineup — but the Embarcadero market is more than p.c. eats, it's the place where my life seems to unroll like some ambulatory alumni magazine. Here one meets everyone, old flames next to new potatoes, colleagues from abandoned careers, a lost friend to remind me of an ancient indiscretion. A famous film critic will be there, cookbook people galore, and at 9 a.m. there's Maestro Michael Tilson Thomas holding court outside the local coffee house, conducting perhaps with a breadstick.

> Halve lengthwise some **crookneck squash, summer squash** and **zucchini**, sculpt as you wish a **carrot** and a bulb of **fennel,** and julienne some **sweet red pepper**. Put all in a single layer on a cookie sheet and top with a few tablespoons of **olive oil** and a sprinkle of your favorite **herbs**. Then bake in a moderate oven for about 40 minutes.
>
> That is the basic recipe. At serving time I like to single out some of the yellow squash for spreading with a mixture of **Dijon mustard** and **bread crumbs**, and spoon a simple **vinaigrette** with finely chopped **anchovy** over the zucchini and fennel or more of your vegeto-rama. Another useful topping is a "syrup" of sliced onions sautéed with olive oil, capers and balsamic vinegar.

ROASTED JAPANESE EGGPLANT VINAIGRETTE
—or with Vegetable Cassoulet—

Meanwhile, yuppies and babushkas alike might find useful notions here . . .

> Halve lengthwise and bake cut side down 2 **Japanese eggplants** per person with a little **olive oil** at high heat for about 40 minutes, until they're crinkly outside and

reasonably soft inside. Some halves, of course, in their recalcitrant serpentine attitudes will refuse to lie flat, so cut them amidships. Cool, and spoon over the eggplants a bit of **Lupo vinaigrette** (see page 19).

NOTE: You can combine these mini-bananas with roasted **sweet peppers** (page 34), and with or without this addition you could translate them from a main course dish to an antipasto misto component.

OR: Lay your eggplants over mini-cassoulet (page 162) minus the sausages. Or — recent brainstorm! — lay them over pasta sauced with a pesto in which you substitute watercress for basil; in this case, somewhat up the lemon content in the pesto (see page 70).

FAVA BEAN AND PANCETTA RAGOÛT

And with this recipe you'll be in step with the increasing population of fava bean eaters, also the new fans of pancetta, Italy's unsmoked bacon available in most good delicatessens. But you must love those fava beans because they're demanding critters, shelling and peeling them will take forever. Of course you can always take a ringside seat for Jim Lehrer while you're slaving, or pop a Mahler symphony into that microwave in your hi fi corner. Seriously, though, you can match cooking times to favorite recordings: two rather large chicken breasts will emerge from their pot of boiling water in perfect condition having marched to their destination neck and neck with Hans Knappertsbusch's Vienna recording of Brahms' Tragic Overture. Baked yams of perfect squishyness equal an average tempo'd Shostakovich Fifth, and lamb shanks, I'd say, will win you stars if matched to an uncut second act of *Die Walkuere*.

Pinoli toasting in a little pan might, however, outrun Chopin's Minute Waltz, which usually takes closer to two.

Shell 2 pounds of **fava beans** and blanch them for about 5 minutes in boiling water; then drain them and when they're cool enough to handle peel the tough outer skin (although some fava bean eaters don't mind it).

In a skillet fry a dozen or so little oblongs of **pancetta or slab bacon**, adding after a couple of minutes half a small chopped **onion** for softening in a bit of **olive oil**. When the bacon is virtually done add a tablespoon of **tomato paste** diluted with 1-1/2 cups of **dry vermouth** and simmer all for 2 or 3 minutes, until some of the liquid evaporates.

Now add the beans, 2 minced **garlic** cloves and some chopped **parsley** and warm your ragoût, with the skillet covered, for 5 or 6 minutes — except that if your favas happen to be senior citizens they'll take considerably longer to soften sufficiently for a good dining experience. Serve the finished product over **French bread** toasts.

ALTERNATIVE: You could reduce the bacon content or eliminate it altogether and frame the tomato'd fave with Italian sausages, even puréeing the beans, adding milk as for mashed potatoes . . . another option is Two Bean Salad: simply mix some shelled, peeled, steamed favas with the string beans and pine nuts of the vinaigrette several recipes back (page 18).

STEAMED CABBAGE AND CHARD WITH SCALLION

This may be what they serve at the gates of vegetarian heaven. A raid on the leftovers bin has rarely produced a more satisfying mélange of green.

Steam half a small sliced **cabbage** and a bunch of **chard**, washed and trimmed but not necessarily cut up. Top the veg with 1 thickly sliced **scallion** and toss with **olive oil** to taste.

Portrait of a Hotel:

It's common, of course, for people to fall in love "across a crowded room." I fell in love with a hotel looking out a train window: passing through Brive-la-Gaillarde, that pleasant market town between Limoges and Cahors, I was drawn, across the way, to a Late Victorian hotel facing the station, four or five stories, a bit ornate, friendly looking and solid in more than the pure engineering sense. I made a note of it, as the telephone informationist recommends when giving you a number. And eight years later, one 10 p.m., I came to know the Grand Hotel Terminus' birdcage elevator, its varnished halls, creaking armoires, bathtubs long as a yacht if not as sleek; and there was the resident cat to join us for breakfast.

Several visits indicated that the Terminus had few clients, and the formal dining room, once proud I'm sure, stood empty at the lunch and dinner hours. Soon the Michelin guide, requiring gleamier, less Titanical tubs, dropped the Terminus as if it were some eccentric aunt not welcome in the parlor. But the hotel continued to answer my requests for a room, assuring us the "calme" we enjoyed in room 16 which overlooked the garden and was assigned to us "comme d'habitude." One year the dining room even echoed to a meeting of hearty locals, Rotary members perhaps; they lunched on good roast veal because the aroma of its juices shot up to our little balcony where we were picnicking on a robust Cantal from the nearest fromagerie (just down a bucolic lane) and looking off to Auvergne, or its environs, in the East. It's ten years now since we included Brive in an itinerary, and I pray that the Terminus with its lovable anachronisms and pianissimo corridors and *Monsieur le Chat* and the voice of the station announcer across the way has not been, well, terminated. Who cares about governments falling?

Let's see, is that number 011-33-5-55-74-21-14?

—*PLATS DU JOUR*—

*— Remember that unless otherwise noted, recipes are for
two generous or three light servings —*

TROUFFADE AUVERGNATE
—potato cake from Central France—

    Auvergne is one of our favorite parts of France, a volcanic area with austere but charming hill towns, idyllic pastureland, six three-star Romanesque churches, scarcely more American tourists, and a rugged cuisine to be sampled by its sloping meadows and hastening brooks. The Auvergnats like to eat near-Germanic things like the stuffed cabbage we had at Madame Komorek's period-piece hotel, teetering, almost, at the slippery-looking top of St-Flour. She also served a meat tart that seemed like France's answer to piroshki. Trouffade, potatoes-and-cheese in one texture or another, is a signature dish of Auvergne, a cake of fried potato slices as our recipe has it. At a Shangri-La like the Remparts in lovely little Salers with its pocket gem of a Grande Place Trouffade was course two in a five act meal, the banquet du jour. In our scheme of things it makes a fine main event, accompanied perhaps by a simple salad, with a light dessert to follow.
    Life at the Remparts one April also meant breakfast with lengths of fresh warm baguette, candy-like sweet butter and juicy homemade strawberry jam. The sun shone, the cows were in position, the Austrian honeymooners not up yet, and there'd be good Cantal at the store: all was right in one of the world's most private corners.

    In a skillet cook 1/2 cup of diced **slab or thick cut bacon,** then remove it with a slotted spoon and reserve. Pour off and reserve all but 2 teaspoons of the bacon fat.
    Now begin slicing thinly 1-1/2 pounds of **potatoes** and spread a single layer of them in the skillet. Cook them gently, without stirring, until they're browned on one side. With a spatula gently lift the potatoes on one side of the skillet onto the potatoes on the

other half. Slice more potatoes and place a single layer to cook in the vacated space. Now turn the cooked slices over onto the uncooked ones, and place another single layer in the vacated space. (I know this sounds like "Who's on first?")

Repeat this process until all the potatoes are cooked, adding a little of the reserved bacon fat every so often. Before the last turn and addition of potatoes sprinkle on the cooked bacon and with a deft hand mix it in. When all the potato slices are cooked, carefully turn and redistribute them into an even layer.

Finally, sprinkle over all: 1/4 pound of diced **Cantal cheese or** coarsely grated **gruyère**. Turn the heat down, cover your skillet and cook the trouffade 10 to 15 minutes longer, until it's crisp and brown. Invert onto a warm platter and serve.

BÛCHERON POTATOES
—and a circle of vinaigrette—

A "New American" chef with a bit of France in his soul might come up with the attendant recipe, someone like that culinary Albee named Jeremiah Tower. Ah, Bûcheron, one's reminded of those straw-paved platters of cheeses fueling the citizens of one French republic after another through the years, not to speak of ardent visitors to Androuetian shores. Cheeses firm and mooshy, austere and hedonistic, clean-shaven and peppered specimens, Camemberts tasting like wine in a new dimension, Roqueforts that have made strong men cry *Mon Dieu*! There they were, and sometimes are . . . Globalization, alas, may be making inroads: it's no longer the case in Paris, Lyon or Marseille that waiters taking away your main course plates will automatically ask that vital question, "un peu de fromage? . . . "

Boil 3 or 4 good-sized **red potatoes** in water-to-cover with several peeled **garlic** cloves. Meanwhile in a saucepan combine 1/2 stick of **butter**, 1/2 cup of **cream** and 1/2 cup of a characterful **goat cheese** and stir over low to medium heat until the mixture is just melted and smooth, a lumpless wonder.

Using whatever kitchen and nature-given equipment seems right, mash the potatoes, along with the possibly vanished garlic cloves, whisking into them the cheese mixture with a little **nutmeg** — 2 turns, say, of the nutmeg mill. Transfer the mash to a shallow flameproof baking dish and broil it about 2 inches from your heat source for about 8 minutes, until the top is golden crisp.

Spoon your potatoes onto plates and serve them ringed with a vinaigrette of roughly 2 parts **olive oil** to 1 of **red wine vinegar**, dotted with diced **tomato or pitted black olives**.

OR: You could serve these potatoes on a bed of rather lightly vinaigretted watercress surrounded by smallish, candy-like pieces of mostarda di frutta (from an Italian delicatessen) arranged, more or less, like numbers on a clock face — but don't feel obliged to stop at a dozen.

PROSCIUTTO-WRAPPED ASPARAGUS WITH TWO SAUCES

I had an old recipe lying about for prosciutto-wrapped asparagus with Béchamel, its provenance wrapped in mystery. Tasty, I remembered, but a shade rich, so the tomato sauce in the adjacent lineup has been applied to maximize the vegetable element. A little red chasing white makes for a pretty dish, too. The ovenproof platter I envision is a silvery oval, the sort on which an oldtime tuxedoed waiter would bring a pile of baby lamb chops decorated with cress or wine-soused filet of sole surrounded by an elegantly fluted ring of mashed potatoes — potatoes converted to royalty! Peering further into the past, I see the great *salle* of San Francisco's Bardelli's where, a young newspaper reporter, I tried not to spill that sole on my notebook while interviewing, over a martini-lubricated lunch, the latest film *vedette* to hit town.

The other and even gorgeouser venue for our amiable grillings of visiting celebs was the landmark Garden Court at the Palace Hotel (we never said Sheraton-Palace, being sentimental anti-corporate San Franciscans in our twenties and thirties who didn't want to be banished to Goleta for a gaffe), a grand and leafery-punctuated space flooded with light, or a little less light when a cloud passed over its glass roof: it was as if the lighting were on some Providential rheostat.

It was in the Garden Court, our table near one of those onyx pillars behind which some operatic conspirator bent on doing in royalty might lurk, that I asked the venerable tenor Tito Schipa for his autograph. A bit remote but courtly, he affixed his name to an old photo of a Marin County garden party at which he and the baritone Stracciari, dressed in Brioni suits and boxing gloves, engaged in some jokey sparring while Two Other Great Tenors, Cortis and Ansseau, looked on. Alas, the menu of their lunch, with bootleg Cabernet of course, remains a mystery. It was September, not asparagus season, but late peaches maybe, or lovely figs . . . And probably there was barbecued chicken, fussed over by a burly retainer . . .

- Trim and steam asparagus stalks and wrap bundles of them with thinly-sliced **prosciutto**; place them on an ovenproof platter. Now drizzle the bundles with Sauce #1, a light **Béchamel** made as follows: melt 2 tablespoons of **butter**, blend in 3 teaspoons of **flour** and stir until golden; gradually add 1/3 cup of **chicken broth** and 7/8 cup of **milk**, plus a little **nutmeg** and grated **dry jack or parmesan cheese**, and stir constantly until the sauce just begins to thicken.
- Then, in a design counterpoint with #1, to create a bi-colored lattice effect, drizzle a little Sauce #2, a simple onion-less Tomato Sauce made by simmering canned **tomatoes** with a little **sugar** and a pressed clove of **garlic** — this could be tomato sauce left over from a meatloaf dinner.
- Using a brush, oil the asparagus bundles at both ends so they don't dry out, and bake them at 350° for 10 minutes. Just before serving, top them with some grated **dry jack or parmesan cheese** and run 'em under the broiler until they're a little browned and crispy.

STUFFED GIANT (or somewhat smaller) ZUCCHINI EGYPTIAN

Inspired by the giant zucchini grown by Papa Louie Colombano, who also provides more green olives than we can keep up with and has a shiny 1915 Ford, the same age as he is. You can also use this recipe for stuffing and saucing green and/or red sweet peppers. An interesting extra is to roll the hull of whatever veg you choose in beaten egg, breadcrumbs and grated cheese before baking — for this touch we're indebted to Rose Zelalich, our daughters' beloved Tuesday afternoon nanny, a stout but sprightly veteran of the '06 quake. How Rose loved to take her charges downtown for Woolworth treats. And like an amiable clock that enjoyed striking sixteen or seventeen times she continued to arrive at our house on Tuesdays for many years after her nanny-ing talents were no longer needed.

I did not discourage her, because she always headed for the kitchen and proceeded to stir up a batch of three-star chocolate chip cookies. This Croatian Escoffier, we eventually discovered, had a tie-in to The Food World: her late husband had been "the salad man" at Sam's Grill downtown. I fervently hope that man got his cookie fix after a long stint over the greens.

- Cut your **zucchini** in halves lengthwise and make hollows for stuffing in each. Steam the zucchini halves to soften them somewhat and drain them for half an hour on a rack, skin side up: they are very watery devils.
- Now boil 3/4 of a cup of **rice**, sauté 1/2 pound of **ground lamb** with a little minced **onion** in a tablespoon or so of **olive oil** just until the meat loses its butcher's-counter pink, and in a small skillet toast 2 or 3 tablespoons of **pine nuts** for a minute or more.
- Combine the lamb, rice and pinoli with 3 tablespoons of **currants**, a little **lemon** zest, **rosemary**, **dill weed**, a pressed **garlic** clove, a bit of **cayenne**, 2 or 3 tablespoons of grated **dry jack or parmesan cheese**, and an **egg**, then stuff the zucchini with this mixture. Any left over stuffing can be parked next to the zucchini on a diner's plate faithful-dog style.
- Bake your stuffed zucchini — along with the leftover stuffing — in a moderate oven for about 25 minutes and serve them surrounded by our house **tomato sauce** (see page 69), into which you've stirred a tablespoon of **cinnamon**, and topped with a ladling of **yogurt**.

SAUSAGE-STUFFED TOMATOES À LA DUMAS

Alexandre Dumas' *Dictionary of Cuisine* is a witty and wonderful book, concise, irreverent, its author's tongue planted firmly in cheek, the prose perpetually on the verge of a guffaw. Listen to Dumas concerning turnips: "The first recipe that comes to hand is for turnips *à la d'Esclignac*. Whatever did M. d'Esclignac do to earn the honor of having a dish of turnips named for him! Nothing offers a more curious study, in this connection, than books written by cooks, and their strange fancy of saucing, grilling and roasting our great men. Here is what you will find under the heading of soups, for example:

Soup *à la Demidov, à la William Tell, à la Dumas* . . ." Some of this pen-flashing gourmet's recipes are a bit odd, like the Cream of Spinach made by mixing, sieving and baking a tablespoon of cooked spinach with 12 crushed sweet almonds, a little lime juice, 3 or 4 bitter almond biscuits, sugar, 2 glasses of cream, 1 glass of milk and 6 egg yolks. But many of them fall into the mainstream very nicely, for instance the light and zesty dish which Dumas calls Stuffed Tomatoes *à la Grimod* and we have re-christened. Dumas' recipe gives the outline of what needs to be done; we have filled in such minor details as ingredient amounts and baking time and come up with the following:

- Cut the tops from 2 large **tomatoes**, and pushing on their interiors with both thumbs make space in each for stuffing, removing the seeds and some of the juice meanwhile. Bake the tomatoes in a moderate oven for at least 10 minutes or so until they're quite soft (or if your tomatoes are truly ripe, skip this step).
- Meanwhile in a smallish skillet sauté a good 1/2 pound of **ground pork sausage** until it loses its raw look, adding a minute or so into the cooking 3 heaping tablespoons of chopped **scallion**, 2 tablespoons of minced **parsley**, 1 large pressed **garlic** clove and a sizeable tangle of **fresh tarragon**. Keep tossing: you'll be occupied thus for a couple of minutes.
- Then stuff the tomatoes with the seasoned (and drained!) sausage meat and bake them for another 15 or 20 minutes. Don't worry if some of the stuffing jumps overboard; you can still serve the dropout crumbles. Serve M. Dumas' tomatoes on cupped plates with a few decorative leaves of lettuce and a wedge of **lemon**: he suggests a light sprinkling of lemon juice.
- P.S.: I'm sure M. Dumas would approve of following his tomatoes — after you spoon up the spicy "tomato soup" in the bottom of your plate — with a simple salad of oakleaf lettuce in a Dijon mustard vinaigrette.

FOUR ONION GRATIN GARNI

The "Alfredo" of onions. Although offered as a headliner this creamy gratin could be used as sidekick to some pork chops. If you keep it in the dominant position — it's fairly rich — then add a little Toscano salami to the side. And by the way, a suspicion of browning in the sauté stage is entirely acceptable.

Now I must confess that truth in labeling requires me to tell you that "Alfredo" doesn't really mean cream in a dish: we have it in black and white from that delightful sage of all things gastronomical between Cherbourg and Catania, Waverley Root. The unvarnished facts of the matter are as follows: a fabulous Roman restaurateur named Alfredo became identified with a damn-the-cholesterolic-torpedos presentation of fettuccine so buttery — and there was lots of grated cheese, of course — that people figured there was cream involved and somehow it came to pass that Italo-American restaurants emptied their cream containers into the misto and the dish took flight on wings of dairy.

Then Spaghetti Carbonara was similarly embroidered, or corrupted.

Waverley Root, music critic/foreign correspondent/food historian/bon vivant, was one of my heroes. I modeled my San Francisco restaurant guide as best I could on his omniscient but unpretentious paperback about Paris dining, and I sent him a copy at his flat on Rue Cherche Midi. His response was original and beyond the call of graciousness. Rather than thanking me directly he simply persisted in listing my guide in the bibliographies of more than one of his many books. What a scandal that his obituary in a San Francisco newspaper appeared under a misspelling of his first name! But to the gratin . . .

In a large skillet in perhaps a tablespoon of **butter** soften over low-medium heat:

> 3/4 pound of small **white onions** (you can halve them if they seem too bulky — they'll take the longest time, so be sure to start them a little before their skillet-mates)
>
> 3 or 4 good-sized **leeks**, trimmed, washed and chopped
>
> 1 large **yellow onion** sliced thin
>
> 2 large minced **garlic** cloves

Stir into the softened onions 1 cup of **cream**, bring it to a boil and simmer until the cream just starts to thicken, season with **pepper** and **nutmeg** and stir in some minced **parsley** and a splash of **white wine**.

Spoon this mixture (along with some slices of boiled new potato if you wish) into a lightly buttered casserole, sprinkle with grated **dry jack or parmesan cheese** and bake at 375° for about 15 minutes.

GRILLED LEEKS (OR ASPARAGUS) WITH BACON AND CAPER CREAM

A sumptuous/piquant souvenir of the checkered first regime at the Boonville Hotel, oasis of gastronomy on the way to Mendocino in the gorgeously tawny and famously scorching Anderson Valley. The Berkeley-oriented chef fled raging creditors but the recipe remains. It does, I must say, benefit from adding lemon juice, a kind of mystical binding force. While leeks make a superb base for a sauce seductive as ten courtesans I need to tell you that asparagus is an excellent alternative: I know this because one night we happened to substitute nice tall stalks for lettuce in our post-grill vinaigrette and when the plate was set before me all I could think was, I don't want vinaigrette on this, I want more of that great Boonville sauce — with lemon added, of course. Another alternative is to add sautéed prawns to the leeks-in-sauce and serve all over pasta — penne, for instance.

Then you come very close to a dish I adore at one of my all-time favorite restaurants, the Rio Grill in Carmel: it's served to me annually by a jolly Brit of a waiter who remembers my dining obsessions with the ease of one of those continental concierges in cutaway and gold chain, someone like the Mr. Memory who filed me in his mystic system at Brussels' Atlanta Hotel in '52 and reminded me five years later of my previous visit. He must have seen me, a novice to continental ways, a veritable young Bean, wrestling a café filtre in his lobby: coffee everywhere and scarcely a drop to drink!

In this early stage of my Going Abroad I thought that coffee was always served with sugar pre-inserted, that sandwiches didn't exist on the continent, that every man on the street had a mistress, that the only kind of bed on offer between Calais and Istanbul was a double. It's a wonder I didn't think berets were issued by the government.

Trim and halve lengthwise half a dozen smallish **leeks**, clean them as well as the proverbial whistle and steam 'em until soft; then transfer them to your broiler, cut side up, and "grill" them for a few minutes until they're quite brown, even blackened a little. Concurrently fry in a skillet 20 to 25 thin oblongs of **slab or thick cut bacon or pancetta**. When these are getting crispy add 1 large pressed **garlic** clove, 3/4 cup of **cream**, 2 tablespoons of **capers** and a good 1/2 tablespoon of **lemon juice**; simmer very briefly until the sauce just begins to bubble.

Place the leeks (or asparagus, which you would simply trim and steam) on pretty plates and pour the cream sauce over them and sprinkle all with minced **parsley**.

TORTILLAS STUFFED WITH PIPÉRADE
—peppers-tomatoes-and-ham—

We didn't have tortillas with our delightfully mooshy Pipérade in St-Jean-Pied-du-Port, but a "Basque burrito" seems not at all outrageous. Our lunch at St-Jean, a cozy April day in '72, was one of those home-free meals capping a brush with adversity. Since Roncesvalles, a relatively de luxe stop on the old pilgrimage route to Compostela, was just over the border into Spain, we thought to have our midday gastronomic binge where Count Roland met his Waterloo. Well, we had a small Waterloo of our own. Perhaps it was only snobbishness on our part that the Spanish countryside looked scruffy, a kind of pastoral wastebasket. But the luggage-slamming customs men halfway up the valley made their East German counterparts look like teddy bears — perhaps they were put off by the Bordeaux plates on our rented Renault, that city being a headquarters for Basque separatists. Then, when we reached our destination, a village silent as eternity — or a comprehensive siesta of noon-a-phobes — all we could find was a forlorn inn presided over by the dourest of hosts, a minor figure out of Goya from whom even a bit of "attitude" might have been welcome. We quickly fled down the valley specked with garbage, and found our living heaven in St-Jean.

Mince 2 medium-sized **onions** and soften them in a tablespoon or more of **olive oil**; add a **green** and a **red sweet pepper**, roughly chopped, with a little more oil and cook 2 or 3 minutes. Stir into this mixture a rather finely chopped **tomato** with **thyme**, **pepper** and 1 large pressed **garlic** clove and simmer all for 30 minutes, covered, stirring occasionally.

Now heat 2 or 3 generous slices of very good quality **ham** (your local equivalent of Jambon de Bayonne would be first choice), 1/8 inch thick. Remove the vegetable mix from the fire and slowly pour in 3 lightly beaten **eggs**; return your developing pipérade to low heat and stir until creamy: this shouldn't take long.

Your last task is to place the ham on top of the vegetables, dot it with minced **parsley** and maneuver all onto steamed **flour tortillas** and roll them up. Proceed with knife and fork.

. . . And what you are eating is, in current quick-food parlance, a wrap — subject, of course, to the winds of change in burritan signage.

CAPONATA

A jack of numerous trades, this sweet-sour vegetable ragoût is good served alone, warm or cool, or as part of a festive antipasto misto selection, or a pasta sauce warmed up with some sliced Polish sausage, or as an accompaniment to (or bed for) lamb chops. This doesn't count Caponata Soup: do the first paragraph of the following recipe, then proceed with half as much tomato, a bit of cumin and pitted black olives, then after 20 minutes of simmering add 3/4 of a 49-ounce can of chicken broth and simmer your soup 10 minutes more before puréeing it in a blender or food processor.

In a large pan sauté in several tablespoons or more of **olive oil** 2 conventional-sized **zucchini**, thinly sliced (start with these, they'll take the longest time); 1 **eggplant**, diced; and 1 **sweet red pepper**, cut into thinnish strips. When these vegetables are almost soft add a sliced **onion** along with 1 or 2 pressed **garlic** cloves; toss all until these newcomers are soft.

Now over the vegetables pour 1 28-ounce can of **tomatoes**, simmer a little, then add a pinch of **thyme**, **nutmeg** (1 turn of the mill), 2 tablespoons at least of **pine nuts**, a small handful of **Niçoise olives** if you have them, and — the decisive flavoring factor here — about 1/3 cup of **red wine vinegar** with a heaping tablespoon of **sugar** dissolved therein. Simmer all, uncovered, for 25 to 35 minutes; cool a little if you're serving the caponata warm, or refrigerate and serve cold.

—24-hour—
EGGPLANT ANCHOVY TERRINE

Caponata elements are interestingly recycled in this meridional terrine. The amount of anchovies you include depends on how wild a gastronomic ride you want. Bear in mind Sicilian anchovies are considerably stronger than those central-casting Portuguese filets common in most markets.

First off, roast about 3 cups of **sweet peppers** (page 34). Then cut 1 **eggplant** into 1/4-inch slices, place these on a cookie sheet, brush them lightly with **olive oil** and broil them on both sides until they're lightly browned. Meanwhile in a small skillet lightly sauté 1/2 cup or so of **anchovies** (the salt-packed, trim-and- wash-requiring Sicilians are best) in a little olive oil: turn them over but don't break them up.

Now line the bottom and sides of a lightly oiled loaf pan with the eggplant slices. Place the glistening anchovies over the horizontal eggplant and top with some of the peppers, continuing upward with more eggplant and peppers. Bake all in a moderate oven for 35 minutes, cool, and refrigerate covered and weighted for 24 hours. Unmold and serve.

EGGPLANT PARMIGIANA OLD TRATTORIA STYLE

Sautéing eggplant does make one a little nervous: it eats up the olive oil like a very aggressive sponge. You remember the story about the new Arab wife who was sent home to mother because she exhausted her dowry of oil cooking a single eggplant. Well, persevere, dishes like Eggplant Parmigiana and Caponata are too good to banish from your rep.

Out of the same pot, so to speak, would be a particular batch of pointy sweet red peppers stuffed appealingly with meat, rice and onions and served to a dear friend in . . . Sofia, Bulgaria. I cannot claim myself to have visited this city with its lovely antique trams, cobblestoned and graffiti-free downtown, its odd mix of a charming poor man's Paris with something on the order of rural America lapping at its faded close-in margins. But our friend Juliana, having landed there thanks to a bus conductor spooning deliriously with his girl and forgetting to call out her intended destination considerably to the South, and a good monk adopting her with the call, "let us go eat with my friends, brothers in Christ," has graciously lent me her vignette.

The genteel taxi driver (female) who drove monk and charge to a dinner christened with milk-laced chicken soup was more business-like than the wayward busman.

- Slice a small **eggplant** into quite thin rounds — actually, for two diners a so-called "Italian eggplant" with its 1 or 1-1/2 inch diameter would fit the bill perfectly — and sprinkle them with a little salt; let them stand for an hour to get rid of any bitterness, then wipe them dry.
- Meanwhile, make our basic **tomato sauce** (page ???), listening to it burble reassuringly like a country brook — or maybe the allemande from Bach's fourth French Suite.
- Next step, sprinkle the eggplant slices with a little pressed **garlic** and brown them lightly in **olive oil** (yes, you'll need rather a lot before you're done), drain them on paper towels and place them on the bottom of an ovenproof serving dish, arranged, for instance, up and down the center of an oval-shaped vessel.
- This way you are setting up what will be a red carpet once the eggplant is topped in turn with:

    mozzarella cheese rounds of good quality

    tomato sauce

    grated **dry jack or parmesan cheese**
- Now bake your pagoda in a moderate oven for about 30 minutes, then run it under the broiler until the grated cheese browns a little.

AND: see page ??? for a robust relation, Veal and Eggplant Napoleon.

ANTIPASTO MISTO

The game of mix-and-match begins here. I propose a practical three or four item selection, but I treasure the memory of more elaborate productions sampled abroad, crowded buffet table symphonies on a Mahlerian scale and serial presentations that were almost bizarre.

Some years ago in Brussels we thought we were finished with the hors d'oeuvres after devouring a plateful of cold meats and pâtés, only to see the waiter advancing on us with a large selection of vinaigrettes and mayonnaisey things; and there was a third act as well, *before* the main course of chicken in cream. This reminds me of my son the computerist's experience while on business in Israel: he and three fellow diners were presented with a platter of six rather copious lamb chops, and then, after a pause, three similarly stocked chargers.

I think my favorite antipasto misto, absolutely manageable, was at a little trattoria in Turin, the Tre Galline — which was listed *last* in Michelin's extensive assortment of Torinese restaurants — and it ran as follows: vitello tonnato, anchovies in a salsa verde, carpaccio, mushrooms vinaigrette, fava beans, salade russe, red peppers with garlic gratiné, ricotta vinaigrette and hard boiled eggs mayonnaise. Perfect!

. . . Speaking of antipasto misto, I recall a lunch at the Osteria al Fico d'India in Palermo that began with a pleasant variation on that Tre Galline theme, a ham risotto seizing the chief laurels. How, I wonder, did we encompass the succeeding midday challenges, pasta con sarde, grilled mullet, peppered pecorino and fruit, a snifter of Sambuca. The best part of this meal was the company, the cast of a Mozart opera in rehearsal at the Teatro Massimo around the corner. I see by my diary that the basso buffo was balancing wine glasses (empty, I believe!) on the head of one of his colleagues, while a baritone/magician was making 100-lira notes disappear into some Mephistophelean vapor. This was not the sort of Sicilian entertainment proclaimed in Fodor or Frommer — but next day we did head out for that lone and not un-operatic temple at Segesta, climbing through gorgeously green meadows, rows of cherry and olive trees in alternation, donkey carts along the enchanted way painted like Renaissance palaces. And there was a picnic, of course: salami, cheese, bread with fennel seeds, olives, oranges.

Then we waited fifteen minutes at the crossing for the Trapani-Palermo local to show up, a small red toy in the landscape.

Essentially you want three different textures, that of cold meat, a mayonnaisy offering, and a vinaigrette — as in an ensemble of:
1. Mortadella or Coppa slices
2. Hard Boiled Eggs with Green Goddess Mayonnaise: commercial mayonnaise of good quality dotted with chopped anchovy filets, a little chopped onion, parsley and tarragon and lightened with a bit of lemon juice — also add 1 pressed garlic clove.
3. Roasted Sweet Peppers Tricolore: Dot short fat strips of **sweet pepper** (red, green and yellow) with discs of peeled **garlic**, apply several tablespoons of **olive oil** and roast at 400° for about 30 minutes, until a few black edges

develop; then stir in minced **parsley** . . . and you can if you wish combine these peppers with roasted Japanese eggplant (page 22).

Now you can work variations on the prescribed trinity, for instance as follows:

1. Retain the mortadella or coppa slices, plus some pâté and Mediterranean olives
2. Substitute for Eggs Mayonnaise:
    Vitello Tonnato à la Don (page 139)
    or Sliced cucumbers (marinated in salt, then drained) with Aveyron dressing, see page 12
    or Marcus' Potato Salad (page 48)
    or Smoked Trout, Basil Mayonnaise (chopped fresh basil in a 3 to 1 mayonnaise to Dijon mustard combination with a little lemon juice)
    or Lightly Vinaigretted Artichoke Bottoms and Potato (boiled with a little lemon juice, pressed garlic and white wine), served with Basil Mayonnaise
    or Vegetable Pudding XXIV December, served at room temperature (page 42)
    or Specifically to mate with the Mushroom Salad in the next section of our chart: Tomatoes stuffed with Sardines, Hard Boiled Egg and Pine Nuts in a Basil Mayonnaise
3. Substitute for Sweet Peppers:
    Caponata (page 32)
    or Bean Tomato Bacon Salad Caper Vinaigrette (page 15)
    or Raw (thinly sliced) Mushroom Salad with Olive Oil, Lemon Juice and Shaved Parmesan Cheese
    or Ricotta and Tomato Salad (page 11)
4. Plus the possible addition of:
    A wedge of Tarte à l'Oignon at room temperature (page 39)
    or Leftover Risotto of an appropriate sort (see risotto chapter) or Lentil Stew (page 147)

Another antipasto combination I can recommend is:

    Rice, Shrimp and Bacon Salad (page 1)

    Tomato halves, with vinaigrette

    Hummus   (Soak 1 cup of dried garbanzo beans overnight, drain them and cook until soft in water an inch above the beans, remove their skins and purée them with 1/4 cup of **olive oil**, the juice of a **lemon** and 1 pressed **garlic** clove.)

Or you can, in summer at least, scrap all the above and focus on our Home Picnic:

    Salami

    Fresh Figs

    Goat Cheese or Taleggio on Toasts

And there must be a place somewhere for prosciutto and kumquats marinated as on page 86.

CORN FRITTERS À L'ORANGE WITH BACON

A variation on a dish from childhood, served, if I remember right, with southern fried chicken (which is, of course teetering on the ropes of gastronomic rectitude these days). I must have thought a lot about this Sunday evening combo in my, so to speak, salad days.

What I know for sure is that, biscuit fetishist that I was, my favorite dream brought delivery of a plateful of inch-high orange rounds, fluffy and golden, a sugar lump pressed into the Rombauerian brow of each, with a saucer of marmalade waiting conveniently nearby. Alas, to get these objects of adoration safely into my mouth before alarm clock or auroran burst intervened was impossible.

My mother's chicken and fritters were frequently "on" during World War II when she ran a virtual USO at our house. My older sisters' uniformed beaux and their friends were much in evidence, romantic figures on leave, just like in the movies I'd see on Saturday afternoons at the old Fox or Paramount. But we were not, of course, in as much danger as Mrs. Miniver with the blitz overhead. Our Target for Tonight was likely to be from the poultry department.

- Drain 1 14-ounce can of **creamed corn** and whisk it in a mixing bowl with 2 **eggs**, 2 tablespoons of **flour**, 1 teaspoon of **baking powder**, a little **nutmeg** and the rind of 1/2 an **orange** cut into juliennes.
- Also fry some **bacon** to serve with the fritters.
- Now heat a skillet — or better, a griddle which aids maneuverability in fritter-flipping — until quite HOT. Add a thin film of bacon fat and spoon the batter onto the cooking surface of your choice in amounts to make fritters about 2 inches in diameter. Add more fat as the previous liquid is absorbed.

NOTE: A chutney is good with these fritters (see page 130).

CORN SOUFFLÉ PUDDING PETER PAN

At the age of twelve I ate something closely resembling this at the musty old Peter Pan Lodge up in Carmel Highlands (the Craftsman charmer burned down some years ago and only the foundation of its parlor eerily remains, overlooking a Pacific horizon), and I can still taste it, as if 1943 were the proverbial yesterday. The guestbook at Peter Pan — where the guests glided into the dining room at an Elysian tempo — was a Who's Who and you expected Somerset Maugham to drop in any time, or Ronald Colman, or maybe Charlie Chan. Well, Hitchcock had filmed *Rebecca* exteriors down by the naughty ocean not so long before. And in Carmel itself, director's chairs and tangles of Hollywood rigging were fairly standard summer features as I remember along Scenic Drive.

One August we rented a spectral stone house on Scenic, complete with cobwebby organ, that would have filled the bill for *Sunset Boulevard*. It's a wonder Erich von Stroheim didn't emerge from the woodwork to polish the silver.

> In a bowl beat 3 **eggs** well. Whisk in 1 tablespoon of **sugar**, 1 14-ounce can of **creamed corn**, 3 tablespoons of melted **butter**, 1/2 cup of **milk**, 3 tablespoons of **flour** and 2 teaspoons of **baking powder**. Pour this mixture into a buttered ovenproof dish and bake at 350° for 30 to 35 minutes, until it's puffed, golden, and comfortably beyond the soup stage.
> Serve your corn soufflé pudding alone, followed by a salad, or with ham or link sausages.

CHEESE SOUFFLÉ; SPINACH OR PESTO SOUFFLÉ

It took me years to get up the courage to attempt the folding in of egg whites required in the adjoining recipes — and to endure the awful suspense of "When will it be done? I can't see inside!" But now I have my invisible diploma, "stamped" by Mrs. Bloomfield my mentor in egg white matters. It might, of course, be withdrawn at any time. Any of the three confections here would make a perfect headliner for your lunch, supper or a light dinner at home, but consider as well playing "celebrity chef" and casting them as gastronomical character actors, so to speak, supporting prima donna lamb chops fried to your taste and bathed in white wine, a little tomato paste and herb of choice.

Cheese soufflés came into my life Sunday lunchtime back in pre-pubescence: this was correct 30s "luncheon" food of modest bulk. But what I remember most from those pre-Cambrian noon meals is that they sometimes coincided with a hot September day, windows open onto the garden, a small plane perhaps put-putting overhead, and my mother would bring in — Proustian download here — a fluted pitcher of warm tea heavy with large lemon halves and tinkling ice cubes. It's not that I was so "into" iced (or near-iced) tea; what resonates across the years is that the contents of that pitcher encapsulated all the fuzzy warmth of my totally protected life, my life as a spoiled proto-nerd ten years short of draft age.

Sundays in my protective bubble continued as my father tore himself away from his medical journals and drove me to the Embarcadero where I ogled the fancy white steamers poised for their glides to Honolulu and the pissing rusty freighters just in from Exotica. Then we hastened to the roundhouse at Mission Bay to study the gleaming orange steam engines resting between trips to L.A. And the climax, a chocolate sundae at Blum's, happy leitmotif of my gastronomical life!

Everyone went to Blum's: the conductor Erich Leinsdorf writes in his memoirs of meeting colleagues there after opera rehearsals, *Lohengrin* and such giving way to Lemon Krunch Cake, Coffee-esta Sundaes and items listed on the cutesy-pie bill of fare under the heading, "Gosh Awful Gooey."

. . . And back home my father would pop into his study to dash off an article on the order of "Variations in the bacterial flora of the upper air passages during the course of common colds."

Melt 4-plus tablespoons of **butter** and stir in almost 1/2 cup of **flour**; blend and cook a little. Then add 2 cups of **milk** and a little **salt**, whisk this "Béchamel" until it's a bit creamy, remove from the fire and cool. Next, separate 4 **eggs** and whisk the yolks into the milk mixture one at a time.

Now add 3/4 cup of grated **Swiss cheese** and a little grated **dry jack or parmesan cheese,** plus some snipped **chives**
> *or*

Add 1 box of frozen **chopped spinach**, thawed, drained and squeezed, and a generous grating of **dry jack or parmesan cheese**
> *or* (best of all!)

Add a good half cup of **pesto** (page 70) and the same generous grating of **dry jack or parmesan cheese**.

Beat the egg whites stiff and fold them in carefully. Then bake your soufflé of choice in an overproof dish lubricated with **canola oil** at 350° for 30–45 minutes, and pray.

TORTA DEL PASTORE TRENTINA

My chief Italian consultant delivered this tempting recipe with the title Soufflé di Patate, but it seems more like a Dolomitan version of shepherd's pie than a soufflé, hence our christening it Torta del Pastore — I almost wrote Torta di Pastore, which would have deposited an unwilling pastoral person in the pie. Typographical (or is it Macintosh?) murder does occur, of course: my favorite example is an oldtime *San Francisco Chronicle* compositor's "Cop au Vin."

Speaking of shepherd's pie: when I used to play hooky from my music critic's job in San Francisco to catch Wagner-in-English in snowbound London, there we'd be, sitting on stools at the bar in the Salisbury, the most gourmet pub in the theater district, fueling up on what my diary describes, with rare simplicity, as "divine meat pie." This is the true British cuisine — like the aromatic ham in cider we had at an inn out near Stonehenge, and those wonderful currant jelly and mint sauces — and long may it wave. Outside, one February, the Anglos were tossing snowballs in St. Martin's Lane when the pub-keeper called "Time, please!" And soon we'd be off to more opera in Stockholm, the BEA pilot mellifluously announcing, like some aeronautical Sir Ralph Richardson, "conditions for landing at Arlanda are quite reasonable this afternoon."

Another year a steep ascent in our social standing propelled us to the Savoy Grill where an old English friend mated us with a taciturn, while friendly enough, Kenneth Tynan, drama critic de luxe. The meal, for which I was not financially responsible, was Beef Wellington and Château d'Yquem, the latter lubricating a stiff occasion notably well. Inscrutable as a cat, Tynan did not overtly suggest the man Mary McCarthy was sure would spout a four-letter word on TV.

Boil 4 or 5 medium-sized **potatoes** and patiently/agressively mash them with the best your culinary Dept. of Defense has to offer, then, wielding a large wooden spoon in a copious mixing bowl, mix them with 1 beaten **egg** and 1/2 cup of **milk** (low fat, of course). The potatoes should now be VERY smooth.

Coat a deep ovenproof dish or large-ish ramekins with **butter** and **bread crumbs**, spread half the mashed potatoes on the bottom, top with a mixture of 1/4 pound of a **highly flavored ham**, thickly diced, and 1/4 pound of a **rather sharp white Italian cheese,** roughly diced, then spread the other half of the potatoes above the meat-and-cheese; sprinkle with a very liberal amount of grated **dry jack or parmesan cheese**, dot lightly with **butter** and bake at 350° for 20 minutes. Before serving — possibly with mostarda di frutta, or Mary Kelley's mango chutney (page 130) — run the torta under the broiler briefly for crisping.

VARIANTS: In the Marche region of Italy they do a cousin of this recipe with baby meatballs sandwiched between layers of sliced boiled potatoes with parmesan on top. In this case the beaten egg goes into construction of the meatballs, along with nutmeg and pepper . . . now if you string a bridge from Trento to the Marche you ought, I think, to be able to combine the baby meatballs of one region with the mashed-potato-cum-egg of the other.

TARTE À L'OIGNON PLACE PEREIRE

This one's a souvenir of Chez Schmitt, Place Pereire, Paris, May 1952: dinner on the terrace with the old open-ended busses snorting by, and the smell of perfume and Gauloises all about, those Gauloises with their take-no-prisoners aroma. If I remember correctly, Schmitt's did an interesting cabbage and cheese-topped veal chop as well. Then it was off to the Théâtre des Champs-Élysées to hear Pierre Monteux conduct the Boston Symphony in a thirty-ninth anniversary performance of Stravinsky's *Rite of Spring* (as usual, he cued the orchestra with mystic twitches of his walrus mustache) or over to the Chaillot for a recital by the venerable Gigli who parked his paunch in the bend of the Erard. I anticipated these concerts happily, of course, but I raced down Avenue Niel with the next onion tart in mind. The metabolism of youth! Now I eat string beans before *Rites of Spring* and concerts by wonderful elderly tenors holding handkerchiefs while they croon Neapolitan *mezze voci*.

Postscript: one evening on Niel I almost bumped into the great conductor Knappertsbusch, as natty as ever in his Churchillian bow tie. He was probably thinking about Brahms. Or was it simply Paris? About this time Kna prepared in Munich a notable production of that most un-Germanic of operas, Charpentier's *Louise*, a love letter to the city of Gauloises and tartes à l'oignon.

Make enough rich pie dough for a single crust 8-inch pie and line a pie plate with it.

The Pie Dough: With a table knife in each hand, wielding them across each other over and over again, cut 1/3 cup of **butter** into 1 cup of **flour** (with a pinch of **salt**) until the texture throughout is even and no pieces of butter as large as a pea remain. Chill the mixture and, separately, 1/3 cup of **water**.

After 25 minutes or more, drop the water teaspoon by teaspoon into the flour mixture, very quickly working it in with a fork. Use as little water as possible and stop adding water as soon as the mixture will stick together. Chill for 15 minutes.

Now turn the dough onto a floured board and quickly roll it thin with a floured rolling pin. Fold the dough into thirds top to bottom and left to right, to make nine layers. Roll it thin again, and lay it in the pie plate, gently pressing it to fit and pricking the bottom with a fork.

Slice almost 2 cups of **scallions**, using some of the green part, and sauté them in 2 heaping tablespoons of **butter** until soft. Beat 2 **eggs** and add the scallions, 1 cup of **cream** and a little **pepper**, stir well and pour the mixture into the lined pie plate.

Dot your tart with little oblongs of **bacon**, the equivalent of one slice in all, and bake at 400° for nearly 30 minutes. Before serving, run the tart under the broiler for 45 seconds to brown a little.

CRÊPES CAUCHOISES
—Ham and Apple stuffed—

Inspired by a meal at Le Beffroi in Rouen, this is the ideal fare for Shrove Tuesday. A "team" comes in handy in the kitchen when you're preparing these nice squishy bundles: person No. 1 to place ham on the crêpes, No. 2 to spoon apples onto the ham, No. 3 to fold the crêpes into nice, leak-proof packets. Random notes from Rouen, that neat, timbered city by the lower Seine: the rather barren but spectacular church of St-Ouen, all grey and black inside as if designed by that demonic operatic master Jean-Pierre Ponnelle; the museum Le Secq des Tournelles with its pre-Williams Sonoma collection of old coffee grinders, pepper mills and Norman waffle irons, kindly cousins as it were to dangerous dungeon equipment; Maison Perier, Rouen's answer to Demel's and Florian, where high tea for a pair of forty-somethings and daughters aged thirteen and eleven included croissants, baked apples, profiterolles, and "banana spleet."

. . . And then we were off to an old coaching inn at Les Andelys up river. This is the place to watch the barges swishing determinedly by, looking like overgrown surfboards with life jackets neatly attached.

Make **crêpe dough** (page 185) and let it sit: this will make about 15 9-inch crêpes. Match this with diners' appetites and you will know how many servings you have.

Cook the crêpes in a 9-inch pan as directed. It's best to make them ahead and stack them between sheets of waxed paper.

For the stuffing: peel, core and slice into half-moon pieces and poach in a little water 1 small **green apple** per person, and dice 1/2 slice per person of a **highly flavored ham** purchased in 1/4-inch-thick slices.

Place 2 tablespoons of the ham and 3 or 4 apple slices in the center of each crêpe. Fold the crêpes in thirds top-to-bottom and side-to-side to make little packages, and line up the packages on an oven-proof platter.

To finish: warm the crêpes in a 275° oven for 10 to 15 minutes, drizzle them with 3/4 cup of **cream** and several tablespoons of grated **Swiss cheese**, then run them under the broiler long enough to melt the cheese and perhaps brown the crêpes a little.

NOTE: For the cream you could profitably substitute crème fraîche, made by warming (not cooking) 1 cup of cream combined with 1 tablespoon of yogurt, covering it and letting it sit out overnight. Or simply buy table-ready crème fraîche at the market.

FALAFEL DE LUXE

And a move Eastward for some play food.

- A. Make patties according to the recipe on the **falafel** box.
- B. Insert in the pocket of warmed **pita bread** shredded **lettuce**, sliced **tomatoes**, and a patty.
- C. Apply a **yogurt** sauce with liberal amounts of peeled and diced **cucumber** and **lemon juice**, along with minced **parsley**, **mint**, **pepper** and pressed **garlic**.

—8-hour minimum—
RED BEAN CHILI MAISON

Herewith our silky and slightly eccentric chili. Chili, of course, is very personal. Laurie Colwin writes about a Nebraskan aficionado who always puts cinnamon and turmeric in his pot, a not unenticing proposition — this, I guess, is sort of a Greek Indian chili, and news to the average gastronome in Delphi or Delhi. Now chili in a hot dog bun I would vote against, but in a tortilla, absolutely no problem; and phyllo might do very nicely, too. Think upon these notions, remembering that chili is one of cooking's great themes, waiting like an innocent ditty for an army of kitchen composers to vary it as they will. To the pots!

Soak 1-1/2 cups of **dried kidney beans** in 4-1/2 cups of water for 6 hours, then bring them to a boil and simmer covered until soft, about 1-1/2 hours, checking the water level after a half hour.

Meanwhile in a large pan soften 1 chopped **onion** in a little **bacon fat**, adding 2 pressed **garlic** cloves after a couple of minutes. Now add 1 14-ounce can of **puréed tomatoes**; 3 tablespoons of **chili powder**; briefly sautéed **cumin, paprika** and **oregano,** perhaps 1/3 teaspoon each; 2/3 cup of **red wine** and a good splash of **red wine vinegar**. Simmer all these ingredients for several minutes before adding the beans with some of their liquid and cooking your chili slowly, covered, for 1/2 hour, adding liquid if skillet-drought occurs.

A little before serving, add 1/3 cup of grated **dry jack or parmesan cheese**, some chopped **cilantro**, a dozen strips of **orange peel** (this dish is almost turning into a beany Niçoise daube!) and adjust the seasoning — which means: is it hot enough? Also spoon up dishes of **yogurt** and **chutney** (page 130), they're excellent accompaniments. And remember: chili gains from being cooked several hours ahead.

VEGETABLE PUDDING XXIV DECEMBER
—with Sauce Mousseline—

(about 10 servings)

A dense green terrine that's especially good as a leftover with cold roast, or as part of an antipasto misto, sans sauce, served at room temperature. It's a staple of our Christmas Eve dinners, but placed, alas, in rather a stepchild position. The eager diner has already consumed one or two helpings of Leek and Potato Soup and three or four of Cracked Crab Remoulade and is distracted by thoughts of the homemade stollen and six kinds of Christmas cookies to follow. No wonder I'm partial to it in its second, and sometimes third day states, when the competition is much less stiff.

Pacing oneself through our Eve-time orgy requires the same sort of long-distance planning a conductor like the iron-fisted Fritz Reiner called into play when he architected the hour and fifteen minutes of the first act of Wagner's *Tristan und Isolde*. Signalling his orchestra with that unflappable pencilette of a beat, he would save his fullest climax for when the lovers unwrapped the sto . . . no, that's not it, I mean for when the potion released these medieval bickerers into the ecstasy of their irrepressible amorous feelings.

Our recipe, I hasten to report, had its origins in Lillian Langseth-Christensen's airily imperial *Old Vienna Cookbook,* our copy of which bears the telltale chocolate-colored spots of many a holiday afternooon dangerously propped near a hard-pressed oven.

- Thaw (but don't cook) 3 packages of frozen **cutleaf spinach** and 1 package of **asparagus spears** and drain in a colander. Then soften 1/2 cup of **butter** and add 6 **egg yolks** and beat until light and creamy; squeeze the liquid from the thawed vegetables and add them to the butter/egg component, adding about 1/3 cup of washed and chopped **mushrooms**.
- Now cut the crusts off 8 or 9 slices of **French bread** and crumble the bread into enough **cream** to moisten it; squeeze out the excess cream and add the bread to the vegetable mixture. Add 1/3 cup of dried **bread crumbs**, about 3 tablespoons of finely chopped **parsley**, 3 or so tablespoons of grated **dry jack or parmesan chees**e and **salt** and **pepper** to taste.
- In a separate bowl beat 6 **egg whites** with a pinch of **salt** until very stiff; fold them gently into the vegetable mixture. Now it's time to generously butter a pudding mold and its cover; pour the egg/veg mixture into the mold and cover it tightly. (At this point said mixture can stand.)
- The last procedure is: put the mold on a rack in a kettle with enough boiling water to reach up its sides and steam the pudding for 1-1/2 hours, then unmold it onto a

platter. Serve this pudding with Sauce Mousseline: beat 1 cup of **cream** until stiff, fold in 1 can of **Aunt Penny's Hollandaise sauce** and heat in a double boiler.

TORTA DI RICOTTA WITH TOMATOES AND PESTO

(3–4 servings)

Something like this torta, I like to fantasize, was on the bill of fare at the simple restaurant run by my probable great-great-great-great-great-great-great-great grandfather near Mt. Etna in the seventeenth century. Now, aha, I know why I'm a foodie: intensive genealogical detective work has revealed that my father's family is not restricted to the likes of German-speaking linguisticians, concert pianists and daydreaming dry goods impresarios who let their less bookish wives run the store, not to mention cousin Otto who coined the term nuclear fission (gastronomical puns on which I will resist). No, we were Sicilian vintners — and it was only an operatic chain of events, including the bubbling over of Etna in 1669 like a very angry cappuccino, that sent the Campofiori family to Germany and their reinvention as Blumenfelds, in, naturally enough, the wine wholesaling business. Well, there were circus jongleurs too, busy at the old Deutschland fairs. The "show business" gene at work! The move northward was facilitated by a vacationing German painter (cast him as a tenor) who conveniently fell in love with the papa vintner's daughter.

Well, this torta is an excellent party dish, and, especially if you have a good pastry maker on your staff, not all that much work. Making up a batch of pesto in advance will, of course, lighten the load. Excess pesto can look forward to a fine career as pasta sauce, piscatorial accoutrement and facilitator of trendy two-toned mashed potatoes.

- First — and this can be done considerably ahead — make a 10-inch pie or tart shell using the same initial procedures as for the Tarte à l'Oignon (page 39) only with 1/2 cup of **butter**, 1-1/2 cups of **flour** and 1/3 cup of **water**, plus the pinch of **salt**.
- Chill the shell for half an hour, line it with waxed paper and fill the cavity with **rice or dry beans** to weight it down. Bake it in a hot oven for 15 minutes, then remove the waxed paper and rice or beans and brush the bottom of the shell with 1 lightly beaten **egg white** or some **milk**. Bake the shell for 10 or 15 minutes more, until golden; let it cool.
- Meanwhile halve 5 or 6 medium-sized **Roma tomatoes** lengthwise and remove the seeds to make hollows. Brush the tomatoes with **olive oil**, sprinkle them with **pepper** and bake cut side up at 325° for 20 minutes — longer if they're especially big. Then put the tomatoes cut side down on a rack to drain for 20 minutes.
- Now, put in a bowl 1 cup of **ricotta**, 1/2 cup of **sour cream**, 1/2 cup of minced **Italian parsley**, 2 whole **eggs**, 2 **egg yolks**, 2 teaspoons of chopped **fresh basil**, **pepper** and **salt**; beat together until smooth.

Fill the pie shell with this mixture and place the cupped tomato halves thereon. Bake at 350° for 20 minutes. Finally, spoon **pesto** (page 70) into the tomato hollows, let the tart cool to lukewarm, and serve.

BEEFSTEAK TOMATOES POMIANE

If the thought of this tomatoes-in-cream as a main course scares you, convert it to an elegant and unusual starter. Only with good tomatoes, however! Now come to think of it, you could combine Tomatoes Pomiane, like so many other things, with pasta. Or rice. Or poached eggs and bacon on toast — that would be an Old English breakfast taken into a new dimension. Dr. Edouard de Pomiane, Polish-born, was a professor at the Institut Pasteur in Paris and author of a book I'd love to lay my hands on, *French Cooking in Ten Minutes*, which is not, I'm sure, about FAST FOOD.

. . . Well, just a few days after writing that sentence I found that this 1930 opus had been awakened from a long slumber by North Point Press; and in it I found not precisely the "Pomiane" recipe Elizabeth David fondly published in one of her books and I for your pleasure on this page had pumped up with added cream and embroidered with herbs — no, what I came upon instead was a tomatoes-and-cream with finely chopped onion added to the pan early on and *sour* cream some minutes later.

So now you can enter your kitchen in a delightful haze of pomodoran possibilities.

Pomiane's enchanting book, the size of a Beatrix Potter, is, he says, designed for "students, dressmakers, secretaries, artists, lazy people, poets, men of action, dreamers, scientists, and everyone else who has only an hour for lunch or dinner but still wants thirty minutes of peace to enjoy a cup of coffee." Sounds very French. And in this book there are revelations — that, for example, Pomiane in 1930 found modern life "so hectic that we sometimes feel as if time is going up in smoke." How would he deal with 2002? Hide in a Trappist monastery, where the cheese is good? Better, become a consultant to Mr. McDonald or the Colonel who, I think, need help.

And back in '30 the French, we learn, were overcooking their pasta and serving it in "a formless mass." So, announces the cheerful Docteur, "Let's cook some noodles right."

But on to those tomatoes . . .

Melt a good teaspoon or more of **butter** in a skillet, place therein 2 large halved **tomatoes**, cut side downward and pricked to let the juices escape into the pan; then warm the tomatoes gently for 10 or 15 minutes, turning them several times.

Stir in 1/4 to 1/3 cup of **cream**, mix with the juices, and when it bubbles maneuver the tomatoes-cum-juicy cream, which you've sprinkled with **fresh tarragon** and **chives**, onto diners' plates — actually I like to serve these tomatoes in soup bowls.

TIMBALE OF CORN, BACON, FIGS AND GOAT CHEESE

When I read in a book about country inns that Todd Muir at Healdsburg's Madrona Manor had programmed a dish rather like this for a fig festival the wheels of inspiration began to turn. The result is the adjacent timbale. Or timballo as the Italians say — I love that word, it sounds like it ought to be the name of a percussion instrument banged lightly in some old baroque suite. The orchestration of this timbale/timballo is interesting, highlighted by the counterpoint of the mildly sweet corn and the somewhat less mildly sweet figs. The bacon provides the basso continuo, and the goat cheese . . . but enough of metaphors, let's eat!

> In a skillet sauté a dozen or more smallish cubes of **thick cut or slab bacon** until they're almost crisp, then add a good 2 cups of **frozen corn**. Continue cooking the bacon and corn for several minutes over moderate heat, stirring almost constantly, after which you should stir in 1/2 cup of chopped **dried figs** (fresh ones in summer!) which you've soaked in warm water for an hour or so, and blend in (a really large spoon helps here) 3 or 4 ounces of **goat cheese.** Note well: you want a moist, well-aged cheese, not too sharp but really flavorful. Best to visit a cheese shop whose staff know as much about cheese as your physician presumably knows about your insides. Next, top all with a thin layer of **bread crumbs**.
>
> Now off the fire stir an **egg** into the bacon/fruit/veg/cheese and spoon all into a buttered ovenproof dish — or individual ramekins. Then top with another film of crumbs and bake at 300°, mostly covered, for 25 minutes.
>
> NOTE: I don't see why this dish wouldn't work well with cubes of leftover roast lamb instead of the bacon; and roast pork would be a natural. In any event you'll doubtless want a green salad as a follow-up.
>
> FURTHER THOUGHT: Since this timbale when served on plates rather than in ramekins looks a bit like a large pillow waiting for some sautéed Calterranean fish or fowl to be laid against it, well, that's your cue . . .

A Considerable Postscript:

Editors helpfully peering over the shoulders of memoir writers often ask for celebrities, celebrities. Well, as a newspaper reporter I did interview Admiral Byrd the South Pole man, very cordial indeed; I had an unfortunate brush with John Foster Dulles squired by a disagreeable contingent of State Department huskies; there was a black-haired, eighty-two-year old Leonid Massine who'd danced with Diaghileff's legendary troupe and answered my questions over tea at the Sir Francis Drake pleasantly but stiffly, in a posture that was arthritically erect, as if he were a talking medallion or de Medici bust; and I knocked on the hotel door of Sir Thomas Beecham, that lovely old tease of a conductor, asking for a few memories of his beloved composer friend Delius, and although it was a nap I think he had in mind he happily obliged, in shirtsleeves. But the food connection with these celebs is non-existent, unless one counts Sir Thomas' remark, heard at one of his Lollipop concerts in London a few years later: "anyone who can identify this next encore will be awarded a ton of chewing gum."

In the food world, though — her world, of course, was much bigger than that — I did have the privilege of knowing M.F.K. Fisher a little. It was never for a starstruck scribe, meaning me, a totally relaxed relationship, but as fielded from her end of the court it was certainly a friendly one, with some good fun and gossip thrown in, especially via absolutely inimitable postcards written in her uniquely laidback rhythm and stocked with that fine quirky wisdom of which she seemed to be the originator. I first met M.F.K. (I never really felt I knew her as Mary Frances) about 1955 when a mutual friend dragged her, I suspect, to my mother's house because my mother was a great fan of hers. Thirty years later another mutual friend thought M.F.K. might look benignly on a literary effort of mine (which she kindly did), and when she invited Anne and me to lunch at her unique studio/house in the Valley of the Moon, preparing for us at the kitchen end of her book-lined living room a very tasty tapenade of olives-capers-anchovies as the centerpiece of a light and perfect meal, sort of Panisse Café-ish, washed down with a simple white wine, she recounted for us everything that had transpired at my mother's house three decades earlier, including a vivid description of my mother's large in-house feline population. I guess those cats struck a chord as they say, but then M.F.K. was as observant as the most sensitive detective, or novelist.

When a large book of M.F.K.'s letters came out not long ago I devoured it, all its knowingness, and I dreamt I told her how much I felt its pull.

—SOUPS—

PURÉE MONGOLE WITH YELLOW SPLIT PEAS AND CURRY CREAM

Soup is: good chowder served from an abalone shell at Pop Ernt's on Monterey wharf back in the 30s — I can hear the kindly weatherbeaten waiter drawling his litany, "Well, tonight we have rock cod, mackerel, abalone . . ." (and I, of course, was much preoccupied with the imminent arrival of the *Del Monte Express* outside our sunporch window); and soup is an unctuous brew of *Cream of Tomatoes* at that San Francisco landmark Jack's, poured from silver urns deep as Wonderland rabbit holes; it's leek-and-potato soups in modest French restaurants of the 50s served with butter floating on the top ("very strange," thought a young GI in Orléans); it's the soup of one's first bouillabaisse in Nice, served in two courses; it's goulash soup high on a hill in Budapest; it's that haunting she-crab brew at Perdita's in old Charleston, S.C.; it's an outrageously ribsticking "Prime Rib" soup in the Oregon Cascades; it is of course that soup so ceremoniously eaten by the mama, papa and working girl in Charpentier's *Louise* (what could it be, a thin veg broth, I'll bet, big on carrots); and it's even the canned, pleasantly doctored soups of one's childhood family dinners.

My mother sometimes used to combine cans of tomato and pea soup with a little curry powder, and that led, some years later, to the frothy item of this page.

In a large pot soften 1 chopped medium-sized **onion** in a tablespoon or more of **butter**. Add 3/4 cup of **yellow split peas**, 1 **ham hock**, 2 diced **tomatoes**, a dash of **dry sherry** and a 49-ounce can of good quality **chicken broth** (or the equivalent of homemade — note that the commercial sort does come with "1/3 less salt").* Bring all this to a boil and simmer, covered, for at least an hour.

Now skim the excess fat off the soup and remove the hock, separating the meat from the bone, editing out the thick skin and fat and cutting the good stuff into fairly small pieces, then put the meat back in the soup.

At this point you're ready to purée your soup, in batches, transferring the results to a serving bowl and stirring in a good half cup of **cream**, into which you've mixed about 2 tablespoons of **curry powder**, commercial or homemade. Then sprinkle all with a nice heap of minced **parsley**.

Serve your Purée Mongol with large croutons: cube slices of **French bread** and cook them slowly in a non-stick pan with a smidgen of **butter**, turning them occasionally, until they're crisp and brown.

* If you use a little less broth you can freeze the remainder, beginning an emergency cache.

—24-hour—
BLACK BEAN SOUP

Here in the U.S. at least, we've been in the Great Black Bean Era for fifteen or twenty years. Few self-respecting young chefs in New American Cuisine restaurants would be caught without a dish or two involving this ingredient seemingly despised by those blind French and Italian masters of cuisine across the pond. Chinese, to be sure, have been sending black bean sauces out of their kitchens since the year 1, and occidentals like the canny proprietor of New York's original Coach House were featuring black bean soups several decades ago. But the crescendo of the 80s was a giant one. Here we offer a fairly basic soup recipe — no chilies, no sour cream, no lime, no rum, just a tinge of tomato, a bit of ham, and with the egg and lemon punctuation that strikes me as rather crucial. If you're feeling down, this is culinary penicillin.

Cars, of course, run more smoothly after they've been washed, and this soup will taste even better if you serve it in large pottery bowls that've been sitting indolently about the house looking decorative and having no idea to what wonderful purpose an inventive home chef de cuisine will put them.

Soak overnight about 1/3 pound of **black beans** in water to cover. Next, in your soup pot soften in a tablespoon or 2 of **olive oil** 1 chopped **onion** and enough chopped **celery** to equal about 2/3 of the onion, along with some minced **parsley** and **thyme**.

Add the beans, drained, and 1 **ham hock**, a 14-ounce can or a little more of **tomatoes** (the "ready cut" variety will save you having to scissor the tomatoes into sufficiently small pieces) and most of a 49-ounce can of **chicken broth** (or homemade if you have it). Bring all this to a boil and simmer covered for 2-1/2 hours at least. Late in this stage water may be added — guardedly! — if the soup is beginning to cook away.

Remove the ham hock and cut the meat into small pieces, then stir them into your soup. Some skimming of excess fat will be advisable. Now serve your black bean soup with chopped hard boiled **egg** and **lemon** slices.

SPINOFF NOTE: The next day when you're debating what to do with the rest of your bunch of **celery**, chop several spoonsful into what I call *Marcus' Potato Salad*, along with boiled, cooled and diced **red or yukon gold potatoes** and those other embroideries, peeled and chopped **cucumber** and **red onion**, some minced **parsley**, and a **dill Dijon mustard mayonnaise** spiked with a few drops (or more!) of **dry sherry**. You can serve this salad with garlic sausages and tomato halves, or as part of an antipasto misto. Don't stint on the mustard and cucumber, and don't overchill . . . and note that this salad is even better if orchestrated with sprinklings of paprika and turmeric.

—24-hour—
SOUTHWEST PINTO BEAN SOUP WITH SAUSAGE

A variation on the preceding, this desert minestrone. It's a bit hotter.

Now the Southwest has been such a force in American cooking lately but I'm afraid I haven't had much experience of its cactal countryside. My one time in Santa Fe I was in a constant fidget under that Big Top of a threatening-and-often-thundering sky that seemed to be administered by an unstable god out of a Wagnerian opera. But the enchiladas at La Fonda couldn't have been tangier, the zigzaggy Native American interior design was right up my alley and my interview with the composer Hans Werner Henze, a rather icy but cordial enough character, didn't go too badly. As for his opera *The Bassarids* which the Santa Fe Opera was staging, well, listening to its trendy aridity was hard work with no time off for good behavior.

Soak overnight about 1/3 cup of **pinto beans** in water to cover. Next phase, soften in a tablespoon or more of **olive oil**: 1 chopped **onion,** a thinly sliced **carrot** and 1 chopped **sweet red pepper** along with 1 pressed **garlic** clove. Add the beans, drained, and 4 cups of **water**, a good teaspoon of **cumin** and a respectable smidgen of **cayenne**, bring to a boil and simmer, partly covered, for 1-1/4 hours.

Now brown (but don't overcook) 1 **chorizo or Italian sausage** per serving, drain the sausages on paper towels and slice them, then add to the soup with a 28-ounce can of **tomatoes** and a 14-ounce can of **chicken broth** (or equivalent homemade); simmer all for 30 minutes. Serve this soup with a sprinkle of minced **parsley**.

BLACK-EYED PEA AND SCALLION ETC. MINESTRONE

This zephyrean meridional brew comes from the extended family of what my friend Alden Gilchrist calls *garbage soups*. If you've recently cooked a roast, steamed a green vegetable and chopped more green onion than you needed to top a sliced egg salad — not to speak of locating a partly-used, three-year-old dried bean-mix packet in your cupboard — well then, you're right in position to produce the following cornucopia of second gastronomical thoughts.

In a soup pot place 1 or 2 cups of a packaged mix of **black-eyed peas**, **garbanzos** and **kidney beans**, etc. Add at least 4 cups of liquid, a combination of **juice from a roast**, **liquid from steaming a green vegetable**, and **water**, plus a teaspoon of **salt**, 1 medium-sized chopped **onion** and several sprigs of **parsley**. Bring all to a boil and simmer for 2 hours or until all the beans involved are soft, adding more liquid as appropriate. Before serving, remove the parsley sprigs and garnish your soup with chopped **scallions**, **parsley** and/or **cilantro**.

ONION GARLIC SOUP CHEZ NOUS

This soup was invented in response to a not entirely unfair complaint about the "simplicity" of a garlic soup I'd been serving my chief companion and cooking consultant: you can thank her for the increase in its weight of onions and the addition of potatoes. Clove-spotting is a bit of a problem when you dish out this soup, the well-softened garlic like some clever animal hiding from a heftier assailant fairly vanishes in the prevailing white of the broth and your dining partner may end up with all the aiolian goodies. But an amicable redistribution should put things right.

Garlic soup, this, or onion soup? Well, it's a far cry from the classic crock of weedy French Onion sloshing beneath a crust of cheese so extensive in its accordion of stringiness you could hang the wash on the Emmentalerian "A" or "E" expanding gummily between bowl and mouth.

In my childhood that soup, tasty or not, was the eternal unidentical twin of consomme or clam chowder appearing just past the *de rigeur* shrimp cocktail on menus about to proceed to Filet of Sole ($1.25) on the tried-true route to Prime Rib au Jus ($2). I knew it well too in my early visits to Paris, and could as a matter of fact have used some the first time I arrived in my beloved second city — parading in its air, this was 1952, an overwhelming mix of perfume, Gauloises and drains — but after a pre-jet age journey involving something like twenty-four hours in the air, not counting an insomniacal night on the nineteenth floor of New York's old Biltmore Hotel, orchestrated with sirens from a detective thriller and the virtuosity of the percussion section of Manhattan's garbage collection agency, I arrived in Paris, of all places, too exhausted to eat.

An expat friend had booked me into a walkup hotel near St-Etienne-du-Mont with a beshawled Defargian granny at the desk and spatting late-to-bed lovers next door to my viewless cell. I escaped, found my appetite several kilometers away and soon was dining at Schmitt's and Valentin and Lipp.

And breakfast on the Place Pereire was croissants with flakes like autumn leaves.

In a large pot soften 2 sliced **onions** in 2 or 3 tablespoons of **olive oil**, adding about 8 large peeled **garlic** cloves a little after starting to cook the onions. Keep stirring! Then add a 49-ounce can of **chicken broth** (or equivalent homemade) and 1 **red potato**, cut into large dice; simmer, covered, until the garlic is soft: this will take about 1/2 hour.

Now whisk together 1/2 cup of **cream** and 1/2 an **egg yolk** more or less; take the soup off the fire and slowly whisk in the cream-and-yolk mixture, having stirred a little hot soup into the mix.

Ladling out your soup at the dinner table, lay a latticework of steamed **French beans** (a tenth of a pound should be enough) across the benign potato bergs rising amiably enough from the aromatic broth. Gaze briefly at the good approximations of Impressionist paintings staring back at you from handsome Italian pottery bowls or whatever you've chosen for your meal, then dust them with nice helpings of grated **dry jack or parmesan cheese**.

CORSICAN SOUP MAXIM

And here a fish-less Bouillabaisse, adapted from an old cookbook well worth looking for, the Art Nouveau-flavored *Chez Maxim's* (McGraw Hill, 1962), and it's not a celebrity tank dish, either. In Provence they call it Aïgo Ménagère as I see from a recipe in *Cooking with Josephine* by the inimitable Josephine Araldo, resident chef to San Francisco gentry and occasional employee of Isadora Duncan (who taught this Bretonne to drink Champagne) and whose grandmother, by the way, was an earlyday fusion-ist, combining fresh cherries with string beans and kumquats with Jerusalem artichokes! Of course there's nothing to prevent you from warming a few mussels in the brew at the last minute (I recommend buying pre-cooked large green New Zealands) instead of poaching the eggs: the fennel and saffron may be pining for such familiar company. If you opt for mussels, eat the soup with spoon and fork.

And speaking of poached eggs: surely their greatest glory must be in a dish served at San Francisco's LuLu, slices of leg of veal draped over a warm salad of escarole, fingerling potatoes and bacon topped with a gushing rivulet of ovoid goodness.

I've been re-reading Josephine's cookbook lately and I must say, it's the most delightful suicide manual I've encountered. The Vintage French recipes are swimming in butter, cream, egg yolks and bacon fat. I do not find this distasteful or immoral, just a bit scary. Josephine's food — including no less than a dozen variations on the melodious theme of Hollandaise sauce — is unctuous, charming, filling, sort of the gastronomical equivalent of Massenet and Chausson with perhaps a bit of Richard Strauss borrowed from over the border. And I rather imagine that if it's consumed without guilt it might not kill you.

Chop 2 medium-sized **onions**, put them in your soup pot and soften them in a little **olive oil**, adding a large pressed **garlic** clove as the onions take on color.
Now add:

    1 28-ounce can of **tomatoes**, mashed

    2 medium-sized **red potatoes**, diced small — here's where your sous-chef comes in handy, if available!

thyme: a bit

fennel seed: a little more

saffron: enough to make a decided impression

the zest of 1/3 of an **orange**, cut into juliennes

1 49-ounce can of **chicken broth** (or equivalent homemade)

Bring all this to a boil and simmer partly covered for about 50 minutes, making sure the potatoes are DONE! Moosh them up some, then break an **egg** into a saucer and carefully slip this wobbly object into the soup; repeat the process to provide an egg per person.

Simmer the soup gently until the eggs are firm, about 2-1/2 to 3 minutes at least. Sprinkle with minced **parsley** and serve each diner a portion including one of the submerged eggs.

AVGOLEMONO

An easy recipe for the tired home chef: I think I know why we have this soup fifteen times a year.

Avgolemono I made friends with many years ago at a homey Greek restaurant on one of those seedy streets just behind San Francisco's Hilton-Hyatt-Nikko land; lamb stew with okra and tomatoes stuffed with delicately sweetened meat and rice were other East Med lures. I remember asking a visiting historian at the next table how he found my "secret" taverna and he responded that it's on just such an unpromising street, with a vagabond reclining perhaps at the door, that exemplary eats may be found. True: Julia herself adopted a Vietnamese bistro around the corner.

In your soup pot bring to a boil a 49-ounce can of **chicken broth** (or equivalent homemade), add 2/3 to 3/4 cup of **long grain rice** and simmer covered for about 25 minutes. (If you want to add chicken pieces, do so exactly halfway along.) Then in a small bowl beat 2 **eggs** to a froth and slowly stir in the juice of at least 1-1/2 **lemons**, mixing in a little hot soup.

With the soup off the fire, slowly whisk the egg/lemon mixture into the soup, stirring until all is well blended. Garnish rather generously with **dill weed** and **tarragon**, preferably fresh (mint and chives are excellent alternatives), and serve.

ZUPPA MARITATA

Another white soup, a creamy old-timer with pasta that seems to be getting rarer and rarer if not totally extinct. Cholesterol counts are surely against it, and tortellini in brodo is about as close as you'll get to it in today's weight-watching world. Fifty years ago Italian restaurants in San Francisco that served only a handful of main dish pastas (along with frog's legs, tripe, squab en casserole and fried cream) might offer Maritata — *Wedding Soup* — as a matter of course. But it was never a staple in North Beach like Minestrones red as fire engines or their delicate sidekick Pastina, that's broth with miniature pasta units therein.

I'm inclined to doubt Maritata aids fertility as the folklore has it; it seems more like the luxuriantly lulling prelude to a first class snooze.

To a 49-ounce can of boiling **chicken broth** (or equivalent homemade) add 1/4 pound of **fettuccine** broken into manageable lengths and cook the lot for several minutes, stirring occasionally. Stir in 3/4 to 1 cup of **cream** and simmer your sea of white uncovered until the pasta is done: this would be about 12 minutes after it was put in the broth.

Just before serving, stir in 1-1/2 to 2 beaten **egg yolks** diluted with a little hot soup. Sprinkle grated **dry jack or parmesan cheese** on the bottoms of your soup bowls and ladle the Maritata thereon. Topping all with chopped **fresh basil** is an aggressively recommended extra, and don't fail to bring more grated cheese to the table.

PERUVIAN SHRIMP CHOWDER FRANCESCA

The core of San Francisco's pervasively Hispanic Mission district with its Languedocian shade trees and busy vegetable markets spilling onto sidewalks is like a foreign country nestled against America, not the Middle variety since this trendy periphery includes a high tech gulch and a sort of East Village West, but America just the same.

In the Mission heartland we eat oozy cheese pupusas at tiny Salvadorean restaurants with jumping Jobimian jukeboxes and the chef's grandkids doing their homework, buy tamales from agitated Nicaraguan produce depots, abandon our resolutions in bakeries dishing up trayfuls of one sugar-dusted goodie after another, attempt the insertion of mile-high burritos (for which Dagwoodian treat the 'hood is famous) into one's hungry mouth, grab a grilled cheese or ham on rye at the counter of the old St. Francis soda fountain-cum-candy shoppe which constitutes, I think, the only slice of "Anglo" culinary culture slid in (well, it may have been there first) amidst the prevailing Hispania . . .

It was in the Mission a few years ago, at a barren but friendly place called Francesca's International Cuisine, that we had huge bowls of milky potato-dotted Chupe de Camarones, a fascinating Peruvian shrimp chowder. It was a red and white soup, more the latter, sort of a cross between Soupe de Poissons and Maritata — with Corsican overtones. Alas, before we could return for further investigation, Francesca's International Cuisine closed. But our daughter Cecily brought a little cookbook back from Peru some months later — in Peru she was served baby tamales for breakfast! — and this prompted a veritable rebirth of Francesca's capacious Chupe.

In a large pot soften 1 chopped **onion** and 1 chopped **tomato** in a tablespoon of **olive oil**, stirring in a pressed **garlic** clove midway along.

Next, add a 49-ounce can of **chicken broth** plus a large diced **red potato** (after the initial slicing you can take a big knife and quickly go buh-buh-buhbuhbuh like Jacques Pépin), 1/3 cup of **rice**, 2 or 3 tablespoons of frozen **peas** and the same of **corn** (somewhat thawed first), a little **pepper** and — indispensable this — 2 or 3 generous shakes of your **saffron** container. Simmer all partly covered for at least 45 minutes, until the potatoes are done for sure.

Now add 1/3 pound of raw **rock shrimp** and cook the lot 2 or 3 minutes more . . . and now a slightly traumatic final lap in which you

1. slip an **egg** per person into the soup for poaching, which takes about 3 minutes,
2. take the soup off the fire and stir in 1/3 cup of **cream** which you don't want to boil,

3. decorate your Chupe with minced **cilantro** and send it off with a blessing to the dining table.

I recommend that your spouse not be in a crucial stage of marmalade making on the same stove during these final minutes: that was the hapless situation I found myself in when I first made this Chupe. But I must say, it survived the ordeal nicely.

TURKISH RED LENTIL AND TOMATO SOUP
—*Kirmizi Mercimek Çorbasi*—

A great mush, this, adapted from a Turkish cookbook, *The Famous Turkish Cookery*, in which, with a logic I see no reason to dispute, an official recipe cup is a teacup and the tablespoon of record a soup spoon. My favorite picture in this engaging paperback is of Terbiyeli köfte, lamb meatballs in a lemon and egg yolk sauce which in its modified whiteness over the puffy walnut-sized balls suggests eggs sunnyside-up but in a light mist.

Red lentils for this Kirmizi-etc. can be found in most supermarkets, health food stores and at some fruit stands out in the country.

Meanwhile, friends always return from Turkey with the same score sheet: the ruins are fascinating, the calls to prayer outdo the best alarm clocks, camel wrestling is far out, and the lamb is excellent but ubiquitous — like a lone leading man in a small theater company who intones his lines with *brio* but could use a relief thespian with a different style.

In a pot soften 1 large minced **onion** in a little **butter**; add 4 cups of **chicken broth**, a cup of **baby red lentils** which you've washed in a sieve and drained, and 1 chopped **tomato**; bring all to a boil and simmer uncovered for about 30 minutes. Serve this soup with minced **parsley** and croutons made by slowly sautéing cubes of **French bread** with a dab of **butter** in a non-stick pan.

OR: Stir into your pot large pieces of leftover lamb roast and you'll have a new dish, a half-soup we hereby christen Lamb and Red Lentils.

CURRIED LENTIL SOUP WITH YOGURT

Brown lentils are the lead player here, a more conventional raw material, but this is not an ordinary soup. The aroma of cinnamon'd curry wafting through your house for forty-five minutes makes great company. And this is a good soup to cook when you have a ham bone hanging about after a party and several nights of leftovers.

Toss it in: a noble shipwreck in a sea of lentils.

Chop an **onion** and soften it in a little **butter**, then stir in 2 heaping teaspoons of **curry powder**, 1/4 teaspoon of **cinnamon**, a large pressed **garlic** clove and the barest smidgen of **chili powder**.

Add 1 cup of **lentils** (the standard brown variety), 1 or 2 tablespoons of **long grain rice** and most of a 49-ounce can of **chicken broth** (or equivalent homemade), bring all this to a boil and simmer partly covered for about 45 minutes. Sprinkle your soup with minced **parsley** and set out a bowl of **yogurt** on the dining table.

—24-hour—
GAZPACHO THANKSGIVING STYLE

Long favored at Thanksgiving in our house but an obvious choice for summery days, which in San Francisco means February or October. With no soup, perhaps, is the last minute tasting for correction of cooking errors so charged; one can easily go on "seasoning" until your guests go home Gazpacho-less.

I'm reminded of earlier backstage conferences in my kitchen life. When, a small short-trousered person in blue suit eager to pass the anchovy toasts to my parents' guests — the men in boiled shirt and black tie, because this was still the Georgian 1930s — I'd spy in the pantry Dr. Horace Gray, eminent Bostonian, who didn't happen to drink himself, fussing at length over his cocktail shaker, on the verge of producing the best Martini in San Francisco's northern arrondissements. The learned doctor (deprived of gin because the top of an ear turned a very improper pink) was like some Professor Higgins about to translate an unruly brew into a masterpiece.

I should say, too, that Dr. Gray with his erudite-sounding sing-song would have had no trouble getting a job as announcer for the broadcasts of the Boston Symphony — "Ah, here comes Dr. Koussevitsky (the voice over the airwaves rising) . . ."

Amazing little parties! I remember the lean long dresses, some worn by forty-somethings who must have been Southern belles not very far in the past, the post-dinner separation of the sexes at brandy time, the general air of cheer.

But these were much more difficult times than this blue-suited innocent with a nervous grip on the anchovy toasts could know. What did the partyers converse about when a Linzer Monster on the far side of the Atlantic was annexing little countries like so much *antipasti misti* to be piled up on a large refectory table constituting a continent, my mother's beloved FDR was locked in dismal combat with a Republican congress, dirigibles were up to no good . . .

My innocence, thanks be, tasted as good as those toasts.

This is a rather free-form recipe in which the main ingredient is a 49-ounce can of **tomato juice**.

First off, in a blender or food processor mince enough de-stemmed **parsley** to accumulate 1/2 a cup, and reserve it. Now with enough of the tomato juice to facilitate puréeing, purée in the same piece of machinery 1/2 of the following items, in batches:

- 1 **sweet red pepper**
- 1 **red onion**

> 1 **cucumber**, peeled and seeded
>
> 2 stalks of **celery**
>
> Next, finely chop the other 1/2 of the vegetables and combine them in a large serving pot with the rest of the tomato juice, the puréed vegetables and the parsley. Before refrigerating your brew overnight for flavor enhancement, season it with a little of each of the following, or to taste:
>
> > **olive oil**
> >
> > **red wine vinegar**
> >
> > **lemon** juice
> >
> > pressed **garlic**
> >
> > **Tabasco sauce**
> >
> > **salt** and **pepper**
> >
> > **breadcrumbs**
> >
> > **powdered chicken stock** (optional)
> >
> > **cilantro** (optional)

LEEK AND POTATO SOUP XXIV DECEMBER

A Christmas Eve perennial, but entirely edible at other times. The only burning question here is: should the potato dice be tiny or somewhat larger?

Forty years ago, my wife and I had a soup of this endearing type at a French auberge about which I entertain the most nostalgic sentiments and have composed a tiny playlet:

Scene 1, spring of '54, I am contracted to the U.S. Army and a buddy and I are returning to base from Mont-St-Michel. As we swing up the West Normandy coast I sight a bucolic village crowned by a large stone house — "Ah," I muse, "if I find a wife when I get home I'll bring her here one day." The name of the village is St-Jean-le-Thomas.

Scene 2, winter of '57, I have found the legal mate I envisioned, not too clearly, three years back, and now from San Francisco I'm writing La Grande Auberge, Michelin's only entry for St-Jean.

Scene 3, a month later, there's no response — Oh dear, was that village a cruel mirage?

Scene 4, a few days later, heavens, we've got mail — "Oui, Monsieur, une chambre pour deux," says the letter which came by slow boat around the horn.

Scene 5, Bastille Day, we're in Europe, we've driven out from Paris, we arrive at St-Jean, many *papillons* in the *estomac*, and there, how about that, a little man appears on the front steps of, yes, the big stone house, and he throws up his hands, exclaiming, as if perhaps we were Columbuses in reverse, "Ah, les Bloom-FIELD! (accent on the second syllable)."

He thinks we're from Carolina, not California, but no matter. What a welcome.

In Monsieur's guest book we saw that General Patton had slept here; in the dining room the waitress was a bit blasé about the fly that settled into our '38 Bordeaux but was deftly fished from its improper perch in the kitchen before the same bottle — not, by the way, from a great year — was duly returned to a pair of queasy but charmed Americans; and in the W.C. we smiled at the little placard that requested us, decorously but strenuously, to please pull the chain *doucement,* gently!

One dared not think of the consequences of failing to heed this admonition.

> Wash 2 **leeks**, slice them rather thin and soften them in 2 tablespoons of **butter** with a not particularly large chopped **onion**; dice and add to your soup pot 2 biggish scrubbed **red potatoes**, cooking them for a minute or so. Don't be afraid to use some of the green part of the leeks — and if you dice the potatoes a little in advance you can reserve your spud-bits in a bowl of water.
>
> Now add about 3/4 of a 49-ounce can of **chicken broth** (or equivalent homemade), bring it to a boil and simmer uncovered for about 45 minutes, until all the veg are soft — you can if you wish moosh down the potatoes some.
>
> Then, just before serving, stir in a little **cream** . . . an added frill, not standard operating procedure at our Christmas Eves, would be to strew some bacon bits over your soup.
>
> AND: Don't ignore the possibility of stirring pesto (see page 70) into this soup. Also — don't be shocked — diced summer squash is an excellent stand-in for this recipe's potatoes. This is not to mention the addition of salt cod fritter "croutons" whose contents will ooze like a sinuous melody into the veggie lake below.

GIGI'S ALSATIAN SOUP WITH CABBAGE, GARLIC SAUSAGES AND HONEY

After Hoi, my mother's cook, abandoned her during World War II — to cook for FDR's "best man" Lathrop Brown at Big Sur — she got right down to business and made things like this hearty number, one of the best gastronomical traffic jams I know. It might be described as a little onion soup that grew up into a meat-and-veg giant.

I think during its long history in our family it's always been a main course production and it should certainly be kept in that central position because as a starter it would kill any course that dared to follow. Dessert after Gigi's soup? Well, a nice tarte aux quetsches or some other item from the majestic battery of Alsatian sweets would be close to suicidal, so opt for a baked apple or maybe the Oranges Terrazza of our dessert chapter (page 179).

My mother cooked on until a series of orthopedic disasters deposited her in the clutches of unrepentant hospital cooks. I think we did take her some care packages. A rebel aristocrat, a raging liberal, my mother died just before all the interesting cultural, and gastronomic, revolutions of the last third of the twentieth century. When she felt hemmed in by boredom or Republicans (she had, by the way, gone to school with Wallis Simpson and thought her dangerous) she threatened to take off with a donkey and a cooking pan.

To the Cévennes, I suppose. She knew her Robert Louis Stevenson.

And I can't help trying to fit her in the picture . . . "The road smoked in the twilight with children driving home cattle from the fields." Elsewhere RLS writes of "plentiful hurrying clouds — some dragging veils of straight rain-showers, others massed and luminous, as though promising snow . . ." No, it wasn't all pastoral peaches and cream, Stevenson would "proot mellifluously" to his balking donkey, "like a sucking-dove," without getting her to storm the interminable hill.

My mother's life was an uphill thing, redeemed in large part by good cooking. Her parents died young, they were even divorced, a terrible no-no a century ago, her brother was a Marine officer killed in a silly insurrection in Haiti, and she gave up Bryn Mawr after a year, I'm not sure why, maybe because of "a boy." Then she scooted off to nursing school in Baltimore, a calling that suited her kindness and her feeling of *not* being an aristocrat. Her aunt, perhaps the one who almost took the Titanic on its famous half-voyage, had a fit when she fell in love with the Jewish doctor at Hopkins who took care of her during the big flu epidemic of '18.

> Pour boiling water over 1/2 a **cabbage** and let it stand in a bowl for 10 minutes, then drain it, remove the hard parts and and cut it into eighths. Next, in a large soup pot sauté a little diced **pancetta** (more practical than salt pork!) for about 4 minutes; then after reducing the heat add a large finely-chopped **onion** and soften it: that will take another 3 minutes.
>
> Add the cabbage, a large pressed **garlic** clove and 3 14-ounce cans of **beef broth** (or 2 of broth and 1 of water) and bring to a boil. Now add **pepper**, 1/2 teaspoon or so of **caraway seed** and a small onion stuck with about 4 **cloves**; cover and cook all these components gently until the cabbage is nearly done, no more than 15 minutes.
>
> Now add 1 large diced **potato**, a little fresh **dill weed** if you have it (left over, say, from a Greek soup), 1 sliced **garlic sausage** per serving and a teaspoon of **honey** and cover and simmer all for 30 minutes. Serve this soup over toasted slices of **French bread** spread with a little **Dijon mustard** — and leave a pot of mustard on the table.

CHICKEN SAFFRON MINESTRONE WITH TOASTS

Ultra Mediterranean, rather robust, and crowned with the elegant saffron mayonnaise you'll find on the next page. If you have trouble as I do making a garlicky mayonnaise from scratch, be advised this "no ordinary substitute" can fill more roles than the lead part in this particular soup. How about with cold roast pork, to enliven a Euro-oriented Cobb Salad, to dress a hamburger in gastronomical tux? I can see it now, the *Saffron Mayonnaise Cookbook, 100 Great Recipes*.

Well, I hope my ancestors in the schnitzel and Schlachtplatte capitals of Europe got to eat some Mediterranean chow now and then, great uncle Moriz whose Tartuffe won praise from Kaiser Wilhelm in pre-Armageddonian Berlin, cousin Heinrich who ran a newspaper in Vienna with the husband of Mahler's girlfriend only to have another Kaiser, Franz Josef, shut it down because of their anti-war stance. The paper's editorials, I imagine, were written on good strong coffee. And do you suppose the standard "side" of whipped cream, the net stockings so to speak of the café table, was deemed a tad frivolous?

> Soak at least 1/2 cup of **cannellini or Great Northern beans** in water to cover (plus a good inch more) for an hour or so; then cook them for at least an hour, covered,

adding more water if necessary. Meanwhile de-stem, wash and dry a cup or more of **spinach** leaves.

Chop 1 trimmed **leek**, 1 peeled **carrot**, 1 peeled **turnip** and 1/4 of a **fennel** bulb, all medium sized, then mince these vegetables in a blender or food processor. Next put them in a soup pot with 2 or 3 tablespoons of sliced **mushrooms**, some **thyme**, minced **parsley** and most of a 49-ounce can of **chicken broth** (or equivalent homemade). Simmer all, partly covered, for at least 30 minutes. Now add a 14-ounce can of **tomatoes** and simmer your soup 20 minutes more, uncovered.

Add the spinach and beans, well drained, and continue the simmering process another 10 minutes. Then serve this minestrone with little **French bread** toasts spread (or heaped) with a saffron mayonnaise that will run all about each diner's bowl, converting a pleasant veggie broth into a sybaritic treat, a . . . well, a mayonnaise soup.

Saffron mayonnaise is made as follows: combine 2 tablespoons of **lemon** juice and several shakes from your tiny container of **saffron** (don't lose that treasure), then stir in 2 pressed **garlic** cloves and several tablespoons of commercial **mayonnaise** of good quality (i.e.: not too sweet) and whisk well.

RED PEPPER AND CORN SOUP WITH SOUR CREAM AND JACK CHEESE

Pink, red and unctuous, this one. And with its tomato-peppers-cilantro orchestration you could perhaps call it a warm second cousin to a gazpacho. By the way, Alice B. Toklas that tongue-in-cheekiest cookbook writer found in her comprehensive gazpachan researches a Malaga version made with veal broth and rice, and a Cordoba specimen with cream. And in Seville a snippy shop assistant told her gazpacho is only eaten by peasants and Americans . . .

In a soup pot in 2 tablespoons of **butter** soften 1 large chopped **onion** and 1 large chopped **sweet red pepper**; add a 14-ounce can of **tomatoes**, several cups of **chicken broth** and the smallest unit imaginable of **cayenne**.

In a blender or food processor purée, in about 3 batches — otherwise you'll have a Niagara of airborne soup — 1 small can of drained cooked **corn** (not the creamed variety) with another 2 cups of broth and stir the mixture into the tomato/pepper brew. Bring all to a boil and simmer uncovered for 30 minutes.

Remove the soup from the heat, whisk in 1/2 cup of **sour cream** (low-fat suggested) and shower it lightly with shredded **Monterey Jack cheese**. Serve with a sprinkle of minced **cilantro**.

QUASI-HUNGARIAN MUSHROOM AND ASPARAGUS SOUP

A Mittel Europa mushroom soup is not easily found in cookbooks but strikes me as a necessary staple. Herewith, then, a little invention in the genre, light and fragrant. It's more, perhaps, for the sick man than the he-man, but no less rewarding for that. This is the sort of brothy nectar you might find in one of the better new hotels in what used to be East Germany, the Art'otel in Dresden, for example, a hilariously modern — and very comfortable — hostelry where the wash stands look like giant ice cream cones, the bathtub is an oval playpen and the lighting fixtures above the beds are unflappably mammary. But I must tell you, our room was so sexy in an abstract, test-tubey way that, if I remember right, we didn't feel very much like being physical therein.

There's competing fantasy in the mosque-like Wilhelmine cigarette factory across the way, improbable, abandoned, but There, Survival royalty. Maybe all the great Dresden *maestri*, Fritz Reiner, Fritz Busch, Karl Boehm, drove by it on the way to work.

In Dresden one goes to the Semper Oper where so many Strauss operas had their premieres, one promenades amazed in view of the Zwinger's ten-star porcelain collections, and one can't help noticing that all the little numbered pieces of a grand church under reconstruction look in their segments of scaffolding like so much Costco merchandise reaching for a warehouse ceiling.

Yes, the apostrophied Art'otel was a shade contrived . . . and the near-miss of its intended bacchanalization puts me in mind of what I offer as the sexiest room ever of our European travels. It was simply a little room with a bed and a view — and a bathroom that was an essay in chipped porcelain. The location was Moustiers-Ste-Marie in upper Provence, and the view down a long valley that had kept its soul intact.

The room was an unknowing vehicle for passion. And an era came to an end there, but I can't explain that until the book I intend to write next.

It helped to arrive in this room in a state of lyrical fatigue: the previous day we'd had to endure a roller-coaster ferry crossing from Corsica, followed by a trying absence of taxis in Nice, and a fall on an escalator, then a long drive up into the Provence hills — which we'd heretofore avoided, because they're written about and glowed over so much.

And a mis-reading of Michelin (this, I'm afraid, happens more often than it used to, now that they're chucking out charming hostelries not sufficiently modernized to the inspectors' taste) resulted in our spending a night in a motel-like place outside Moustiers itself. Anne knew I'd be a lot happier if I went out and found a simpatico hotel in town, the less modern the better, and the faience shops hadn't opened when I strode into the Belvedere and presented myself to the bartender who seemed to be in charge of bed and board. He was welcoming — and unquestionably gay and wanted to visit San Francisco at the earliest opportunity.

The vibes, in short, were right. I summoned Anne and we dragged our bags happily to the room with the chipped loo and the view and the soul . . .

> Soften 1 small chopped **onion** in a little **butter** along with a couple tablespoons of finely grated **carrot**. Add a cup of sliced/chopped/julienned **mushrooms** (oyster and shiitake, for instance) and 3 or 4 trimmed and rather finely minced **asparagus** stalks, **paprika** the veg lustily and toss them until they're nicely integrated.
> Now add 1 49-ounce can of **chicken broth,** a splash of **dry vermouth or white wine**, a pressed **garlic** clove and some **dill weed,** bring your soup to a boil and simmer it mostly uncovered for 30 minutes. Before serving, stir in a cup of **yogurt** off the fire.

CIUPPIN GENOVESE
—a puréed fish soup—

The most delightful moment in the preparation of this orange-brown ciuppin comes in our first paragraph, just when you notice the aroma of anchovy and celery getting acquainted. Such unions build up super interest in our olfactory memory banks.

Now back in '78 when we were in Genoa and ate at the incomparably named Nino da Nani e Mumo (with that fiery little Toscanini-sized conductor Molinari-Pradelli at the next table) we had fish soup of course, but it wasn't this one, no, Nino's ran another gamut, from calamari to gamberi, plus croutons.

People warned us away from Genoa, suggesting a menu of muggings would be our fate before the first pesto was tasted, but we emerged from its picturesque alleys (and numerous vowels) unscathed. Also charmed. Naturally a San Franciscan feels at home puffing his way up and down this sloping city with its funiculars headed for the stars. Then of course there's pesto, cima and pansoti between climbs, and those incredible Van Dycks at the Palazzo Rosso — paintings with eyes so penetrating they could see straight into a soufflé and all its frothy secrets. Meanwhile from the palazzo windows one looks through tombstone forests of TV antennae to the sea.

But our Genoese epiphany occurred one winter 6:30 a.m. when we took a rainswept walk along the narrow avenue of the palazzi, no one about but us and the streetsweepers.

- In a large pot in a tablespoon of **olive oil** — and stirring frequently — soften 1/2 **carrot**, 1/2 **onion** and 1/2 **celery rib**, all finely chopped (the carrot really ought to go in several minutes before its less slow-pokey brethren), adding to the mélange after a couple of minutes 1 large pressed **garlic** clove, 3 or 4 drained and finely chopped **anchovy** filets and about 1/4 cup of minced **parsley**, standard or Italian. Keep stirring for a good minute.
- Now add 2/3 cup of **dry vermouth** and cook your mush enough to palpably reduce the liquid content; then add 1 14-ounce can of **tomatoes** ("ready cut" is best), 3 or so cups of **fish stock** and some **salt** and **pepper**, bring all to a boil, lower the heat and simmer for 25 minutes, mostly covered.
- (The fish stock you can produce as you start this recipe: while softening those first paragraph veg boil a pound or so of **fish bones** from the market with 1/4 cup of carrot-onion-&-celery pieces in 4 cups of **water**, reducing the liquid by about a quarter and straining it).
- Now you have a viable soup, a lovely and slightly sea-influenced vegetable tomato broth, but continue, else you will have an Unfinished Symphony on your table. Add at least 1/2 pound of fileted **halibut and/or butterfish** in chunks and simmer the soup another 10 minutes, uncovered. Then cool it for 10 minutes and, in batches, briefly purée it in a blender or food processor. Include the fish pieces in the purée or not as you please.
- *Finalmente*, return the ciuppin to a second pot or large saucepan and warm it for several minutes, until the consistency is half-way-to-creamy. Serving this soup with croutons (see page ???) is strongly recommended.

PURÉE OF CAULIFLOWER AND WATERCRESS

Two-toned and delicate, and vaguely related to Leek and Potato, this is an excellent cream soup for a cold winter day, or when your mind lights on a nostalgia for things Northern, a panelled Luebeck rathskeller, say, or a dowdily luxurious Amsterdam salle.

Or perhaps a restaurant like the sprawling and sparsely populated one in Copenhagen's Tivoli where, one evening long ago, a nine-piece palm court orchestra lit gamely into the Finlandia hymn with such fervor this DC7-lagged tourist couldn't help weeping into his soup. Such fun! Well, it had been twenty hours from San Francisco, with a stop at Winnipeg then a leisurely drone-and-rattle through the spacious twilight of the North — complete with SAS's cooked-to-order scrambled eggs served with courtly Nordic precision by the brass-buttoned pursers to one and all.

Such airborne eggs of yesteryear I can scarcely fathom in this era of millennial cattle cars. Now Amtrak, that's where the proper cooking of an egg is a grave responsibility, a matter of nothing less than kitchen honor. Figure in the fluffy biscuits and you have something close to breakfast heaven, with Lake Erie and its gulls or a Nevada morning at your side.

> Break off the flowerets of a medium-sized **cauliflower** and steam them until they're almost limp, then reserve 'em. Meanwhile in a large pot soften 1 small chopped **onion** in a good tablespoon of **butter** along with 1 small diced **red or white potato**; add 3/4 of a 49-ounce can of **chicken broth** — you can freeze the remainder — bring it to a boil and simmer, covered, for 20 minutes, until the potato is done.
>
> In a blender or food processor purée the broth and the cauliflower in batches, adding 1/2 bunch of washed and de-stemmed **watercress** in the later stages. Re-heat the soup in another pot or saucepan, stirring in 1/4 cup of **cream**, then serve it with a light sprinkle of grated **gruyère, cheddar, dry jack or parmesan cheese**. Croutons would not be ill-advised.

LEONIDA'S FARINATA

Leonida Frediani, Don's mother, was, not long ago, a lovely little lady of 93 who still cooked up a storm of "old country" dishes. She was still driving to the market from her hilltop house to choose her provisions with an unfoolable eye: for the right peach, the best pear, the freshest Blue Lake bean — if, that is, she wasn't picking lunch or dinner from the huge vegetable garden just below her kitchen window: such fussiness, alas, has become socially unacceptable. I suspect Leonida was so tuned to the heart of the gastronomical matter she didn't notice that three-star view over the Russian River valley and down to the distant stream of traffic on Highway 101, a million feet, it could have been, below her Shangri-La.

Meanwhile Mr. Frediani, if he wasn't off hunting — he'd invested well and retired from his Plymouth agency at fifty-five — would lounge in the well-stuffed and very red leather chair he was allowed to retain amidst the fine crisp lines of a modern house son Don had commissioned from the architect Mario Corbett.

Now a polenta minestrone such as Leonida's Farinata is a rare thing in cookbooks and in restaurants too — San Francisco's Fior d'Italia used to offer it sometimes at lunch — but well known in old Lucchesan families either side of the Atlantic. Here are cabbage and sausages again as in Gigi's Alsatian soup, but translated from Strasbourg to the bucolic Garfagnana just north of Lucca the meat-and-veg change their colors, so to speak. Whatever its provenance, this is your perfect soup for a winter day, the ideal meal-in-a-bowl, a singing porridge to please the soul as well as tum.

Leonida and my mother got on very well. They came from quite different backgrounds, *garlic* and *non-garlic*, etc., but they were both perfectionists in "quality of life" concerns — and, because of that, they had their cranky moments, not at times un-operatic I should add. When Don Frediani was a Navy officer in Korean waters, my mother wrote him faithfully: letters Victorian in their formality yet utterly up-to-date in their feistyness.

In a large pot simmer for an hour, covered:

- 1 small **ham hock** with the skin left on
- 2 **Italian sausages** cut into thick rounds
- 1 small head of sliced **cabbage**
- 1/2 bunch of **chard**, trimmed, washed and torn into manageable pieces
- 1 14-ounce can of **tomatoes**
- 2 cups of cooked **cannellini beans**, drained (the canned variety has Leonida's stamp of approval)
- 2 cloves of **garlic**, sliced thin
- **pepper**
- 5 cups of **chicken broth**

When the soup is virtually ready to serve take out the ham hock, skin it and cut the meat into pieces and put them back in the pot, then slowly add a cup of coarse **polenta**, stirring constantly until it's well mixed into the soup. This is prelude to simmering the soup for 25 minutes more, stirring it every 5 minutes or less to prevent the polenta sticking to the pot.

Serve this Farinata with a teaspoon of **olive oil** drizzled over each serving plus a little shower of grated **dry jack or parmesan cheese**.

LEFTOVERS? Reheat the soup, topped with a little olive oil and a lot of grated cheese, in a skillet coated with oil, then run it under the broiler until brown. The result is no longer a soup, it's a polenta cassoulet!

ZANZIBAR CHICKEN SOUP WITH AVOCADO AND CAPERS

And here is our version of the piquant Colombian soup we ate at a vibrant little tapas palace in San Francisco's gastronomically formidable Mission District — off a tabletop suggesting perhaps too vividly the spots of a leopard.

Save a piece or more of chicken, some carrot and all the remaining broth from our **Boiled Chicken and Vegetables** (page 104). Skim the fat off the broth, heat it and cook in it the kernels of a small ear of **corn**. Then skin and bone the chicken, cut it into juliennes and warm them in the soup for a minute or so.

To complete the ensemble, top the chicken-and-broth in each diner's bowl with a little **yogurt**, **avocado** chunks and **small capers** to taste, and serve with a relish-like, minimally liquid salsa verde made with small amounts of **olive oil** and **red wine vinegar** (about 2 to 1) along with a little minced **onion** and rather a lot of **parsley** rat-tat-tatted into mince with a big sharp knife such as you see on the TV cooking shows.

And was it sprouts or a second-rate slaw Leonida Frediani from her verdant mountain top dismissed as "lawn trimmings"?

Remembrance of Things Lost:

My sister Julie who's ten years older than I am (older enough, that is, to have pretended she was making gin in the bathtub during Prohibition) reminds me that back around 1931 Pop Ernt was still alive and joyfully presided at a tableside Rite of the Crêpes Suzette at his enchanting restaurant at Monterey Wharf. There was more, in short, than clam chowder and the mackerel-abalone-rock cod I remember Pop's lanky son reciting. But all would eventually be lost; by my college days Pop's sons, the tall one and the short one, had retired, selling their restaurant to a piscatorial entrepreneur of considerably less cachet. And then, shortly after, as if old Pop had posthumously released some ancient Hanseatic malediction, the successor restaurant burned, well not to the ground but down to the mud of Monterey Bay.

As for the *Del Monte Express*, my beloved Pacific-powered puffer that would steam into the station across the way at 6:52 p.m., proud bell ding-donging into the summer mist: well, first it was the maestro of the snacks and drinks in the parlor car who retired after thirty years' service (and the SP kindly named the car after Oliver Millet), then it was the train itself that became history, victim of California's love affair with Fords, Chevys and Toyotas that don't have a big number like 2-4-8-2 stamped on the side in large white letters a small child could read from a hundred yards.

There must have been a printed menu at Ernt's, but the regulation litany seems to have been all we needed for ordering. I'd give a royalty cheque to have a copy of Ernt's *carte* for my menu collection, which ranges from the much comma'd laundry list of old Jack's in San Francisco — before it was pulled kicking and screaming into a millennial yuppification — to the flights of graphic fantasy favored by Benoit in Paris or André Daguin in Auch-en-Gascogne. Occasionally chefs penned inscriptions, and my favorite is the one by Jean Peronnet of the long-gone Chapeau Rouge in Feurs, a little town west of Lyon we visited in '73. M. Peronnet had as many Michelin rosettes as the urbane M. Daguin, but he looked one morning in his smock and beret more like the proprietor of a country hardware emporium than a celebrity chef.

No inscriber for my menu cache has come close to his lovely (and something is lost in translation): *"With my compliments, hoping to see you again, have a safe trip, be healthy."*

—*RISOTTOS*—

Risottos are hard labor, and rich, but essential. Your goal is a creamy texture — as Carlo Middione says, "like a loose mud slide." Be sure to have 35 or 40 ounces of broth at the ready.

RISOTTO: basic steps

In a skillet soften a chopped **onion** in a tablespoon of **butter**, then turn up the heat, add 1 cup of **long grain rice** and sauté it for 1-1/2 to 2 minutes, until opaque, stirring constantly. Reduce the heat some, add a cup of **chicken or vegetable broth** and a liberal sprinkle of **saffron** — repeat, liberal! — then during the next 30 minutes stir your maturing risotto almost continuously, adding more broth as the liquid is absorbed: this you will do six or eight times at least.

Accursed procedure? Perhaps, but YOU are the sculptor in charge, the constant hands-on creator of what will be a lovely finished product. Brahms lovers while circling their skillets with a motivated arm might think of the soft tidal opening of the fourth symphony, at a rather leisurely tempo, say, of sixty-six half notes to the minute. The writer Jane Kramer used to stir to "the solemn rhythms of late Eliot," but needing something "more hypnotic than sublime," switched to the *Argonautika* of Apollonius. Whatever your driving force, don't be afraid to steal a standing wink or two along the way.*

AND an assortment of finishes:

RISOTTO WITH DRIED FRUITS AND PINE NUTS

Soak several tablespoons of assorted chopped **dried fruits** in boiling water and drain. When the rice is almost done, stir in the fruits and 2 tablespoons of toasted **pine nuts** (sautéed a minute or more in a small pan without fat) and a little grated **dry jack or parmesan cheese**. Serve in soup bowls and pass more grated cheese.

RISOTTO WITH BABY GRAPES AND BASIL

De-stem a generous supply of **Corinth (baby) grapes** and chop a liberal amount of fresh **basil**. When the rice is almost done, stir in the grapes and basil and some grated **dry jack or parmesan cheese**. Serve in soup bowls and pass more grated cheese.

* We're on a bit of a limb adding the broth straight from the can at room temperature rather than ladling it from a simmering pot, but your skillet will be so warm from sautéing the rice over high heat that the broth will boil instantly.

Risotto with Salami and Nectarines (or Mangoes)

Cut **salami** into juliennes and dice **nectarines or** peeled **mangoes** sufficient to make a good textural contrast to the rice and stir these into the risotto when it's almost done along with grated **cheese**. Salami and dried figs, by the way, are awesome with yogurt and Mary Kelley's mango chutney (page ???).

Risotto al Limone

Beat an **egg** with the juice of 1/2 a **lemon**, adding some grated lemon rind. When the rice is almost done, take it off the fire and add the egg-lemon mixture, minced **parsley** and grated **dry jack or parmesan cheese**; return the risotto to the fire and cook another minute or more.

Risotto with Portobello Mushroom Sauté

Trim, wash and slice into 1-inch lengths a **portobello mushroom** and sauté it in a good tablespoon of **butter** with a generous amount of **lemon** juice, minced **parsley** and pressed **garlic**. Stir the mushroom sauté into the risotto at the last moment along with grated **dry jack or parmesan cheese**.

Risotto with Shrimp and Bacon (or Juniper Berries)

Fry some oblongs of **thick cut or slab bacon** and add them — or the juniper berries — to the rice at the last minute along with some **cooked shrimp**: figure on about 10 bacon "bits" per serving and at least 3 tablespoons of shrimp. Adding grated **cheese** goes without saying.

Risotto Verde

Gently sauté 2 small sliced **mushrooms** with a little finely grated **carrot**, several tablespoons of chopped raw **spinach** and a few shreds of **prosciutto**, capping all with a pinch of **nutmeg**. Add these items to the rice at the last minute along with the ever-necessary grated **cheese**.

Risotto Meneghina

From a Milan trattoria with too much attitude but excellent rice.

Stir into your rice at the last minute several tablespoons of lightly whipped **cream**, along with minced **parsley** and grated **dry jack or parmesan cheese**.

Risotto del Cambio

From an eighteenth century Turin ristorante with lovely mirrors, columns and chandeliers far outweighing attitude — but don't arrive too early, you'll be seriously outnumbered by a chorus of attentive waiters.

Same as previous recipe plus a good shot of **red wine**. And you could dress up this risotto by stirring in 1/2 pound of rock cod 3 or 4 minutes before estimated completion time. In this case the cream is optional.

SUN-DRIED TOMATO RISOTTO

And this recipe has its own first steps.

Soak an ounce of chopped **dried tomatoes** in a cup of water until soft, then reserve the liquid and combine it with several cups of **chicken broth.**

Soften a chopped **onion** with 1 pressed **garlic** clove in a tablespoon of **olive oil**. Stir in 1 cup of **rice**, toss it for 1-1/2 minutes over rather high heat, then reduce the flame, add the tomatoes and proceed with the usual additions and stirrings of, in this case, a chicken broth with dried tomato cooking liquid.

When the risotto is ready, sprinkle it with minced **parsley** and serve with the **dry jack or parmesan cheese** you must always grate before beginning a risotto: to add broth, stir rice, fondle your tiny bottle of saffron and grate cheese more or less simultaneously would lead, I think, to dire psychological consequences.

REMEMBER: Risottos can be made ahead and reheated without flavor loss: just stir in a little fresh broth. A boon, this, when company comes for simple chicken and portobello risotto. Another idea: salmon steak with mango risotto minus the salami. Or how about pesto-flavored risotto fritters? Or risotto with pancetta and water-packed chestnuts from M. Faugier's tin . . . And there's always that Piemontan last minute drizzle of truffle and olive oil, half a tablespoon each, wonderful with a mushroom risotto.

Sartorial Note:

We are not all that fond of posh places to eat, but sometimes research must be done on the lobster-&-truffles circuit, a thin wallet palpitating in the process. Well, it's not always convenient to dress up, and I'm happy to say Madame Point accepted us in picnic clothes at her multi-rosetted Pyramide and the folks at Sacher's in Vienna let us in without a green light from Mr. St. Laurent. Nor did we rent striped pants-and-trimmings when a count and countess invited us to lunch one springtime in Florence.

But I have experienced what it's like to be left at the door.

Currently a friendly place, the Clift Hotel in San Francisco was owned in the ribald 70s by an ultra-conservative Santa Barbaran who refused admission to any gentleman whose hair fell the slightest distance below the water line of one's Brooks Bros. collar top. I qualified very well at the time and was thus deprived, at least during the reign of this Jesse Helms of a hotelier, of the delightful lamb curry offered in the French Room, a silvery salle that seemed to float, oblivious of the seedy arrondissement lapping at its back door, like the first class dining saloon of a Titanic or Lusitania that had made it, somehow, into modern times.

In Chicago not long ago, eager for a look at the Pump Room where the movie stars used to enbooth themselves between compartmental nights on the old *Super Chief* and *Twentieth Century* — which carried them, through their joint steamy efforts, from L.A. to Chicago and the "Windy City" to New York — I was advised by the hostess, a young woman in pants, that my blazer and regimental tie had failed utterly to conceal my crisply pressed jeans, Land's End's best, which were, alas, not part of the Pumpean dress code. Now perhaps if the Pump people rolled out a cashmere carpet in my direction . . .

—PASTAS—

IN GENERAL...

Unless otherwise noted, the recipes in this chapter are for the saucing of good quality commercial dried fettuccine, about 1/4 pound per person for main course dining.

You want to drop the pasta into boiling water (a large pot of it!), stir it occasionally to prevent sticking, and remove it after exactly 12 minutes — well, it's all right to be five or ten seconds off — this allowing time for the water to return to a good boil after the pasta goes in. Twelve minutes should give you a golden mean pasta, neither chewy nor mushy. (For shells and tubes, check the timing on the box and add several minutes).

When the pasta reaches the zero hour, so to speak, drain it in a colander, letting a bit of liquid cling to the strands, then pour it into a serving bowl where it will impatiently await your sauce, along with grated cheese: either the robust dry jack we favor or the daintier, more traditional parmesan (one man's sand, I guess, is the other's parmesan). Now stir your sauce in well.

And always leave extra grated cheese on the table — you know what it feels like in a restaurant when the waiter whisks the cheese away or parks your bottle of wine in a bucket a small football field from your rapidly emptying glass.

Before proceeding, I should add that the Bloomfields occasionally dine on a pasta dish not included in the formal precincts, so to speak, of this chapter, because, well, it's scarcely a recipe, merely pasta — tubes, preferably — tossed with butter and grated cheese . . . except that I should add that lots of freshly ground black pepper, a significant issue of nutmeg, and a medley of herbs gathered more or less at random from pots on your deck or in your garden will bring this minestran offering to star status. Very little effort is involved here, and you won't be reduced to succumbing to the charms of your upscale supermarket's take-out counter, or the promise of a pizza delivery person at your door.

Alas, pasta with butter and cheese pure and simple, unadulterated by imagination, proved a thing of comedy, and not a very high variety, when Anne and I traveled one night on the ferry from Naples to Palermo. Here we were, bobbing about on presumably Italian waters, and what could the kitchen come up with but bowls of pasta, pats of cold butter and containers of grated cheese, these ingredients to be assembled by the diners aboard the M.S. Sicilia as if they were children hooking together pieces of Lego.

Our consolation was that next morning, like Paul Theroux, we beheld the Bay of Palermo "in a sunny Sicilian dawn . . . mountains on either side and a great harmonizing background of stucco-colored peaks behind the ancient buildings."

PASTA AL POMODORO
—house tomato sauce—

This is a "mother" sauce, our trusty house tomato, and the Busseto and Agrodolce that follow are offspring involving diverse elaborations — if they're siblings they're radically different in personality, one suave, the other frisky.

Stout and tranquil, Carlo Bergonzi himself was behind the bar when we visited the beloved tenor's Due Foscari in Busseto in '71: in this civilian role he shed all vestiges of footlight glamor. I'm not sure now exactly what the tomato/cream balance was in Signor Bergonzi's pasta sauce; for years we've been enjoying it as about 75 or 80 percent tomato to 20–25 cream. Well, recently our daughter Cecily was preparing a good tomato/cream pasta recipe (with sautéed sliced zucchini!) and in this one the balance was inverted, in other words it was a cream sauce with flecks of tomato, and since we didn't have enough cream on hand about a quarter of the "white element" was milk. This resulted in a marvelously light and fragrant sauce, and the chance to offer you a Busseto I and II. Also note: several pinches of red pepper flakes, while not precisely Busseto-esque, are amusing in these recipes.

- Soften 1 thinly sliced **onion** in 1 or 2 tablespoons of **olive oil**, adding 1 clove of pressed **garlic** as the onion colors.
- Stir in 1 28-ounce or 2 14-ounce cans of **tomatoes** (even with the "ready cut" variety you may want to use a potato masher to un-kink your sauce) and season them with several pinches of **sugar**, a little **oregano,** and a splash of **dry sherry** — it needn't be a distinguished one — to give a little "complexity." A nice sec or demi-sec white wine would be a more than ordinary alternate.
- Now simmer all uncovered for 20 minutes or more: you want the sauce to reduce a fair amount but not become really thick before it's combined with your boiled **pasta** and a small avalanche of grated **dry jack or parmesan cheese**. Note here that Greek black olives are an amusing occasional extra . . .

and
PASTA ALLA BUSSETO
—souvenir of Carlo Bergonzi's albergo (two versions)—

I
- The same sauce as above, into which you stir toward serving time 1/4 to 1/3 cup of lightly reduced **cream**, plus a few thick-sliced **mushrooms** (brown or "boutique" would be best) you've sautéed in a little **butter**.

II

Make about half as much of our tomato sauce and stir in a good cup of the "white element," mostly **cream** with some **milk** . . .

**and
PASTA AL AGRODOLCE**

While simmering the above basic tomato sauce add 2 overflowing tablespoons each of **yellow raisins** and **pine nuts** along with a few **chocolate chips**, plus about 1/4 cup of **red wine vinegar** and 2 teaspoons of **sugar**, gastronomical opposites whose in-sauce sparring will be conducted for your benefit — best, by the way, to combine all these ingredients first.

PASTA AL PESTO
made with pine nuts, walnuts or pistachio nuts

There are some quirks here from the purist's point of view, but we lap this up every two or three weeks throughout the year with virtually unfailing pleasure.

I think "the Auguri man" would have liked my pesto. Those three words, alas, are all that's left of him in my diary for '71, but he was a haunting figure, like an ancient beggar/philosopher in some oldtime opera. We were leaving Signor Bergonzi's inn the morning after the pasta of the previous page (thinking, perhaps, of Bergonzi's exquisite phrasing in the big third act aria of *Forza del Destino*) and there he was, venerable enough to have known the great Verdi himself, who hailed from Busseto, hobbling about with a cane, saluting our industry in coming to this untouted corner of his country, insisting our journey would be full of joy and meaning.

The pistachio version is the most intense of my three, but not unduly so. It was over a plate of it the conductor John Mauceri revealed an ingredient in Brahms' Third I'd never realized was there: the passionate opening of the slow movement's coda is a quote from the finale of Wagner's *Goetterdaemmerung* — Wagner had just died as Brahms was preparing for his symphony's premiere.

John, I must report, cleaned his plate.

In a blender or food processor mince 2 or 3 tablespoons of one or another of the above-listed **nuts**; then in the same apparatus purée with the nuts:

    1 cup of chopped **fresh basil**

    a short 1/4 teaspoon of **lemon** juice

    a smidgen of **nutmeg** (for that mysterious added richness, as if the sauce were beginning to turn a corner to . . . ?)

    1 large pressed **garlic** clove

3 or 4 tablespoons of grated **dry jack or parmesan cheese**

2/3 cup of **olive oil** ("pure" is fine!)

Now stir your pesto into boiled **pasta** with more grated cheese.

AS A MATTER OF FACT: This pesto is also good without nuts, pine or other.

PASTA AL PESTO TRAPANESE

A Sicilian cousin of the above, as delectable with poached salmon as boiled fettuccine. And note the charm of this pesto swirled into a corn soup made with a little onion, chicken broth and lime.

Signor Cipollina, the padrone of the U.S. Restaurant in my hometown's North Beach, is from Trapani, accent on the first syllable. He tells me that yes it's true, on a clear day you can see North Africa from Erice, the ghostly hill town near his city. I must salute Signor Cipollina here for the utter calm with which he and his staff glide about their open kitchen, carving bolliti like culinary Michelangelos and spooning up fine red sauces with the deftest of hands. Restaurants are only as good as the concept behind them; the idea of building on Serenity as well as clean silverware is, for this foodie at least, an impressive one.

For this pesto repeat the previous recipe substituting ground **almonds**, omitting the nutmeg and adding 1 large chopped **tomato**.

PASTA AL GORGONZOLA

This rich and captivating sauce is versatile. It would be excellent with the tortellini several pages on in this book as well as our habitual fettuccine, it's been seen in recent years in concert with poached pears and fried polenta, and — don't sneer — I can taste it with bacon and tomato draped over an English muffin old coffee shoppe "Rarebit" style: Wallace and Gromit, can you hear me?

Tuning my memory more precisely, I remember eating a *comme il faut* cheddar-blanketed rarebit at a decidedly down-market corner house where I, a young critic on one of San Francisco's Siamese twin dailies — joined in the workrooms of their common printer-circulator — used to eat in the silent company of Skid Row gentlemen. I did so because the bustle and gossip of the only nearby alternative, a newspapermen's pub, were not in sync with my midday regimen, to wit, the imbibing of verbal fertility pills in the form of Rarebit-side reading matter, choice paragraphs, say, by V.S. Pritchett or Graham Greene.

Three decades later, gentrification has, of course, turned Newspaper Row into a gourmet ghetto to be reckoned with: confits de canard are elbowing those ketchup-drenched burgers. My corner house, by the way, issued from its cafeteria display a tapioca pudding that was a minor work of art, all bubbles and solidity.

Over a low flame heat about 1/4 pound of **gorgonzola or a good Wisconsin blue cheese**, 1/3 cup of **milk** and 3 tablespoons of **butter**, mashing all together well. Cook this mash until it's creamy-smooth, adding a little **pepper**, **nutmeg**, and fresh **chives** if you have them, finely minced. Set aside.

Just before your **pasta** is done, turn the sauce on, over a low flame, adding — and integrating nicely — 1/2 cup of moderately whipped **cream**. Work in 2 or 3 tablespoons of grated **dry jack or parmesan cheese**, plus 1/4 cup of **white wine**, before combining sauce and boiled pasta, then add more cheese.

ALTERNATIVE: Substitute goat cheese for the blue, delete the chives and work in a little radicchio lightly softened in a bit of butter.

PASTA AGLIO E OLIO

For some odd reason it's considered improper to serve this pasta with grated cheese, whether parmesan or our beloved dry jack. I can understand why the proprietress of a trattoria in Bergamo once refused us such a frill atop pasta ai quattro formaggi, that would have been gilding a lily in full bloom, but it seems to me the forbidden parmigiana mates exceedingly well with oil and garlic, giving this piatto its third dimension.

Bergamo is also where a vigorous all-night fountain outside our albergo window misled us into thinking the heavens had opened.

And it's the town where we enjoyed casoncelli Bergamasca, with melted butter, pancetta and sage. Casoncelli are crescent-shaped pasta hats suggesting a baseball cap pointing both ways or the zanily protuberant headgear of Don Basilio the disreputable music master in *Barber of Seville*. The puffed-up area in the center of these edibles crafted, it seems, by some mad hatter holds the filling of choice.

Our imminent arrival in Bergamo was amply heralded. Speaking as it were into an ear trumpet to the deaf nonna manning the front desk of our intended Bergamo inn, the trim, tart concierge at the Duca di York in Milan intoned operatically, for all in his lobby to hear, a geographical illumination of B-l-o-o-m-f-i-e-l-d: BOLOGNA, LIVORNO, OTRANTO OTRANTO, MILANO (a breath here), FIRENZE, IMOLA, EMPOLI, LIVORNO (and crescendo!) DOMODOSSOLA.

I was sorry we weren't eligible for POGGIBONSI, a battle cry of sorts.

While your 1/2 pound or so of **fettuccine** is doing its 12 minutes in the pot, slowly sauté in a skillet, in a pool of 3 or 4 tablespoons of **olive oil** (or more, because it will cling to the pan when you need it at serving time), about 10 or 12 peeled and sliced **garlic** cloves. When they're a little brown turn the heat up for about 45 seconds, add a heap of minced **parsley** and sauté all until crisp but not burned. Don't fail to combine pasta and aglio-olio with grated **dry jack or parmesan cheese**.

THRILL RIDE: To capture the deep woodsy flavor of a good Piemontese *Bagna Calda* while cutting out the signature cream and avoiding six hours of stirring, not to mention a trip along heartburn lane, you could slow down that final 45 seconds of the above recipe, stirring in along with the parsley fairly generous portions of chopped

anchovy and **dried porcini or mixed "boutique" dried mushrooms**, the funghi soaked briefly in a little water.

AND: Mrs. Bloomfield reports great satisfaction with leftover pasta aglio e olio stirred into leftover broth from roasting a chicken. The entrancing bouquet of this inspiration — my wife did not graduate with honors for nothing — I can vouch for.

PASTA ALLA CARBONARA DELLA CASA

Was there really a time before Carbonara? I tend to forget that fifty years ago one of San Francisco's top Italian restaurants could offer in the pasta department (they called it "Italian Paste") Chicken Ravioli, Egg Tagliarini, Spaghetti and Lasagnette, and that was it. So many oldtime places served a pallid reddened Bolognese a tale developed that it was pumped down from a great vat in Coit Tower, looming a little mockingly, one suspects, over North Beach.

Then we read about Carbonara, the charcoal burners' pasta, in a column by that intrepid traveler Stan Delaplane, just back from Italy. It was a new dish sent us on a silver — well, ceramic — platter. We ran with it and have not stopped serving it since. Recipes vary some: garlic is sometimes added, which is acceptable, or cream, which rather changes the dish's character. The pasta is sometimes added to undrained bacon for stirring over the fire, but this can coat your "paste" with too much fat.

Carbonara, I might tell you, did me a very good turn, about ten years ago, nourishing me with a pile of High Comfort fare when I was locked into the period in my life I now refer to as my "blue period." It was an appalling time, I was drowning in the unruly sea of a complex literary project beyond the powers of a single mortal to bring, as it were, into port, and a lingering journalistic commitment, from which I should have bailed out, had me placing one inappropriate word after another in a public print when I had lost the will to write and thought I would never dream up a metaphor again.

But Carbonara, which I cooked, in my sleep more or less, every week without fail — and pan fried trout was a friend, too — helped considerably to make life somewhat bearable: I suppose it was the bacon and eggs, those pillars of our traditional American breakfast, brunch and perhaps midnight snack, that dribbled crumbs of happiness into the big void, while Fate was evolving me (without pills, I want to stress) toward a rosier future than I thought possible.

P.S.: There was a time before pesto too. I've just found a Morrison Wood column from a 1960 food page in which his Italian neighbor offers him fresh basil for pesto and he responds, "Pesto? What on earth is that?" In San Francisco today that would be the equivalent of asking, who's Joe DiMaggio?

In a mixing bowl combine 1 whisked **egg** per serving with a lively hailstorm of **black pepper**, a pinch of **nutmeg**, 3 tablespoons of grated **dry jack or parmesan cheese** and some minced **parsley** (or better, **fresh rosemary** needles).

Fry about 8 or 10 oblongs of **thick cut or slab bacon** — or **pancetta**! — per serving, drain them on paper towels, then stir them quickly into the egg mixture after you've drained your boiled **pasta** and put it in a serving dish. A little curdling is inevitable, and will not reduce the yumminess of your completed Carbonara.

PASTA "TRASIMENO" WITH EGG, COPPA, PEAS AND LEMON ZEST

This is a cross between a lemony Elizabeth David "Pasta Giovanna" with chicken livers (which I've jettisoned as a trifle heavy) and a dish half-remembered from the Trasimeno restaurant visited on a brief and heady trip to Perugia in 1966. As you see, it's a distant relative of our old friend Carbonara. The pasta at the Trasimeno must have been homemade because I see by my diary that the waiter expounded: "You must make it yourself with arms."

Another year we established ourselves as interns in pasta studies at Perugia's nearby La Rosetta and inventoried such regional specimens as spaghetti with black truffles and a light shower of breadcrumbs, tagliatelle attended by a garlicky black olive and anchovy purée, and, our graduation number, delicately-stuffed tortellini tucked into patty shells and blanketed to the ears with a tomato-cream sauce. This was the minestran equivalent of encasing the Taj Mahal in the Empire State Building.

From Perugia it wasn't far to Spello, a household word, as it were, to those vocal few who consider it one of Umbria's gems. Spello is a tilted horseshoe of a hilltown, one street up and one down. Three quarters of the way up one stops at the Cacciatore hotel and dines on tagliatelle with truffles and homemade ravioli stuffed to the edges.

Speaking of elevation levels, I'm reminded that not all my Umbrian reminiscences are food-related: there were, for instance, the steps of Gualdo Tadino. Two friends from Zurich and I were on our way from Perugia to Urbino in a Volkswagen bug and, logically enough, drove to the top of this interesting hill town to, well, see what was Up There. But no roadway down could be found, only a wide staircase pointed toward Square One so to speak, and so we bumpity-bumpity-BUMPED slowly down this medieval pre-Volksian thoroughfare in the lowest gear modern science could devise (lucky we weren't in a finned Cadillac of that era), our unintended escalierian exhibition causing the locals to audibly mutter, "Zurigo, pazzi," that meaning, these mad people from Zurich (the license plates gave us away).

Slinking out of town as best they could, the three Zurigans did achieve lovely Urbino, dined on arrosto misto in Ferrara — a town I would fall deeply in love with thirty-two years later when I saw it by daylight! — and reach Venice and the humid bedsheets of the Pensione Calcina near midnight. Venice should always be entered at night, that way one hears the eternal lapping of its waters at their best.

In a mixing bowl combine 1 whisked **egg** per serving with a dozen juliennes or more of **mild coppa**, 1 tablespoon of grated **lemon** rind, 1 pressed **garlic** clove, 2 tablespoons of thawed and briefly warmed **frozen peas**, generous **pepper**, a little **nutmeg** and **rosemary,** and grated **dry jack or parmesan cheese** to taste.

Then as in all these pasta sauce recipes drain your 1/2 pound or so of boiled **pasta** in a colander, pour it into a serving bowl and mix in the sauce, drawing meanwhile on your reserve arsenal of grated cheese.

PORTOBELLO PASTA WITH SAUSAGE AND CREAM

These sautéed portobellos which are a running theme in this collection (portobello ritornello?) are also delicious served on toast — which I always think of as Toast aux Champignons because I first experienced this combination in a French-speaking situation. Oh dear, it was a deadly grey afternoon in Brussels, forty-seven years ago, and I was just getting it into my head that the pretty-ankled pianist I was eating mushrooms with was never going to be as excited about me as I was about her.

Next day as it happened a stellar rainbow presented itself to me standing in the corridor of the Paris train and I fully saw the light. But back to the toast. Place your portobelli on a "pane integrale" of the Berkeley school and you ought to be in heaven. Well, that blonde pianist in Brussels did introduce me to the lovely Cygne on the Grande Place with its heady selection of sole cooked every which way — sole searching? — before I put my shy and worshipful love, so bloody amateur, to rest.

I have no regrets, this pink-ankled keyboardist was not for me. It was interesting, though, to hear from a mutual friend just recently that the Mademoiselle in question, although American, would never have considered marrying anyone who wasn't French. Well, I suppose a non-Flemish Belgian might have been, to use an international word, o.k.

Now was it Ravel's Sonatine she used to play so well?

Gently fry 1/3 pound of **ground pork sausage** just past red, drain it and reserve. Meanwhile, trim, wash and slice into 1-inch lengths a **portobello mushroom**, then in the same pan sauté them in a good tablespoon of **butter** with a generous splash of **lemon** juice, minced **parsley** and a fairly large pressed **garlic** clove.

When the portobello is well on the way to browning, add at least 3/4 of a cup of **cream** and reduce it to a rich but not pasty consistency — with a nice jigger or more of **dry sherry** for heightened personality.

Now toss your eight ounces of boiled **pasta** with the cream-and-mushroom sauté, the sausage, a little **nutmeg,** and grated **dry jack or parmesan cheese** of course. Fettuccine are recommended as usual, but also penne or shells.

PASTA NIÇOISE

This Niçoise was inspired by a picture in a French airline magazine. It sang! Really juicy farmers' market-type tomatoes are strongly recommended, also those big Sicilian anchovies if you have a good Italian deli in range. You'll have to wash their salt blankets off, and trim them, but this is a small price to pay for the added flavor.

Divide 1 **tomato** per serving into eighths and combine it in a skillet with **olive oil**, **lemon** juice and **red wine vinegar** (plus pressed **garlic**, **rosemary** and **oregano**) in an approximately 4-1-1 balance — our Lupo vinaigrette, in short. Warm the tomato wedges, tossing them gently for 3 or 4 minutes before adding several fileted **anchovies**, drained on paper towels and chopped, for a little joint sautéing. Combine with your boiled **pasta** (shells are especially recommended in this case) and grated **dry jack or parmesan cheese**.

PASTA WITH BACON, SAUTÉED LEEKS AND TOMATO VINAIGRETTE

Now several *contemporary* pasta preparations — first, a sort of Matriciana seen through the modern foodie's glass. Note that doggie-bagged Smoked Tea Duck from a good Chinese restaurant may be fruitfully substituted for the bacon element (and in this case you may need a little olive oil to lubricate the cooking of the leeks) — this Asian touch, I suspect, makes the dish even more modern.

- Cut 2 slices of **thick cut or slab bacon** or 2 thick rounds of **pancetta** into approximately 1-inch lengths and fry them, subsequently draining them on paper towels; then gently sauté 2 washed, trimmed and thinly sliced **leeks** in the fat remaining in the skillet in which the bacon was cooked ("cipollini" onions would be a fine alternative).
- Next, stir the leeks and the bacon into your boiled **pasta**, along with a vinaigrette of 2 tablespoons **olive oil** to 1-plus of **red wine vinegar** dotted with a large chopped **tomato** ("hothouse" or other farmers'-market types preferred).
- Also in your pasta-tossing include lots of **pepper** (and chives if you're using onions instead of leeks) and a near-reckless helping of grated cheese — I recommend in this case that rugged individual, pale, dour **pecorino**: it's quite sharp in taste, rather aggressively salty, and addictive. True pecorinans never say *basta*.

PASTA WITH BEURRE NOIR AND BALSAMIC VINEGAR

This is the easiest pasta in the world to fix, and tastes wonderful, especially with a regular blizzard of grated cheese. Even Mr. Bean could make a go of it — preferably, of course, if he didn't have a finger caught in the toaster and a puppy lapping at the soft-boiled egg he spilled at breakfast.

- Simply brown 4 tablespoons of **butter**, add 2 teaspoons of **balsamic vinegar** and stir these ingredients into your boiled **pasta** along with grated **dry jack or parmesan cheese**. Linguine are an excellent stand-in for fettuccine in this case: you might look for narrow green Japanese noodles, they'll fill the bill perfectly. Not absolutely necessary, but an interesting extra, is a light topping of breadcrumbs, browned with the butter.

— for basic pasta boiling and topping see page 68 —

PASTA WITH THREE ONIONS AND ALMONDS

Never underestimate the power of onions: Graham Greene fell in love with Lady Walston when they were eating onion sandwiches and he put those onions, if not the bread, into *The End of the Affair.*

The pasta of this page is a variation on a dish at the lamented Ironwood Café in San Francisco's Cole Valley. I remember sitting there beneath a poster of a dour Cologne baker stirring up what looked like a pot of envy for Iago to feed Otello at their next meeting, but this put no damper on the Ironwood's vibrant cuisine. The almonds are my addition and make the dish seem so Asian you might want to use Chinese egg noodles instead of the standard "pasta." And watch for any lurking cupids.

By the way, I fell in love with Anne watching her eating a piece of apple pie. Well, it might as well have been onions . . . Fate had dictated that my blind date for the Symphony — arranged by a ketchup-loving matchmaker friend being chased around town by that sly old dog, the conductor Victor de Sabata — fell through. And then, continuing its work at fever pitch, Fate sped Anne and her escort to the same hamburger heaven where I'd repaired after the concert (Brahms' Second Symphony and Bach's Third Suite, conducted by Eduard van Beinum).

They had hesitated outside the heaven's door, but seeing a famous bearded bandleader in the window, were magnetized inside. So, Mr. or Ms. Fate, and The Beard as well, thank you very much indeed.

- Using a pair of wooden spoons for 8 or 9 minutes of virtually uninterrupted tossing in a commodious skillet, soften-don't-brown over low heat in about 4 tablespoons of **olive oil**: several chopped **scallions**, 2 sliced **yellow onions** and 1 sliced **red onion** torn into rings, and 3 tablespoons of **sliced or slivered almonds:** in the wonderland of one of my favorite groceries the contents of the packages of slivered looked sliced and the sliced slivered, sending this writer into a momentary tizzy amandine, but we'll let that pass.
- Meanwhile, don't be afraid to work your way up the green part of the scallions as you chop: this is not gastronomically Off Limits.
- The next step is to combine the above with boiled **pasta** and grated **dry jack or parmesan** to taste.

PRAWN SAFFRON PASTA

When I'm waiting in line at the supermarket behind some misguided soul investing in a TV dinner, I want to tap, no, rap said person on the shoulder and shout, Try this, it'll be on the table before you know it. The Yellow Pasta!

- Shell 4 to 6 uncooked **tiger prawns** and sauté them for 2-1/2 minutes over low medium heat in 2 or 3 tablespoons of **butter**, along with generous helpings of **lemon** juice, minced **parsley**, pressed **garlic**, **white wine** and **saffron**. Combine with boiled **pasta** and **dry jack or parmesan** to taste.

VERMOUTH ZUCCHINI PASTA

And this is our interpretation of an old culinary song a Neapolitan mama taught her son in Brooklyn before he carried it to a homey San Francisco trattoria where we enjoyed it while Messrs. Domingo and Pavarotti serenaded us from a kitchen cassette. The dry vermouth seems to be the defining ingredient here, giving the sauce a velvety finish. But the vinegar is no less crucial — I know this to be the case because before it went in (the trattoria's waitress didn't list it among the ingredients) the sauce didn't sing at all.

And now this little restaurant is no more, having slipped quickly into the night without benefit of reviewers' attention, and this rather elusive dish seems more phantasmal than ever.

Roast pieces of a **sweet red pepper** with some discs of **garlic** and a tablespoon or more of **olive oil** for 25 minutes at 350°, steam 2 sliced **zucchini,** and toast (for a minute or more in a small lightweight skillet) a handful of **pine nuts**.

Then in a large pan over medium heat toss the zucchini and the oiled and garlicked pepper choppings for 4 or 5 minutes in 2 tablespoons each of **olive oil**, **red wine vinegar** and **dry vermouth,** stirring in the pine nuts a minute or so before combining your vegetable sauce with boiled **pasta** (shells are recommended here) and grated **cheese**, rather a lot of it.

PROSCIUTTO-STUFFED TORTELLINI

We, like many San Franciscans, tend to buy our tortellini at the Rolls Royce of the city's Italian delicatessens: Molinari's, "since 1896." The staff are the soul of friendliness, kind to novices from Eureka and Minneapolis, but the air of AUTHORITY hanging over the peppers-sausages-cheese-olive oil-vinegar-biscotti is so thick you could cut it with the nearest knife. Molinari's is so bloody old-fashioned (and why not!) their tortellini boxes come with a phone number including the original elegant exchange, Garfield by name, not two impersonal digits.

Buy a box of good quality **prosciutto-stuffed tortellini**, boil them — the ones we get take perhaps 13 or 14 minutes — then drain them. Figuring about 1/4 pound per portion, serve the tortellini one of the following ways:

1. Hot, tossed with browned **butter** with **sage** crinkled into it to taste, and grated **dry jack or parmesan cheese**, of course.

2. Warm or cool, with a minced **shallot**-decorated Lupo vinaigrette made with 2-plus parts **olive oil** to 1 of **red wine vinegar** and **lemon** juice, plus 1 pressed **garlic** clove.

3. Baked (following boiling) with our house **tomato sauce** (page 69), a bit of **cream** and lots of **grated cheese**: 15 minutes in a moderate oven is ample.

MOCK CANNELLONI

Well, I was trying to approximate the unctuous enchiladas we ate in Carmel fifty years ago, the work of a friend's faithful Mexican retainer and always delivered to our rented house in a pyrex dish that seemed to contradict the luxuriance of the savory oblongs nestled inside. But inadvertently I used flour instead of corn tortillas, and came up with something remarkably like cannelloni, squishy, comforting, and no pasta boiling necessary.

Our friend was in cattle ranching and could dine at the Ritz, but enchiladas fit her humility to a tee. She had a squeaky voice, and a world class collection of cowbells in her rambling white Victorian that tinkled (sopranos) and thunked (altos) — hearing them as a child meant I was in my vacation paradise.

Ever generous, Miss Doud would take us to a pretentious restaurant in a charming adobe in Monterey where we ate the steaky 40s fare surrounded by well-whiskied swells just off the course at "Pebble," Pebble Beach that is. The proprietor answered to the aristocratic name of Gallatin Powers and his maitre-d' stood at a rather forbidding lectern, but he was not about to turn away Miss Doud.

Her extended circle of friends on the Monterey peninsula rather resembled a cast for *Rebecca*: tweedy Englishmen driving exotic roadsters, eccentric spinsters, maybe a rake or two, and count in actors, painters and priests as well.

My parents came to know the Doud family about 1928 when my father the internist apparently "saved the life" of Miss Doud's baby sister. The family was eternally grateful and showered us with thanks whether in the form of the annual enchilada haul or the occasional gift of a painting by the wonderful Arthur Hill Gilbert whose poetic, powdery cypresses can make you weep with pleasure.

Little ones like me were not forgotten and I remember as a child of eight being taken by another Doud sister for lunch — grilled cheese sandwiches, I'm sure — by the side of the pool at the spiffy Del Monte Hotel. Transportation was via a roadster straight out of MGM.

I was thirty-five or more years older on our last visit with Miss Doud. She was beginning to mix up the various female Bloomfields, but she was still such a stately, and warm, figure — a *grande dame*, almost, out of A.J. Liebling.

First, make a **tomato sauce** (page ???) with chopped onion and puréed tomatoes, simmering it for only 5 minutes. Also grate coarsely 1 cup of white **cheddar cheese** and slice 3 tablespoons of **black olives**. And very briefly fry 3 to 5 **flour tortillas** in a little **olive oil** (one at a time in a large skillet) until they begin to crisp.

Now in a baking pan lay out the tortillas one by one and spoon cheese and sauce onto 'em, then roll them up. Cover the "cannelloni" with more sauce, shower with olives and bake in a moderate oven for 10 or 12 minutes. Sprinkle with grated **dry jack or parmesan cheese** before serving.

FULLER DRESS VERSION: Abandon the olives and add shrimp, avocado, cilantro.

LASAGNE BOLOGNESE ALLA NOSTRA MANIERA

Another staple on which a book might be written concerning recipe variations. You could, for example, substitute ground veal for the beef and add a little white wine before the milk. You could add chicken livers along the line, cream, balsamic vinegar, ricotta, peas! I don't know if I'll ever settle on a definitive version of this one — the gastronomic equivalent, so to speak, of Giulini's Bach B minor Mass or Tilson Thomas' Schumann *Rhenish* Symphony. Meanwhile the light and meaty little number on this page satisfies me, and it isn't dunked in Coit Tower sauce, no question about that.

Lasagne Bolognese we didn't try in Bologna, that comprehensively arcaded city with its dazzling per capita array of restaurants and barber shops and unvisited by many American travelers hypnotized into Tuscany next door. But we did feast on beet pasta flamed in brandy at the trattoria just behind the gas pump across from the Teatro Communale.

This intimate old opera house (you could fit two and a half or three Communales in the Met) is where we came in very close contact with Verdi's *Forza del Destino* one Sunday afternoon, in the company of a thousand somberly dressed Bolognans who might have been attending a funeral: well, *Forza* isn't exactly cheerful stuff. The thump of the overture with its howling strings, electric brass and manic cymbals came straight up through those delightful eighteenth century floorboards, giving one the feeling of sitting, tibias all-a-tremble, smack on top of a first-class earthquake.

We were happy to be sitting, an imperious pinstriped godfather having informed us shortly before curtain time — he could have been one of those rulebook gods in an *opera seria* — that we were in his *posti*.

> In a large skillet soften 2 heaping tablespoons each of minced **onion**, **carrot** and **celery** with about 12 little dice of **thick cut or slab bacon**, stirring frequently — you should put in the bacon a minute or more before the vegetables to produce some cooking fat. Then add 2/3 pound of **ground beef** (or the more willowy veal!) and, over higher heat, sauté it just until the look of rawness is gone, along with a fistful of thick-sliced **brown mushrooms.**
>
> Now lower the heat and add 1/4 cup of **milk** and a turn or more of the **nutmeg** mill; cook, stirring constantly, until the milk is almost evaporated: this will take very little time. Then add a 14-ounce can of **tomatoes** and a few **rosemary** needles,* bring all to a boil and simmer, mostly covered, for 30 minutes or more, stirring often.
>
> Meanwhile boil a little less than 1/2 pound of **lasagne**: it will take about 6 minutes longer than fettuccine, say 18 minutes. When all the components are ready, toss the lasagne gently with the Bolognese sauce (which in our current interpretation emerges almost more a hashy topping than a sauce) and grated **dry jack or parmesan cheese** ... And this is as good a place as any to tell you it's fun to scoop up grated cheese in your hand from a big bowl and let it shower therefrom over your pasta. Sensuous indeed.
>
> * I added them, then found out it's a Tuscan tradition in the preparation of "Bolognese" sauce.

RAVIOLI STUFFED WITH SQUASH, MACAROONS AND MOSTARDA

This is "that pasta with cookies" which is turning up in every Italian restaurant in sight. It *is* a bit sweet, the veg, cookies and mostarda di frutta scarcely coming under the savory heading, and it must be restrained from turning into Total Dessert; this is where the grated cheese and sage butter come in.

Now making ravioli from scratch is a dreadful bore, and buying sheets of pasta for cookie-cutting into ravioli wraps is not always practical. Besides, the sheets tend to be too thick for the purpose. So I suggest you use the greatest new toy I've found in my old age: won ton wrappers, available in most supermarkets (above the broccoli at ours). You simply spoon your stuffing onto the middle of wrapper 1, run a watery finger around the edge, fit wrapper 2 on top and press the edges together, and *voilà*, a perfect sandwich.

And as we near the end of a chapter devoted in large part to Italian delights I must draw your attention to a high school commencement address by the delightfully quirky columnist Adair Lara who, besides telling the seniors of a Sonoma county school, "do not supply the rocks that are to be thrown at you [in life]," she exhorted:

"Go to Italy. I can't stress this enough."

De-seed 1 small **butternut squash**, brush on a little **canola oil** inside and outside, and place the squash upside down in an ovenproof dish, surrounded by a 1/2 inch deep pool of water; bake at 350° for an hour or a little more, until the squash is nice and mushy and beyond the need of a blender or food processor's services.

Scoop out the flesh and combine it with:

> about 1/2 cup of crushed **almond macaroons**
>
> about 2/3 cup of chopped **mostarda di frutta** from the jar, with some of its syrup
>
> 3 or 4 tablespoons of grated **dry jack or parmesan cheese**
>
> a pinch of **nutmeg**
>
> a fairly generous amount of grated **orange** peel
>
> (and toasted **breadcrumbs** will do no harm)

Spoon stuffing onto **won ton wrappers** as explained in the preceding spiel. Boil the completed ravioli for no more than 4 minutes (in batches if they stick together in the water) and serve with browned **butter** rather liberally punctuated with **sage**. As always in our house/bistro/trattoria, pass extra grated cheese.

RAGOÛT OF PASTA LE NORD

And this is a slightly modified version of a "nouvelle" pasta served us at Le Nord in Lyon, 1984. It originally included string beans which I've decided are a "non contributing" element here, to borrow a term from my wife's architectural history reports.

Frankly, this ragoût with its pretty pool of orange, green and white seems more Berkeley-esque than Lyonnais.

Of course when we're in Lyon, a city I'm much fonder of than many Americans, we always take a crash course in the "real local thing" as old Henry James might have put it: tripe one way or another, herring salads, sausages galore. Lyon specialties are muscular stuff, stevedores of the menu. Patti Unterman, astute doyenne of American dining critics, says eating in Lyon reminds her of digging into the hearty fare of Chicago — the details of the menu may be different (I don't think tripe is in yet on North Dearborn), but both cities are trenchermen's territory for sure.

But Chicago doesn't have the Three Rivers. I heard that old line my first dinner in Lyon, forty-five years ago, a snowy January when Place Bellecoeur looked like an abandoned stage set: the waiter in the empty dining room of the Royal Hotel couldn't have been jollier as he intoned, bottle in hand, "You know, there are three rivers here, the Rhône, the Saône — and (pouring now from the bottle of Guess What) Beaujolais!"

It was next to the second of these attractions, along the world's greatest farmers' market, the one on the Quai St-Antoine, that I had my chance to play Cartier-Bresson. Camera in hand, walking with teenage tower-climbing son, I spied, just ahead, a neatly mustachioed octogenarian gentleman, top-coated and mufflered, a retired accountant perhaps, newspaper in arm, beret almost halo-like on his quintessentially Gallic head, looking intently on many baskets of flowers lined up for his inspection.

Widower, or wife at home? Happy, or sad? Well, he was a sort of Everyman, but a very, very French-looking one. And the republics and non-republic he'd lived through! I snapped quickly, and now Monsieur St-Antoine has a second home next to our front door in a San Francisco Victorian.

> Cut a peeled **carrot** into thin slices and steam them; cut several slices of **coppa** into thin strips; then warm the coppa with the carrot slices in a rather generous amount of **butter** with **dill weed**.
>
> Meanwhile boil a little less than 1/2 a pound of **pasta shells** and drain them in a colander; also, heat gently 2 cups of **chicken broth** combined with a 1/2 cup of **cream** (or crème fraîche) and topped with some chopped fresh **basil**.
>
> Toss the warmed veg/coppa rounds-and-juliennes with the pasta and some grated **dry jack or parmesan cheese**, then fill soup bowls about halfway with the broth/cream and ease in the pasta/veg/coppa. Give each ragoût-eater a fork and spoon to fish the goodies from their minestran lily pond.

Postscript Hollandaise:

I cannot abandon matters minestran without reporting that one of the best pasta dishes I've had on-the-road was a tagliatelle with whitefish and a Champagne dill sauce at the Pays Bas Hotel in Utrecht. And Utrecht, birthplace of that wild and wonderful conductor Willem Mengelberg, is a lovely little city, full of amusing canals and streets going all higgledypiggledy. Note echoes of London and Baltimore in the row houses agile Dutchmen reach by steps worthy of stepladders.

We traveled to leafy Utrecht one rainy afternoon for a concert of university students conducted by a budding maestro who happens to be my fourth cousin, one generation removed. Otto (not the nuclear fissionist, that's his first cousin twice removed) conducted beautifully, but my epiphany in a crowded room of apple-cheeked young Hollanders came following the program when members of the orchestra rose in turn to sing their university songs. This was not quite Berkeley or Cambridge, Mass. When *Gaudeamus Igitur* rose lustily through the quasi-beer hall in which we were gathered I had the feeling I was caught delightfully in the bloodstream of Brahms' *Academic Festival* Overture. And that Champagne dill sauce had, I'm afraid, been upstaged.

But the *bec fin* in me had a field day next year in Holland when my Berliner cousins introduced us to poffertjes, those bulbous, fluffy pancakes constructed in large measure out of baking powder. One consumes platter upon platter of these addictive domettes at Wassenaar beach, a much-umbrella'd venue that sets you down in the middle of an Impressionist painting peopled by careening kiddies and reclining parents. Our poffertjesian orgy followed as it happened attendance at a concert of the Residentie Orchestra in The Hague. A hirsutely advantaged maestro named Pehlavanian made much of Beethoven's *Eroica*, and as we negotiated our way past the skate-boarders outside the concert hall I felt fulfilled.

But that was before the poffertjes . . .

— FISH —

We begin with . . .

**GOOD DINNERS WITHOUT GREAT EFFORT:
A HANDY GUIDE TO THE GARNISHING OF THREE BASIC FISH**

These are the fish we've found most available, delicious, and receptive to our repertoire of accoutrements. Salmon, of course, is the richest, and halibut, with its tendency to seem, as Mrs. Fisher put it, a "strong, meaningless fish," asks for the richest or most elaborate garniture. But there are no hard and fast rules as to which goes with which: you won't be hauled into court for combining salmon and avocado vinaigrette.

Wipe dry and **flour** fairly generously:

    1. Whole **Trout**

    or

    2. **Salmon** steaks

    or

    3. **Halibut** steaks

Pan-fry the fish of your choice in a very hot skillet in a tablespoon of **canola oil,** longer and over a higher flame on the first side than the second, and between sides you can briefly stand up steaks at right angles to the pan so the heat gets to raw places not otherwise so well zapped.

Then serve your fish with — or, more likely, under — one of the following, bearing in mind that mashed potatoes compliment vinaigrettes very nicely and sliced-boiled are the better accompaniment for butters . . .

TOMATO BASIL VINAIGRETTE

    A 2-to-1 **olive oil** to **red wine vinegar** dressing with chopped **tomato** and **fresh basil** to taste — but don't stint.

DICED AVOCADO VINAIGRETTE

    The same dressing as above with diced **avocado**

RAVIGOTE DE LUXE

    A **mustard vinaigrette** (page 1) with chopped **egg, parsley, onion & capers.**

SICILIAN SALSA

    A salsa of roughly equal amounts of minced **red onion**, toasted **pine nuts** and **raisins**, plus a heaping teaspoon of **orange zest** and a tablespoon of **red wine vinegar** for moistening. Make this salsa an hour before serving if not inconvenient.

BROWN BUTTER WITH LEMON, GARLIC AND PARSLEY . . . NOT TO MENTION OPTIONAL "GRENOBLOISE" CAPERS — OR A GOOD SPLASH OF WHITE WINE OR DRY VERMOUTH

2 or 3 tablespoons of **butter** browned with **lemon** juice, minced **parsley** and pressed **garlic**, none of them added timidly. Early insertion of the parsley will, of course, result in crispy greens: I can swing either way on this decision.

BROWN BUTTER AND SAGE

2 or 3 tablespoons of **butter** browned with a good crinkling of **sage**.

CILANTRO PESTO

An odd but wonderful notion is to serve halibut with this or the red pepper sauce below AND a poached egg.

This is our basic **pesto** as on page 70 with **coriander** leaves (cilantro) in place of the fresh basil. Note also the first cousin of this sauce: the puréed salsa verde on page 144.

RED PEPPER PURÉE SANTA FE

Don't forget this purée has another identity: sunset-colored swirl in a green or yellow cream soup . . . and should you be having eight or ten for dinner: offer three, count 'em, three sauces, this one and the above pesto and salsa, to accompany a boned and horizontally split salmon sprinkled inside with thyme, stuffed with a few lemon and garlic slices, bathed in previously reduced white wine (1/4 cup, say, from 3/4 cup) and baked in foil until tender, probably not much longer than an hour in a moderate oven.

Mince 4 medium-sized **shallots** and soften them in a good tablespoon of **olive oil**; also roast 2 cut-up **sweet red peppers** with 2 pressed **garlic** cloves in a light coating of **olive oil** (3 or 4 tablespoons, say) for 30 or more minutes in a moderate oven. Then in a blender or food processor purée the peppers with the shallots and 2 tablespoons of minced **parsley**. Pour the resultant sauce into a pretty bowl and stir in **balsamic vinegar** to taste: play with half to a whole teaspoon.

AND A SPUD NOTE: With halibut steaks and this purée you could serve baked sweet potatoes, contrasting white with two shades of orange.

PISTACHIO NUT SAUCE

These nuts will smell like pastry as they're toasting! A versatile sauce, this one, it's lettuce-friendly and good on pasta, too.

Spread almost 1/2 a cup of shelled **pistachio nuts** on a baking sheet and toast them in a 375° oven for 8 to 10 minutes; cool a little. Then purée the nuts (you want a sandy texture) in a blender or food processor and stir them into a "dressing" of 1/3 cup **olive oil**, 2 tablespoons of **lemon** juice and 1/4 cup of **orange** juice, plus the grated zest of an orange.

RHUBARB CREAM BROTH

This was inspired by a tart and rosy salmon preparation we ate at Giovanni Leoni's Buca Giovanni at the foot of San Francisco's Russian Hill. This is an Upstairs, Downstairs restaurant: one eats in a cave, the kitchen is up at street level, and the chef, like a captain on his bridge, keeps in contact by the latest in tele-communication.

Wash a large stalk of **rhubarb** and cut it into 1/4-inch slices. In a saucepan almost cover it with water and boil it for 5 minutes, then add 1/4 cup of **white wine or dry vermouth** and cook the brew for another 2 minutes, stirring and mashing all the way.

Next, remove the saucepan from the fire and stir in 2 tablespoons of **cream**, then several sprinkles of **sugar** (don't be too shy about this!) and after that, 3 teaspoons of **balsamic vinegar**: you must nurse the seasoning along at this point, because this sauce is terminally taste-deficient until suddenly it erupts in a surge of flavor, piquant yet rich. Poached halibut would be my first choice to surrender to the racy charms of this sweet-and-sour coating.

ORANGE SAUCE CATALONIA

In case you're not in the mood for a night flight to Barcelona: a sauce for scallops, tilapia, bluenose bass . . . and note that the citrus element here can be dramatized by replacing juice-and-sugar with kumquats soused for the day in an orange liqueur and dry vermouth.

In a small skillet reduce by a quarter 2/3 cup of **white wine** and the juice of a large **orange** plus a few grains of **sugar**. When you turn over your fish in its larger skillet add the wine/orange mix along with a tablespoon of **butter** and stir this lubrication vigorously while the fish finishes its quick voyage in the pan. Garnish the final product with **slivered almonds** briefly toasted in the skillet vacated by the wine and orange.

SUCCOTASH NOUVELLE

A very seductive succotash, very pretty with its yellow, brown and red on salmon's pink, and if you use Japanese pottery plates and add a dab of mashed potato at the side you have a color symphony extraordinaire.

I'm reminded of other modern succotashes, that's to say, without the lowly lima of olden times. The Rio Grill in Carmel, for instance, does a grilled pork loin with a succotash of corn, sweet red pepper and black beans, not to mention three platemates, Jarlsberg potato cake, roasted scallions and barbecue mayonnaise. Does all this give you ideas? . . .

Fry about a dozen smallish oblongs of **thick cut or slab bacon or pancetta** until they're on the verge of crisp; then in the same skillet over low-moderate heat sauté the bacon with 1-1/4 cup of **frozen corn**, 1 diced **sweet red pepper**, some **rosemary** and a good splash of **Madeira or dry sherry** for 5 or more minutes, until all inhabitants of the skillet have grown, as Sylvia Townsend Warner would say, to love each other.

OR: You could substitute peanuts for the bacon: they taste wonderful with corn and you'll still have an impressive color combination. Obviously they'll need less cooking. (I counsel a sandwich of seared tombo tuna over this nut-succotash and under an artistic dribbling of the aforementioned cilantro pesto).

and

BACON VINAIGRETTE AND STEAMED CABBAGE

Steam a small trimmed **cabbage** cut into wedges, fry a dozen or more little oblongs of **thick cut or slab bacon** and drain them on paper towels, and make a dill Dijon vinaigrette by stirring 1 part **red wine vinegar** into a little **Dijon mustard** and adding 2-plus parts of **olive oil** and a sprinkle of **dill weed**. Combine the bacon with the vinaigrette and spoon the meaty dressing over fish and adjacent cabbage wedges (well drained!)

Remarks:

Sometimes when I serve boiled potatoes with fish I break them up a little: I call these "hash whites." Another option is our frothy Quick Gratin: pile thinly sliced boiled potatoes into a ramekin, apply generous melted butter, chopped scallions and grated cheese and run under the broiler for 6 minutes. There's also mashed potatoes with 2 or 3 tablespoons of pesto (page ???) mixed in. Or forget potatoes altogether because steamed crookneck squash is wonderful with fish, it's pretty as a Vermeer lute and not too rich. Remember, these days potato or veg (or risotto!) go under not next to your fish.

And fish served with the pistachio or Catalonia sauces I like to accompany with oranges which you peel, trim thoroughly and bisect into handsome cartwheels.

BAKED BUTTERFISH WITH MUSTARD (OR WASABI) GRATINÉ

If one evening company announced by phone, fax or whatever its unexpected and imminent arrival on our doorstep in a state of gastronomic expectation, well then, I might run down to the fish market with a thought to throwing this into the oven. It's an easy dish to prepare, quite stylish and even rather original. Almost any fileted white fish would do. Bear in mind the recipe here is for two servings and must be multiplied for those instant guests.

And note that wasabi, Japanese horseradish that comes in a toothpaste tube, is a trendy alternative to the mustard. It has the zap of a Birgit Nilsson high C in *Die Walkuere*.

Butter quite generously an ovenproof platter and arrange **butterfish** filets or similar raw material — snapper, perhaps — thereon; spread the fish liberally with **Dijon mustard**, adding a little **lemon** juice and 1 pressed **garlic** clove, then sprinkle it with **dill weed** (fresh preferred!), add a light covering of **breadcrumbs** and dribble over all enough **olive oil** to moisten the gratiné lightly.

Bake your filets at 375° for about 20 minutes, basting occasionally with the accumulated juices, and serve with 1) just bread, and a light salad to follow, or 2) mashed potatoes, or 3) reduced portions of our pasta with beurre blanc and balsamic vinegar (page ???). Yet another option: caponata (page ???).

BAKED FILET OF RED SNAPPER IN A TOMATO OLIVE SAUCE OR WITH INDIAN SPICES

A quintessential bistro bake: I see the filets rather haphazardly arranged on your plate in a nice fluffy bath of black-specked tomato sauce or our spicy-creamy Indian purée. The latter was inspired by a visit to a congenial Indian trattoria near 16th Street and Valencia in San Francisco's latest Bohemia. This is the intersection of a gastronome's dreams: within a few yards are Thai, Indian and Salavdorean restaurants (the last cum thumping Wurlitzer extraordinaire), a Breton crêperie, a Basque tapas house and a taqueria or two, all first class.

> Make the house **tomato sauce** (page ???) with **cream** and **saffron** to taste and add a dotting of 3 tablespoons of sliced or chopped **pitted black olives**. Pour your tomato/olive sauce over **red snapper filets** and bake in a **buttered** casserole at 350° for 20 minutes or a little less.
>
> . . . For the Indian snapper-covering, brown lightly 1 chopped **onion** in a little **olive oil**, add 2 teaspoons of **turmeric**, a bit of **ground cloves** and **cayenne** to taste, cook for a minute, then add a near-purée of 2 cups of chopped **tomatoes**, 2/3 of a cup of **yogurt**, 1 large pressed **garlic** clove, 2 or 3 teaspoons of **cumin** and a little chopped **ginger** before simmering all for 10 or 12 minutes. Pour this sauce, **cilantro**-topped, over the fish and bake as above.

Serve either of these bakes alone or with rice; the Indian fish won't sneeze at a chutney.

BAKED SALMON WITH A SHRIMP MUSHROOM YOGURT STUFFING

My sister Julie cooked us this velvety salmon about thirty years ago, we were quite charmed, and then the chef and her satisfied guests proceeded to forget all about it — like Hitchcock's famous lady, the recipe vanished. It rather sounds as if Sunset Magazine could have been its provenance (there was sour cream in the original, by the way), I'm just not sure. In any event, a belatedly alerted subconscious dialed into this long lost piscatorial rhapsody not long ago, and I've reconstructed what it might have been, more or less.

Mind you, it's not exactly millennial food (although surely less antique with yogurt), but must we always eat with the times? Appetites should roam the decades, I think, looking for what pleases.

Time-traveling beats TWA any day: I like to play CDs of old symphony broadcasts, Bruno Walter's angry Brahms 1, for instance, from March 18, 1939 ("We greet you from Studio 8-H," says the announcer Gene Hamilton in his gently Southern *legato*) and try to conjure what I was doing (read eating) that day. Since this was the period of my Cucamongan captivity at a prep school in sinus-clearing pre-smog southern California I suspect I was in a large dining hall eyeing a raisin snail topped with a fetching silvery glaze.

. . . Now I'm reading in Mr. Root's Paris dining guide about a divinely retro dish of sole poached in white wine and doused with a sauce of cream, butter and grated cheese, a specialty of the Escargot-Montorgueil in the first arrondissement, and I wonder if my great aunt Fannie and uncle Sigmund forked into that one when they dined there with the harpsichordist Wanda Landowska ("bright and vivacious," wrote Sigmund) September 16, 1923.

Re-winding Sigmund's cornucopian diary I find that, seventeen days previous, Fannie who was known as "the Sarah Bernhardt of the piano" and Sigmund the defender of the Haymarket "anarchists" were in Munich and had the Bruno Walters to lunch. That night it was *Walkuere* at the opera and, opines Sigmund, "Knappertsbusch dragged the Magic Fire terribly."

It was a generation later I saw Herr Knappertsbusch striding down Avenue Niel in Paris wearing a wide-brimmed hat worthy of the Wanderer in *Siegfried*. You don't suppose he was heading for Chez Schmitt and their onion tart? . . . And Bruno Walter, I was to meet him in 1951 as one of eighty-five Stanford *bassi* reaching for that crazy high G in the finale of Mahler's Second. At our first entrance he instructed us gently from the podium:

"My dears, the sound must be as if on a distant horizon . . . "

> As for Julie's salmon: On a large piece of foil place side by side 2 halves of a horizontally bisected **salmon filet** adding up to at least 3/4 of a pound in weight. On one half spoon a mixture of approximately 3/4 cup of thinly sliced **brown mushrooms**, 1/2 cup of **rock shrimp**, 4 tablespoons of **yogurt** and a good sprinkle of **dill weed** (fresh preferred).
>
> Place the other filet half on top of this stuffing, wrap the foil around the "sandwich," place your wrapped package on an ovenproof platter and bake it in a 300° oven for 30 to 35 minutes. In-wrap juices may be spooned over your servings of the finished unveiled product.

RAIE (SKATE) BEURRE NOIR(OR SAUCE MOUTARDE

This old French favorite has over the years traveled no better than the deliciously blunt and purple metaphors of Simone de Beauvoir — although James Beard reports that dogs on Oregon beaches adore to roll on top of skate flotsam coming their way — but it seems to be gaining new friends in American bistros with a Francophilic bent. An alternative sauce to consider is the mustard-vermouth brew on page 167, incorporating a little of the thyme-flavored water in which you boiled the skate.

> In a skillet combine a cup or more of water with some **thyme**, **bay leaf** and (optional, this) a little thinly sliced **onion** and **carrot**; cover, bring to a boil, then insert your **skate** and simmer it for about 15 minutes.
>
> Drain the fish, place it on a platter and come close to drenching it with browned **butter**, adding **large capers** to taste and minced **parsley**. Then, making sure not to stand too close, because the fumes can be quite disconcerting, pour a little **red wine vinegar** into the pan in which the butter was browned, and, after it has boiled up — this will be about two seconds later — pour the acidic "brown bits" over the fish.

RAIE IN A WARM SALAD WITH CURRANT VINAIGRETTE

In 1986 we drove through Beaulieu-sur-Dordogne on the way to St-Flour and fell in love with this idyllic market town parked neatly by one of the world's prettiest rivers. Soon as we could we returned, booked into the Central Hotel (they were having a strawberry fair outside, featuring indecently giant specimens, *fraises de Mars*) and proceeded to enjoy Bernard Bessière's cuisine. This skate salad is a slightly modified version of one of his starters. The Central we also remember for the professorly older gent who took breakfast in the front parlor in his dressing gown. Resembling as he did a famous elderly conductor, he will always be for us "Dr. Klemperer."

Poach your **skate** (raie, of course, is a more attractive name for this homely but seductive fish) as in the previous recipe. Then carefully arrange rumpled beds of **boutique lettuces** on your raie-eaters' plates, place slabs of fish on the greens and spoon over all a dressing made by combining 3 parts **canola and walnut oil**, 1 part **red wine vinegar** and a heap of **currants**.

NOTE: This recipe is also tailor-made for quick-fried halibut steaks.

—*several hour*—
HALIBUT MOUSSE WITH CUCUMBER VINAIGRETTE

For some reason this delicate oldie makes me think of garden parties and pretty women in floppy hats. Vanessa Redgrave as Mrs. Dalloway would be Exhibit A, followed by any number of Masterpiece Theater duchesses and flappers of your choosing.

Or how about Mrs. Woolf's "laughing girls in their transparent muslins who, even now, after dancing all night, were taking their absurd woolly dogs for a run."

. . . And sensuous mousses and Glyndebourney vinaigrettes summon for me that humid, nostalgic waltz in Prokofieff's third symphony that conjures billowing skirts and aches with a mysterious *something* that's almost excruciatingly erotic . . .

The recipe here — once you've dodged the ravings above — is a bit of a chore but you could toss off a near-novelette while you're waiting for this-that-and-the-other ingredient to chill, and the end result is exquisite.

In a bowl soak 1 short tablespoon of **gelatin** in 1/4 cup of water for 5 minutes, then add 1/2 cup of boiling water and stir until the gelatin is dissolved. Now add 1/2 cup of **mayonnaise**, 1 tablespoon of **lemon juice**, 1/2 tablespoon of grated **onion**, and a smidgen of **paprika**; chill this mixture for perhaps 15 minutes, until it begins to thicken. Next, whip 1/3 cup of **cream** and fold it in; now chill the mixture again, very briefly, until it's about to set.

In water to cover with some **dry vermouth** gently poach about 2 cups of **halibut** (buy a pound of fish at the market), then flake and pound it into shreds — fine ones! — being sure to get rid of all bones and skin.

After this hazardous waste is dealt with, fold the fish-bits into the gelatin/cream/mayonnaise, place your mousse-to-be in a lightly **oiled** mold and chill for several hours. Now, several tennis matches or a couple of Donizetti operas after you started, unmold your dainty mousse and serve it with a vinaigrette of 2-plus parts **olive oil**, 1 part **red wine vinegar** and a good dotting of chopped **cucumber**.

CALAMARI FRITTI ON GREENS, SAFFRON MAYONNAISE

The darling of New Bistro chefs, this tangly fritto. I would be the first to admit this concoction is more gracefully produced in a restaurant, where the chef, I'm sure, doesn't have the sensation of flying blind over a veritable Atlantic of boiling oil. But if you like squid don't give up.

Squid I certainly didn't know about in my non-Italian childhood. I think my awakening must have been at Il Cenacolo, a delightful Italo-American lunch club that still meets every Thursday at Fior d'Italia restaurant in North Beach. I was a member for several years a long time ago, until my consumption of too much good Louis Martini wine at lunch incapacitated me for metaphors in the afternoon. Also, my damaged leg from a monumental accident was mending, and filled with a seeming barrel-full of Louis' Barbera I walked two miles back to the office one day in a fit of joy and cracked a bone or some such thing unapproved by Dr. Niebauer.

A lawyer named Fleishell, I believe, was a regular at the Fior and he had inspired the chef to cook up an addictive dish in which fried calamari was entwined with sautéed onions. It used to be called Calamari Fleishell, now it's Calamari 1886, that being the date Fior opened, at a slightly different location.

Mr. Fleishell and I collaborated not only on a love of good squid but a "quality of life" issue on the streets of San Francisco. My native town forever contrives to be the most sophisticated and the most inept city on earth, and at that time, when my fellow squid-lover was heading a "beautification" program out of City Hall, I alerted him to the fact that the corner containers for garbage in our mecca were merely old oil drums, produced from heaven knows where. He leapt into action, and the improvement is still visible all about the town.

First off, sift 3/8 cup of **cornstarch** and 1/4 cup of **flour** into 1/4 cup of cold water and whisk until a thin paste is formed.

Then pat one pound of **cleaned squid** very dry with paper towels, slice it, coat it with the paste and fry it, in batches, for a minute or so in an inch of very hot **olive oil**, stirring vigorously — try to stand a mile away from the splatter! Serve over lightly vinaigretted **greens** with our **saffron mayonnaise** (page 59).

SALMON AUBERGE ST-JACQUES

Back in the 1950s when I was stationed with the U.S. Army in Orléans, near the Loire châteaux, we would troop on special occasions to the Auberge St-Jacques down by the river, two stars in the Michelin guide. I remember so well Monsieur Fournier, the *patron*, sitting in his little raised cashier's box rather like a judge, or perhaps a lifeguard surveying his beach, as if maybe one of his clients was in danger of drowning in a sea of Coq au Vin.

The most enchanting meal I had at the St-Jacques was beautifully symmetrical: between the opening soup and closing cheese and dessert came a pair of courses, first a simple salmon mated with creamed spinach in a little symphony of pink and green, then a small steak with boiled potatoes, pristinely skinned torpedo-ettes. Such a satisfying distribution of fish-meat-and-veg!

And when I returned with Anne several years later M. Fournier was still in his box . . .

Thirty years later I was waving at the St-Jacques from the *Capitole* roaring down to Brive-la-Gaillarde. Ten p.m. and we creaked upward in a birdcage lift at Brive's faithful Terminus, pure 1910. "Great old place," I announced, and the kindly concierge, trained, one suspects, for radio, responded euphoniously, "Ah, Monsieur, c'est *solide*."

He, too, was there the next time.

Continuity, it's wonderful! I remember entering the lobby of a hotel in Innsbruck nine years after an earlier visit and thinking: well, there was a very nice concierge here, kindly, helpful, about forty-eight I'd say, and he'll probably still be here, in his black jacket with crossed keys, with about *so* much grey at the temples — and I had judged his ageing process with total accuracy.

But our favorite perennial along our European way was the stout croissant-bearer at the Angleterre in Paris whom we christened *Madame Bonjour* because of her inimitable "GOOD Morning," in French of course, with the accent rising to a great height on an arching, ever-chipper first syllable. Madame's breakfast room welcome was as enveloping as the ample skirts of some fairy tale granny living in a non-Ferragammo shoe.

> This is simply our basic quick-fried **salmon steak** proposed at the start of this chapter (along with a little browned **butter**, **lemon** juice and minced **parsley or dill weed**), plus a good creamed spinach, prepared as follows:
>
> Slowly cook 1 package of **frozen chopped spinach** enough to thaw it — this can easily take 10 minutes — then drain the de-chunked veg through a sieve with maximum thoroughness, squeezing out the excess water with the back of a spoon; then return the spinach to your saucepan, add a healthy pinch of **nutmeg** and 1/2 cup of **cream**, stirring it in well, and re-heat the wavy green. Be sure to thaw your veg without butter, oil or water. And remember, there's no such thing as over-draining spinach.
>
> Come to think of it, the Auberge St-Jacques' spinach was probably puréed, but a bit of "leaf" in the epinardian texture is, I think, appealing. As for adding flour . . . !
>
> But you might consider a few pinches of turmeric for a whiff of Bombay: I'm writing, of course, as a cruiser in San Francisco's multi-ethnic restaurant world, my Orléans I only visit in dreams.

Postscript in D flat:

When one dines at the storybook La Provvidenza in Ferrara, that gracious, gardened city with its muted echoes of the tragic Finzi-Continis, the antipasto table will if the stars are in correct position include a dish of the tastiest herring imaginable, accompanied by large brown beans, and nearby there should be salami, frittata and endive with raisins and toasted pinoli before you go on to the macaroni pie which is Ferrara's culinary signature tune. Perfection!

I should say, though, that La Provvidenza while it is surely a destination experience was not my prime reason for traveling to Ferrara on an unusually hot spring day not long ago, arriving, as it happened, to the epiphany of encountering a vibrant Italian *passeggiata* fully operative in the vicinity of cattedrale-castello-mercato at twenty-eight degrees Celsius.

My mission was to meet a distant cousin, the Russian pianist Stanislav Bunin, who was giving a concert — for a delighted but wilted audience, it turned out — in the venerable opera house across from the castle which for readers of guidebooks is Ferrara's logo so to speak, its Transamerica Pyramid or Empire State Building.

I had sent Stanislav a tape of Chopin played by my great aunt the pianist Fannie Bloomfield Zeisler, and was intrigued when he told me that Fannie's performance of the D flat nocturne revealed at one point a particular interpretive choice made by no other pianist he knew of, except himself and his grandfather the fondly-remembered Heinrich Neuhaus of the Moscow Conservatoire.

Clearly providence was nurturing connections in this pianistic gene pool as well as smiling on the Ferrarese restaurant organizing for its clients such a harmonious assortment of singing antipasti. Need I tell you that a wish in my mind for Stanislav to cap his all-Chopin program with an encore or two from Schumann (we'd just been to the house where Schumann was born, in Zwickau) was answered as if by the surest telepathy.

—CHICKEN—

POLLO ALLA CREMA

There were no creamy sauces in my childhood, if one excludes the wonderful milk-and-drippings "country gravy" my Maryland mother served with southern fried chicken, and the creamed diced potatoes that seem in retrospect sluggish fare indeed. Thrown into the world, though, I found veal chops in cream in little French bistros, fettuccine in the Alfredan sauces of Milanese trattorie, "ranch" salads on the road at home, and that was only the beginning.

Perhaps my apex-de-crème was reached at the fabled old Pyramide south of Lyon, a three-star challenge we tackled one winter Sunday in '69. We arrived from Geneva a half hour late, but a kindly retainer calmly ushered us to the powder room, then steered us into the famous salle where the veteran sommelier (I'd seen pictures of him in books) sized us up as less than patrician, took tactful pity on us and recommended a refreshing, inexpensive Condrieu.

Here, surrounded by the pleasantly dowdy aristos of the region, we polished off great breasts of chicken in near-torrents of cream and Champagne, mushrooms and shrimp added to the sybaritic mix. And not a green veg in sight! Then the cart rolled up with oozing cheeses. (By the way, Mme. Point had no way of knowing a baronial footstool was inadequate housing for my left leg currently encased in a full-length cast: I was simply getting the same treatment Cocteau or Colette would have received if they'd come to lunch in plaster up to the hip.)

And now, of course, cream is under a cloud. Except in Belgium.

The "alla crema" chicken of this page is very old-fashioned, very Sam Chamberlain, and very good. You can be a little reckless browning the onions.

In a skillet brown light or dark **chicken** pieces quite vigorously, without added fat — don't worry, they won't stick — taking longer and using more flame on the skin side than the less handsome reverse. Meanwhile, to the side, in a little **butter**, sauté 1 thinly sliced **onion** until it begins to crisp.

Remove the chicken-and-onions to a casserole, drain off unwanted fat and deglaze the skillet with a good slosh of **white wine**, scraping up the good brown bits as they're called.

Now over the chicken-etc. pour the vinous drippings mixed with 3/4 cup of **cream**, add rather a lot of minced **parsley** and bake uncovered at 300° for about 40 minutes, stirring occasionally and, a few minutes before serving, working in a tablespoon of **light sour cream** — decadence will almost drown you. Serve this pollo with plain rice.

BAKED CHICKEN WITH PORTOBELLO MUSHROOM AND CREAM

Luscious, a trifle unhealthy, and very satisfying . . .

And my adventures in chicken-&-cream I pick up in Hamburg '65, my memory tickled while reading Ron Chernow's riveting tome on the Warburg banking clan. Expats Siegmund and Eric Warburg, dipping gingerly into the postwar version of their hometown (I find it rather daunting, by the way, that the formidable Sir Siegmund was the first cousin of my moderately distant relative, the beloved city planner Hans Blumenfeld), were dining one evening at "their favorite restaurant, the Ehmcke, sitting beneath portraits of Bismarck and Moltke" . . and that set it off, I seized my Jeeves of a diary and found the entry for: "EHMCKE, lovely old panelling and gold-flocked wallpaper, tulip chandeliers, grandfather clock, epauletted imperials on the wall — First War generals I suspect — Spode china, quiet, a friendly low-key host working this amazing room . . . and Hamburger Stuben Kueche, delicate, crisp young chicken in cream gravy," which I'm tasting as I write.

Tyrannical Siegmund and I could, I'm sure, agree on that North Country poulet.

De-stem, wash and slice into 1-inch lengths a **portobello mushroom** and sauté them in a little **butter** with a teaspoon or so of **lemon** juice and 1 small pressed **garlic** clove. When the slices show signs of browning stir in a good 1/2 cup of **cream** and pour the mushrooms-cream-etc. over **chicken breasts** positioned in a casserole.

Bake the lot uncovered at 350° for about 55 minutes — an unlikely number, somehow, but that was the key to success in our tests of this recipe (note, by the way, that dark meat, an attractive option, will raise the time to 60 or 65 minutes, and there is, of course, the disturbing possibility your oven may run faster than mine) — then top with minced **parsley** and serve.

A simple green pasta with butter and grated cheese is an excellent mate for this chicken.

TRANSFORMATION SCENE: Just as surely as Liszt could transform a theme in his B minor sonata to *something else*, you can vary the texture of this dish quite interestingly — and, in the process, come up with something more Tuscan, that being the current adjective for paradise — by doing the following: add some pieces of chicken liver to the mushroom in the sauté process, along with a bit of dry sherry, and a little extra cream, then halfway through the baking stage incorporate some virtually cooked rice along with a little of its cooking liquid.

CHICKEN EN COCOTTE

This is a Grandmère-type preparation, rather spectacular and not much work. It also comes under the "Contadina-style" heading beloved of San Francisco Italian restaurants run by chefs from New York, New Jersey and related culinary climes. With its mix of fresh country flavors I think it would appeal to our new friend Erminio in Ravenna. Erminio is the proprietor, the menu and the soul of a restaurant called Al Rustichello. Reading about this pullman car bistro in *Gourmet* didn't quite prepare us for the stentorian presence of Erminio, a plate-toting, order-announcing Figaro who orchestrates your meal with the zest of a standup comedian, the knowledge of a Waverley Root and the finesse of an Alice Waters, male Adriatic equivalent thereof.

It took us two extended evenings to complete Erminio's prix fixe.

Night 1 we attended to an antipasto platter, pasta with fresh asparagus and dessert, followed by grappa on the house; night 2 was devoted to a medley of pastas, another of meats (gigot, osso buco), more dessert and prosecco courtesy of this maestro who dotes on the few Americans appearing at his door. Evidently Erminio thought our gastronomic intentions good — and when we said our next stop was Ascoli Piceno, which just happens to be his hometown, our stock rose even higher.

So we were in Ravenna and I haven't mentioned the mosaics. Well, if in doubt, they *are* awesome. And if you're driving from Venice, having survived the minotaurian labyrinth of autostradan spaghetti, I mean all those sudden left's and right's on the way out of Mestre, then you must stop by the imposing abbey of Pomposa and sip hot chocolate muddy enough for a hundred Turks.

Marinate **chicken** pieces in a little pool of **olive oil, lemon** juice and lots of **rosemary**, then place the nicely glistening fowl in a large pot with:

- 1 slice of **thick cut or slab bacon** in 1-inch lengths — or better, the equivalent in fat **pancetta** dice
- 2 **red potatoes**, diced (and previously blanched for a few minutes in boiling water)
- 1 **sweet red pepper**, in short strips
- 2/3 of a **portobello mushroom**, washed and de-stemmed, in inch-long slices

several (or more!) peeled **garlic** cloves

1 large **carrot**, previously steamed, in 1-inch lengths

Bake all at 350° for close to an hour, covered at first, then with top removed, basting frequently — I'm indebted to our friend Dorothea Douglas for pointing up the need of faithful lubrication. Then top the lot with minced **parsley** and serve, spooning up any good juices. No accompaniment is appropriate in this case since there are so many elements in the pot; simply follow the chicken with a green salad.

OR: Translate Chicken en Cocotte into a major salad: slice the chicken into strips after it's done, soft-pedal the juices, add a few boutique greens and a light helping of Dijon mustard mayonnaise and serve your chicken-veg-etc. cooled.

CHICKEN SAUTÉ WITH GARLIC BUTTER PASTA ONSLOW-FORD

This lovely combination is a souvenir of lunch at the home of a British painter who had sat, metaphorically at least, at the papa Surrealists' feet but loved to paint crisply galloping galaxies in a stark black and white. But there was nothing stark about Gordon Onslow-Ford's kitchen. Since that Tomales Bay déjeuner thirty-seven years ago we've used this chicken-and-pasta for parties more than anything else in the rep. I've lost track of how pervasive the lemon element was in the original, but I know that it's been making a crescendo, *poco a poco*, over the years, to excellent effect.

Onslow-Ford's San Francisco dealer was a lovely lady, soft-spoken but a tiger of a salesman, who showed his work in an intimate Russian Hill apartment, with a wonderful view of course. Visiting there, you felt you'd been invited to a salon for two. Rose Rabow also featured the uniquely gentle and vibrant paintings of Fred Reichman, a vastly underrated artist, with their forest units and still-life bouquets floating in the most eloquent "negative" spaces, and the exploding post-Monet tangles of Richard Bowman done up in his special fluorescent paint. I'm afraid I still feel a little sheepish — especially after that superb chicken-&-pasta — that I much prefer Fred and Dick's paintings to Gordon's.

- In a very hot skillet without fat brown **chicken** pieces vigorously, longer and over a higher flame on the first side (the meatier one) than the second: this to aid in producing the classic condition of "crisp outside and tender interior." Then drain the accumulated fat.
- Deglaze the pan with **dry sherry**, then squeeze **lemon juice** over the chicken very generously. Continue cooking for about 15 minutes over a lowish flame, with more time allotted the meatier side and the cover of your skillet not fully on in order to enhance crispness.
- Meanwhile mash together a good tablespoon or more of **butter** with at least 1 large pressed **garlic** clove and some **rosemary** needles, also snipped **fresh chives** if you have them. (Thank you, Bill Eddelman, for letting me raid your rosemary patch.)
- Boil enough **fettuccine** (for 12 minutes) to give each diner 1/8 of a pound thereof. Toss the pasta with the garlic herb butter and grated **dry jack or parmesan cheese** in a serving dish and, still tossing, combine with the just-mentioned ingredients the chicken pieces as well as the "good brown bits" if you have them. You can if you wish deglaze with sherry again just before emptying the skillet . . . and occasionally I add some chopped dried figs, marinated in a bit of sherry, to the simmering chicken.
- Serve with extra grated cheese, and lemon wedges for supplemental squeezing.

CHICKEN SAUTÉ WITH BALSAMIC VINEGAR, GARLIC AND TOMATO

A variant here on a dish served at the Jackson Fillmore, a noisy San Francisco trattoria suitable for use in *Moonstruck*. How lucky for us to live two blocks from this foodie's moonbeam.

Eating at the counter here, the epiphany level is high. Six platters of antipasti — tousled smokey red peppers, soft charred muffins of eggplant and so on — sit at attention on a display shelf, ready for ordering. Our enthusiastic waiter, brisk in apron-over-jeans, brings crisp fat toasts topped with tomato, onion and garlic. A neighbor meanwhile attends to a mélange of prawns, mushrooms and an enticing cream-toned sauce we must command on our next visit.

And the *padrone*, some Godfather's nephew it seems, strides toward the kitchen with a worried look, as if the roof of his culinary excellence might fall in. But worry not, neither the gastronomy nor the dancing vibrations of this trattoria will fail: the place runs like a skilled fantasist's clockwork, style and abundance and imagination all about.

(Except in the bare-bones loo, a statement of sorts about where this *casa's* unvarnished priorities lie. Believe me, the style of the rest room is a true key to a restaurant's personality.)

... Now I've just found out that this balsamicized chicken, virtually never found in a restaurant at home or abroad, was a staple at the old Blue Grotto on Broome Street in New York. Doubtless the brainchild of some Village granny. With its zippy flavor it's like walking through a garden sprinkler overshooting its turf.

- In a skillet without fat brown **chicken** pieces aggressively, taking more time and using more flame on the first side as is customary in Bloomfieldian pan frying. Then be sure to drain off the accumulated fat.
- Spread the chicken with a large pressed **garlic** clove, deglaze the pan with **balsamic vinegar** and pour at least 1/2 cup of the same vinegar over the chicken; continue cooking over a lowish flame, cover on the skillet, and with the addition of 1 small diced **tomato**, for 15 or 20 minutes. Add minced garlic and **parsley** to taste before serving.
- Mashed potatoes are recommended in this case, or serve the chicken alone, with a large juice-catching crouton tucked underneath. In any event you'll probably want a simple salad to follow — if you don't feel like making a dressing just put bottles of oil and vinegar on the dining table and pour from one then the other over your greens, judging the proper balance with the eye (one hopes!) of one of those tuxedoed salad cart pilots such as we used to find in San Francisco restaurants like Orsi's and Ruggero's.
- Your reward will be a "dressing" in which the oil and vinegar are distinct lines in the salad bowl orchestration but well harmonized too: the culinary equivalent, this, of a performance conducted by the legendary Pierre Monteux.
- PLAN B: Before serving, whisk in 2 or 3 heaping tablespoons of **crème fraîche**: here I'm borrowing, more or less, the courtly Gilles Lentin's sauce for confit de canard as served at his enchanting auberge, a converted 17th century farm in one of France's neglected, un-Mayled areas, Haut Languedoc. Look for Les Bergeries de Pondérach, just outside St-Pons a couple of hours east of Toulouse.

POULET À L'INDIENNE WITH CUCUMBER SAUTÉ

This tawny-colored chicken is based on Samuel Chamberlain and represents a somewhat Western view toward the culinary East, but it's not, I think, hampered by a low exoticism rating. Dateline-crossing blends are, in fact, very *in* these days, converting my uncertain steps toward the Asian kitchen into properly completed voyages. Dining out recently, we began with all-American slabs of salmon wrestled craftily into exquisite spring rolls, proceeded to veritable Shanghai noodles topped with fatless duck that read as scallopini, and finished with gingerbread in mandarin orange sauce. Only the wine, from Sardinia, seemed uni-cultural. The headwaiter was "fused": a genial Chinese fellow who reminded me of no one so much as A.J. Liebling.

- Brown **chicken** pieces in our standard exuberant manner, without fat, softening 1 small minced **onion** in a dab of **butter** at the edge of the skillet after the chicken is turned (and after you've poured off any disagreeable fat).
- Deglaze the pan with a splash of **white wine or dry vermouth**, add 1 cup of **chicken broth** and 1/2 cup more of the alcoholic element, then simmer all uncovered for 15 or 20 minutes, letting the liquid reduce by at least a third.
- Shortly before serving this poulet in soup bowls or cupped plates stir 3 teaspoons of good quality **curry powder** (i.e.: sufficiently intense) into 3/4 cup of **cream** and add this mixture to the chicken, stirring it in well.
- Serve this "Indian" chicken with plain **rice**, **raisins**, **chutney** (see page 130 for a first-class mango number) as well as not-very-Indian-but-ultra-refreshing **cucumber** strips tossed in a little butter for 2 or 3 minutes over rather high heat.
- Peeling, and seeding, the cucumber goes without saying. And I might add that toasted pinoli generally marry well with tossed cucumber.

NEXT DAY: Leftover sauce you might consider stirring into scrambled eggs.

MARCUS' RED THAI CURRY

Our former de facto son-in-law Marcus Colombano, who happens to be Josephine Araldo's great great nephew, issued a little cookbook with Alison every few years. From the 1988 edition, *Grapefruit on the Beach* (complete, logically enough, with a photo of same on the cover, sitting like a school of pudgy, phlegmatic golf balls) I have seized on one of Marcus' coconut milk rhapsodies. It's hot stuff all right, Marcus being no sissy in the face of armed attacks by lurking peppers, so you might want to tone it down here or there, but I assure you, this is a magnificent curry, as tasty as it is authentic.

. . . Now I'm browsing in the 1991 edition, minus the grapefruit that seem to have wandered out of Marcus' consciousness. I note here this hearty eater likes to put butter in his chocolate sauce, which is the kitchen equivalent of those seven ripe trumpets blowing heavenward in Scriabin's *Poem of Ecstasy*, and his "killer" buttermilk pancakes measured in this vintage year eight inches in diameter. On a clear morning one could, I imagine, see to their far side.

Also included is a Q-and-A session at the Ace Café, two strangers asked to recount their most sensual eating experiences. One reverently recalls munching mustard-coated *frites* in Brussels out of giant cones constructed with a page of daily newspaper, the other fondly remembers eating barbecue in Texas off butcher paper with his bare hands.

You don't suppose it was the Food Page?

Sauté **chicken** pieces until golden brown, without fat, and just before this process is complete soften 2 chopped **onions** in a little butter at the side of the same skillet (having drained the accumulated fat from the fowl).

Now add a mix of:

> several cored **hot chilis** sliced thin (optional!)
>
> ground **roasted unsalted peanuts**, 1/8 cup
>
> **cayenne**, a smidgen or more
>
> **cardamon seed**, 1/8 teaspoon, achieved after peeling the skin off a few pods — or use the ground variety
>
> Asian **sweet chili sauce** (on exotic foods shelf at your supermarket), 2 tablespoons at least
>
> **ground coriander**, 1/2 teaspoon
>
> **cumin**, 1 teaspoon
>
> **ground cloves**, 1/8 teaspoon
>
> chopped **cilantro**, 2 teaspoons
>
> **coconut milk**, 1 cup

Simmer all for about 30 minutes, covered, adding more coconut milk (total of 1 cup) now and then to maintain liquidity. And a little before serving — with rice, of course — add chopped **scallions**.

CHICKEN WITH MANY CLOVES OF GARLIC

For a WASP American growing up in the 30s and early 40s there was no garlic in the air. Many are the tales of our parents and grandparents living out their lives with no more knowledge of garlic than heckelphones or Sanskrit. But then came garlic bread, the rage post-World War II (at a slight extra charge, please). And gradually the aiolian mysteries of Provence and other aromatic territories spread over our land.

Thirty years ago this chicken with — "forty" is the usual titular number — many cloves of garlic was still something of an oddity, but today it's standard rep. The garlic cloves almost disintegrate, of course, in the braising process, making a kind of coating. Writing this, I remember that back in the early 30s my parents frequented a San Francisco bistro, the St. Germain, whose waiter, Gaston by name (and I'm not making that up), promised with solemn regularity that the proprietor would make them his special garlic soup, not on the menu, of course.

Well, you can guess the punch line: said potage never materialized. Was it, I wonder, the chef or my father who balked?

Another favored restaurateur of that era, Fred Solari in Maiden Lane, would stand by his door like a station master with a bag of mail and virtually toss a platter of reenforcement oysters at our hurrying Buick when more tuxedoed guests than originally expected were about to knock on the family door.

A few years later and Hoi's night out (Hoi was our resident *chef de cuisine*) I was joining my parents for lamb chops and salad at Pierre's, a pullman-car bistro on Pine Street done up in renter's green, the waiter not long from Limoges or Lyon. Scallopini mills like the Riviera on Washington Square and the St. Julien downtown (where one ate to the monumental clatter of noisily bussed dishes) were less to my taste. But then we found Lambro's, bearded Charles Bardelli in the kitchen and a hostess passed cheese puffs as we waited in the bar.

Off to Stanford and living in professors' houses where meals, Michelinesque or otherwise, were not on offer, I'd sneak out to a shack on El Camino Real where the chicken-in-a-basket shone. This dive made a virtue of grease, blanketing its fryers with a crackery coating overwhelming in its tempurian machismo. It took me a year to outgrow it.

> In a skillet brown **chicken** pieces without fat, then drain the fat inevitably, alas, produced. Meanwhile peel a good 16 to 20 healthy-sized cloves of **garlic** and when your chicken is brown scatter them over and around the fowl, along with some **rosemary**; reduce the heat as much as possible, cover the pan and simmer all for about 35 minutes, turning the chicken pieces halfway along and spooning some of the accumulated juices over them.
>
> Serve this chicken with all the juices in the pan, and parsley mashed potatoes and baked tomato halves glistening with olive oil specked with breadcrumbs and herbs.

CHICKEN WITH LEEKS, DRIED FRUITS AND CREAM

The genesis of this "invention" was my swooning a little over a picture of Jeremiah Tower's braised rabbit with leeks, prunes, cream and pink peppercorns. The recipe on this page is a shade simpler to prepare; still, you want to be observant, and turn your intuition to High.

I'm reminded of how my father (he was, that puffy wit Alexander Woollcott told George S. Kaufman, the best man for tickers west of the Mississippi) taught medicine. Standing, I'm told, at the door of the subject patient's room, rocking elegantly, he'd ask his Stanford plebes to diagnose said subject at ten paces by "using all your senses."

Colleagues have reminisced fondly and at length about my father's dedication, genius and essential warmth, noting, however, that he was positively Victorian in his formality — a formality in which, I think, there was a certain subtle wit, for my father was as much a literary man, a student of manners, as a science type. I have to quote Dr. Gunther Nagel: "As with the English gentlemen whose caravans passed each other in silence in the vastness of the Arabian desert, because there was no means of formal introduction, there was never a greeting when passing Dr. Bloomfield in the hall."

But back to our quasi-Jeremiahan chicken. It has also, I'd say, become a bit more robust in translation, closer, for instance, to the homey fare at my beloved Perraudin on Paris' rue St-Jacques than the trendy delights of a San Francisco power-luncheria such as the one Jeremiah used to oversee from his mighty stove.

Perraudin is a gift! A few years may elapse, but Madame is always ready with a smile that could melt a Professsor Moriarty. She is not about to forget her Californians. Her aproned lieutenant is a mite gruff, but perhaps only shy: she warms noticeably when a diner groans with delight over the custard-oozing tarts strategically placed, prize-winners all, at the bistro's busiest traffic junction.

- Soak 1-1/2 to 2 cups of cut-up packaged **dried fruits** in water to cover for an hour or so, then drain.
- Now in a rather large skillet brown lightly — for a change! — **chicken** pieces without fat. Deglaze the pan with a little **brandy**, add a tablespoon each of finely chopped **onion** and **carrot** and 1-1/2 cups of **chicken broth** and simmer all over a low flame for 15 to 20 minutes, until the liquid is half reduced. After two or three minutes your nose will tell you chicken and alcohol have found each other: this is a compatible-ingredients marriage, no special license necessary.
- Add the fruits and 4 or 5 small well-trimmed **leeks** (partly split lengthwise) and cook another 7 minutes, covered, then add 1/2 cup of **cream** and continue the cooking yet another 3 or so minutes, until the leeks are soft and the sauce is light middleweight or a tiny bit thicker in consistency.
- It should be as smooth as the milky back of a Watteau nymph — well, almost.
- Then in your arrangement of diners' plates — use the biggest in your cupboard — go to town with chicken in the middle, fruits atop, and the leeks neat logs in the moat of cream surrounding your poultry castle. If that doesn't suit, drape the leeks over the fruit like railway ties.

LEMON MILK CHICKEN FREDIANI

A friend of Don and Renata Frediani served them this almost Chinese-tasting "pollo al latte" in Italy. Each year brings a fresh supply of recipes spilling from the Fredianis' Alitalia bag — crêpes with chopped spinach in the batter, for instance, to roll around pieces of smoked salmon, or a puff pastry red onion tart with the onions and pancetta browned in olive oil and white wine. Or consider a Flemish salad of slivered cabbage, celery and carrots in a mustard vinaigrette.

The latest revelations: baby artichokes cooked in chicken broth, and chicken with a thin pancetta casing roasted in parchment (which you should open 30 minutes before serving). Lemon Milk Chicken with its Asian overtones you might want to eat with chopsticks.

> Skin **boneless chicken breasts**, cut them into cubes, **flour** them well and brown without fat; drain off any fat that accumulates. Now add 2/3 cup of **milk**, the juice of 1/2 a large **lemon**, a little **rosemary** and **pepper** and simmer all, uncovered, for about 10 minutes, stirring frequently: you want a sauce with a consistency just past thin.
>
> Serve Lemon Milk Chicken in cupped plates, or even soup bowls, scattered over stepping-stone slices of fried potatoes — "broasted" potatoes, actually, which are made by boiling rather thin potato slices until they're almost done, then transferring them to a large skillet and slowly sautéing them in a little butter, turning them often, until they're rather crisp . . . if you have a space problem in the skillet, push the first installment to the side, drop in a bit more butter and "broast" a second batch.

CHICKEN WITH BASIL, GINGER AND ORANGE

More fusion cuisine.

Most of the ingredients in this possibly schizoid invention were inspired by a dish at a wonderful little Chinese restaurant on San Francisco's Clement street, but the cooking method — except for the manic blackening of the basil — is identical with that of the Italian chicken just above.

> Skin **boneless chicken breasts**, cube them, **flour** them lightly and stir-fry them and about 18 **fresh basil** leaves over high heat; a minute before moderate browning is complete throw into your skillet 2 tablespoons of peeled and chopped **ginger** and another of chopped **garlic**, also a few 1-inch lengths of **scallion** and a pinch of **cayenne**. Deglaze the pan with **dry sherry**, reduce the heat to low-moderate, add a short cup of sherry, 1/4 cup of **orange juice,** a good teaspoon or more of **soy sauce**, a few strips of **orange peel** and simmer all, uncovered, for 15 minutes, stirring frequently. Serve with plain rice and perhaps some chutney.

CHICKEN, WHITE BEANS AND LEEK-FETA-SOUR CREAM SALSA WITH TORTILLAS

Another symphonically textured burrito — or you can as I like to do keep the chicken/beans/salsa outside the tortilla, treating the latter like bread to be used for mopping up operations. Burritos, of course, are the envelope of the hour, especially in California where one finds them cradling goat stew, tongue, Mu Shi pork, name your stuffing. In this era of the Great Take Out they've become the ultimate if somewhat oozy meal for people with an appetite, good taste, two hands and scant time for committing knives and forks to a dishpan.

Place almost 1 cup of **cannellini or Great Northern beans** in a saucepan with water to cover, bring to a boil and cook 1 minute, remove from the heat and set aside to soak for an hour, then drain.

Now you can brown your **chicken** pieces in a large skillet without added fat — and be sure to drain the unwanted fat that accumulates during browning. Then add the beans to the chicken along with 2/3 cup of **dry vermouth** and 2 cups of **chicken broth** with a tablespoon of **tomato paste** dissolved therein, plus 1 or 2 pressed **garlic** cloves and a little **thyme** and **pepper**; simmer all for an hour partly covered.

Now reserve the chicken while you continue cooking the beans-in-sauce until they're done — that's about another 45 minutes — stirring occasionally and adding water (vermouth, too) as needed to prevent your sauce reducing away. Finally, return the chicken to the pot to warm, then serve your chicken-and-beans with or in steamed **tortillas** (use cupped plates or large soup bowls) along with the following Salsa:

Chop finely 2 smallish **leeks** after the essential washing and trimming. Whisk 3/4 cup of **sour cream or yogurt** until it's smooth, add 3 tablespoons of **milk**, 1 tablespoon of **lime** juice and whisk again; now blend in 1/3 cup of crumbled **feta cheese**, resorting to a potato masher, the ultimate show of force, if necessary. Combine the leeks and feta/cream, adding **dill weed**, a pressed **garlic** clove and **chili powder** to taste: I'd say quite a bit, perhaps 2 teaspoons.

BOILED CHICKEN AND VEGETABLES WITH SAFFRON MAYONNAISE

Decorating instructions here: one could place the chicken over the veg, and a ribbon of mayo, or perhaps a light Hollandaise, on the chicken. Minus these fairly innocent accoutrements this bollito is just what the doctor ordered when the old tum is on the blink. But in sickness or health I've become addicted to this nursery *plat* in its simplest dress . . . and my memory spins back to nursery days when, a five-year-old with endangered ears, I sat in bed awaiting the tray with my dinner concealed inside a silvery metal cover, a bowler hat of a "cloche."

The inserted tip of an index finger in the little hole at the crown of this pristine object permitted said hat to be pulled dramatically off, as if by a headwaiter revealing a Michelin-blessed spécialité. What on earth was inside, on a plate divided into separate wedges for meat-potato-veg. WASP food c. 1936, I guess. It comes to me now, an *amuse-gueule* of square crackers spread with marmalade, probably homemade. And maybe there was a lamb chop, French of course, diced up as if for the pilaf I'd love twenty years on. Well, I was eating as well as the seven cats my mother hovered over in her old age.

In a large covered casserole in several inches of **chicken broth** boil some short juliennes of **carrot**, dropping in a few minutes later several **boiling onions** and some rather thickly sliced **potato**; finally, for exactly 13 minutes which will pilot your bollito to the exact moment of truth, cook the **chicken breasts** that will form its centerpiece (pieces). Figure on half an hour from the first carrot insertion to platter-on-the-table.

And be warned that unusually hefty chicken pieces could take more than that 13 minutes on which we seem to be staking our kitchen reputation. And dark meat if you substitute it will take longer too.

Potatoes employed in this recipe must be peeled. The health advantages of still-jacketed spuds are all very well, but in this context ragged edges are anathema, a dirty brown adds nothing to the color scheme of an attractive bollito.

Remember that the homeliest Dutch or Swiss hotel will attack its boiling potatoes in an orderly kitchen-police manner and send them forth in that virginal academician's white that's so enticing.

You can serve this bollito with a pot of Dijon mustard or a Dijon mustard vinaigrette (page 1); it is, of course, more festive with our saffron mayonnaise (page 59). As a matter of fact, the simple mustard accompaniment can be positively magical if you spoon a little of the cooking broth over your chicken and let the mustard run into the juices, creating thereby an instant sauce of which any Paris bistro might be proud.

ASIAN NOTE: Coating your about-to-be boiled chicken pieces with some five spice powder will give that Far Eastern touch. Recently in Chinatown I succumbed to "taking out" one of those quintupely spiced chickens looking so pristine in the deli window. "But cut off the head, please," I requested — I hadn't noticed it tucked coyly out of sight. "Chop chop?" the counterman responded, as if mimicking something very politically incorrect, and soon my "take home" bird was in thirty pieces.

MILANESE BOIL À LA CRISPI, OTHERWISE KNOWN AS BOTTAGGIO

Ah, Milan, city of designer sausages and *with-it* haberdashery, inflated opera productions and endearing trattorie, the Alps in sight to the north, the bland but suggestive expanses of the Po Valley just to the south of the city's tedious apartment blocks.

And this is an interpretation of a dish we ate at Crispi on Corso Venezia thirty years ago: it was served from a great kettledrum-like tub wheeled up the aisles and included, if I remember right, boiled meats, cabbage and something red, tomato or sweet peppers. There may have been potato and/or white beans too. And it was called bottaggio.

Alas, Crispi was a great throbbing brasserie where waiters scarcely had the time or patience to communicate recipes — the bill of fare contained 107 items, eighteen in caps, typewritten in the amateur chiaroscuro of an apparently ailing Olivetti — and I didn't take a proper inventory of the tub. So I've winged it here. And what does the word bottaggio mean? Is it the cooking pot? I consulted Renata Frediani, who is Milanese, and she threw up her hands: "Why, that must be a dialect word, I've never heard of it." And a similar blank was drawn at the Italian Cultural Institute.

Well, no Poirot of the stewpots would stop there: a fax to Italy brought the news that bottaggio is a Renaissance word, occasionally used now as a colorful alternate for Cassoeula, that long-cooking stew of pork products and cabbage. Bottaggio, I also learned, is very close to the modern Italian word for barrel. And, our Milan contact informed us, Crispi's — *ahimé* — is no more.

In a large covered pot in 2 inches of water boil a fork-pricked **cotechino sausage** for about an hour, adding 15 or 16 minutes before your 13-minute **chicken** pieces some **potato** chunks, fat strips of **sweet red pepper** and a rather generous helping of thinly sliced **cabbage**.

Serve this "bottaggio" with salsa verde, roughly 2 parts **olive oil** to 1 of **red wine vinegar** plus a blinding ton of minced **parsley**, crushed **capers** and **anchovy** filets to taste and — optional but amusing — some very, very finely minced **onion**.

The earlier you make your salsa verde the better, it's a sauce that always seems to start out like strangers at a party, the ingredients not quite comfortable about mingling. In fact, they're almost snarling at each other.

And if you have some mostarda di frutta in the larder, serve that, too: with boiled meats I always say the more sauces the merrier. Let them run together! I'd also recommend arranging your bottaggio-cum-sauces on a bed of large limas: cook them separately as in the first paragraph of our recipe on page 161.

WATERZOOI DE BRUXELLES
—boiled chicken with leeks, cream and egg yolk—

Souvenir of the Taverne du Passage in Brussels, where the waiters were to a San Franciscan Jack's-or-Tadich-like, that's to say, a trifle brusque, the food very rich indeed, and the manicured man oozing pin-stripe in the banquette opposite looked like a *ministre de finance*. No power lunch for him, though; he was simply bathing in chicken with many cups of cream. Fortified as well with velvet poultry, two Bloomfields were able to face the terrors and hilarities of the journey fate dictated for them the following day in '86.

All Brussels-Paris trains cancelled by a strike, we picnic-ready vagabonds heeded a laconic stationmaster's advice to get moving *somewhere more or less in a southerly direction* and hopped the 11:18 local for Courtrai (translation: outer space, reached via a bucolic landscape suitable for knights and maidens), hailing therein a long-distance taxi that carried us across the border to Tourcoing, whence, following a protracted ticket-counter transaction, executed by a functionary in crisp jeans, we rattled into nearby Lille on a dinky interurban and just caught a Paris *rapide* that proceeded to dally like a contented cow by a pretty field near Amiens, like this . . . . . but did in fact deposit us in Paris with two minutes to spare, on a steamily hot afternoon, before our connection for Toulouse glided down the quai at Gare d'Austerlitz. With great thuds of relief we collapsed into seats 35 and 37 in car 6 of the *Capitole*.

And my diary fails to mention the menu of our picnic May 20, 1986.

In a large pot in whatever amount of **butter** it takes to do the job soften the following chopped items: the white parts of 3 **leeks**, 1 **carrot** and 1 **onion**. The carrot being a monolithic critter to the core, it will take longer, so put it in first. Season all with a little **thyme** and **nutmeg**.

Now lay over the vegetables your **chicken** pieces with a small pinch of **salt** and pour over all enough **chicken broth** to cover; cover the pot and simmer for 25 to 30 minutes.

Remove the chicken to a tureen, put the cover on to keep the chicken warm, and strain the broth into a saucepan: place the pan over high heat, reduce the broth by about half and take it off the burner.

Then drape the chicken-in-the-tureen with the remaining vegetables which in traditional waterzooi recipes are cavalierly discarded, thereby depriving the finished product of a lovely dotting of orange.

Finally, beat together 2 **egg** yolks and 1/2 a cup of **cream** and stir this mixture into the broth with the juice of a small **lemon.** (A true cholesterol-defying Belgian would, of course, use 3 yolks). Add the cream-broth-lemon to the chicken-and-veg in the tureen, topping all with minced **parsley**. And serve your waterzooi in commodious soup bowls with plain rice and provide knife, fork and spoon, this is multi-implement food.

MULLIGATAWNEY MENLO PARK
—a half-soup—

A lightened update of a festive "bowl" from *Sunset* Magazine 1963. One tends to disparage Old *Sunset* cookery these days, but there were some inspirations in those pretty pages. It was not, as a friend used to quip, a case of "everything cooked with sesame seeds."

In a covered pot boil 3/4 of a cup of **long grain rice** in several cups of water, adding after a few minutes your **chicken** pieces to allow them their 13 minutes' proper boiling time. Meanwhile in a skillet soften 1 chopped **onion** in a teaspoon or more of **butter**, seasoning same with a heaping teaspoon of **turmeric**, a little **poppy seed** and **ground coriander**, 1 pressed **garlic** clove, a small amount of **ground cloves** and a touch of **cayenne**.

If you want to graduate from "mild" spicing to "medium," be sure to up these amounts, in proportion.

Add to this onion mix 1 14-ounce can of **garbanzo beans** (be sure to drain them), stirring in several cups of **chicken broth** and a small splash of **dry sherry**; simmer for 15 minutes, then turn up the flame and reduce moderately.

Serve your Mulligatawney in the biggest bowls you can round up, placing pieces of boiled chicken and mounds of rice strategically/artistically in the chicken-garbanzo soup. Place 2 or 3 **lemon** wheels per person on the chicken and decorate your finished product with minced **cilantro**. The mango chutney of page??? would certainly be an appropriate condiment.

Now from our handbook of eating instructions: fork, knife and spoon will be necessary, and note the chutney is best with bites of chicken and rice, while squishing those lemon slices into the liquid is essential for flavoring the ochre soup in which the fowl sits.

And speaking of chicken and rice . . .

I was on the Amsterdam-Interlaken express in 1999 reminiscing with a Dutch woman across the aisle about Lucerne and the Pension Montana where, forty-five years earlier, I'd enjoyed such a dish, steaming and good, and lo, she knew the Montana, and its rice chicken, very well indeed. Yes, continuity hath charms.

POULET DIABLE

À la diable or *alla Diavola* means cayenne or crushed red pepper flakes in the recipe. Well, I seem to have shoo'd Satan away, finding a little relatively innocent black pepper sufficient. For me it's the luxuriant mix of mustard, breadcrumbs and pan juices that makes this Hadean chicken sing. Also in its favor is the relative ease of preparation.

But I wouldn't overlook completely a more difficult "Diable" I've read about in Alma Lach's excellent and little-known *Hows and Whys of French Cooking* (University of Chicago, 1974). There's no mustard in this recipe, only the crumbs and melted butter, but you add a sauce made by simmering shallots in white wine and vinegar, drastically reducing this, then adding brown sauce, tomato paste and a "dash of cayenne," simmering all for a while before finishing with lemon juice, Cognac, butter and parsley!

Meanwhile I notice that the pages in Mrs. Lach's tome which have seen the most action are those devoted to Meringue Timbale, Seven Minute Frosting, Meringue Butter Cream, Coffee Flavored Meringue and Butter Cream Frosting. Archaeologists seeing many spots before their eyes will have no trouble deducing from this evidence the interests of a certain Webster Street kitchen.

- Brush **chicken** pieces on both sides with **olive oil** and **pepper** and broil them for about 25 minutes, turning once.
- Spread the undersides of the chicken well with a mixture of **Dijon mustard** and **breadcrumbs** — lots of mustard and just enough crumbs to grit up the texture a bit; then baste with pan juices (using a baster rather than a spoon, this to help your sanity level) and continue broiling for 10 minutes.
- Now turn the chicken, spread with more of the same mustard/crumb mix, baste, and broil another 10 minutes.
- Serve your Diable with tomatoes baked for 15 or 20 minutes with a topping of herbs of choice, pressed garlic and olive oil, along with some watercress to make for a nice tri-colorization. The baking of your tomatoes can, of course, run concurrently with that final broiling-and-basting of the fowl, one flight up if you're looking at our not so mighty Kenmore, an ancient and ultra-dependable appliance which, if it had hands, could write a book.

NOTE: Leftover Diable is wonderful cold with mayonnaise.

—*24-hour*—
POULET MADAME

(Recette Paillard, Paris le 26 Avril 1983, 33 Av. des Gobelins)

Madame Paillard was Cecily Bloomfield's landlady in Paris spring of '83, a pleasant and very talkative hostess in a book-lined salle, across the boulevard from the Gobelins tapestry museum. From Mme. Paillard's it was a bracing hike to "town," out of the unheralded thirteenth arrondissement, into the famous Fifth, up the storybook Rue Mouffetard with its busy morning market. Most evenings, by foot or Metro, we trekked to a good restaurant, research for an article I was doing on "regional" cuisine in the melting-pot of Paris.

For Lyon fare the destination was spiffy little Benoit by the Tour St-Jacques (hot sausages and wilted escarole), for Provençale, Le Paillon in the scruffy Tenth (sardines in olive vinaigrette). Alsatian sauerkraut we found, of course, at Balzar, down from the Sorbonne, and Pyrennesian pipérade was just around the corner from Madame at Etchegorry. No Mouffetardian Hemingway associations in the Thirteenth, but the Basque chow will do.

City eating done, we glided south on the crack *Capitole*, dining at 170 kilometers an hour. Our waiter was a gem, offering us cheese in a courtly singsong that went up (MON . . .) and down (SIEUR . . .), while the countryside lay flat as a slab of jambon.

- In a large pot place 1 finely chopped **onion** and over the onion put your **chicken** pieces, light or dark, which have been coated with **Dijon mustard** (be very generous!) and a little **thyme**. Reserve the chicken, covered, overnight — or at least eight hours — in your refrigerator.
- Then, dinnertime approaching, cook the chicken in the still-covered pot over a low-medium fire for 35 or 40 minutes, occasionally spooning the accumulating juices over the chicken and rearranging the pieces if some are too far from the pot's warm bottom.
- Before serving, stir in 1/3 to 1/2 cup of **cream** along with some chopped **parsley**: the sauce should be a rich and soupy light brown, with the onions verging on crisp.
- Serve Madame's poulet with plain rice as she did, or poached apples (sliced and cooked in a little water until soft) or with fresh green tagliarini with a little butter and grated cheese. Infinitely compatible as well are parsley mashed potatoes. And there's even a medley of baked white beans and tomato halves, flecked with herbs of course — be sure to simmer the beans until they're nearly cooked prior to baking.
- AND NOTE: Leftover Madame sauce stirred into an omelette will give you a mellifluous lunch dish suggesting a daily special at some comfy old grand hotel, Metropole or Carlton by name.

FRICASSÉE DE POULET A L'AUVERGNATE

A piquant, hearty first cousin to Blanquette de Veau. But prepare yourself: the stirring/adding/thickening of the later stages of this recipe happens quickly, it's as if you're in an orchestra that's playing *allegro con spirito* and is not, *bien sûr*, about to stop. A nice bonus, though: as you're cooking this farmhouse treat you can munch on surplus raw carrot sandwiched with excess bacon you've fried to a hedonistic crisp.

Orléans, seat of my Army adventures in the distant 50s, was great blanquette country and it was fun to lap one up after a long stint at the *République du Centre*.

That was the French newspaper where our little *Com-Z Cadence* was printed. Every Thursday two of us staffers would peer over the shoulder of stocky Roger Gentil as he fit sticks of type into the page forms, ash from his teeth-clenched Gauloise spilling onto our prose as he read backward the English he could not truly understand. Meanwhile Marius the aristocratic copy-cutter presided at a lectern nearby in his grey smock.

Once we played a dirty trick on Roger: instead of filling an incomplete column with some traditional "bulldog," as in "there are 3040 elephants in Timbuktoo," we asked him to encase in a little box "Gladys Glover," the screwball Judy Holliday film character who wanted to see her name in lights. "Thees Gladeez Glowvair, what ees dat?" An explanation came soon, from our captain!

In a large pot in a good 2 cups of water braise **chicken** pieces at 350° for about 40 minutes with:

> 6 or 8 inch-long slices of moderately pre-cooked **bacon**
>
> 10 or 12 very thin **carrot** juliennettes, previously steamed
>
> 4 or 5 thin slices of **onion**
>
> a sprinkling of **thyme**
>
> 2 or 3 **parsley** sprigs
>
> 2 pressed **garlic** cloves
>
> 2 **cloves**
>
> 2 good tablespoons of **red wine vinegar**

Meanwhile in the skillet you used for cooking bacon, in a little **butter** and any leftover bacon fat, gently sauté 5 or 6 fairly large good quality **mushrooms**, not too thinly sliced. Reserve, covered.

And half an hour later . . . In a larger pan over minimal heat blend 1-1/2 or 2 tablespoons of **butter** with 1 tablespoon of **flour** and gradually stir in at least 1-1/3 cups of broth from the original casserole — out of the oven now — then add the chicken and veg bits (minus those seaweedy sprigs) and simmer all briefly.

Next add the mushrooms and their juice and a small heap of minced **parsley** and thicken the fricassée with a beaten **egg yolk** into which you've poured 1/8 cup of the hot broth. Stir your quick-developing sauce attentively, you don't want this ode to Auvergne to get too thick — but be careful, the sauce must have substance. Within a minute or so, add 1/2 teaspoon of **red wine vinegar** for crucial flavor enhancement.

Momentarily your braise with all its aura of eternal Gallic verities will be ready; serve it with the only possible accoutrement, plain rice.

CHICKEN WITH ROQUEFORT AND RAISIN STUFFING

When we visited the Roquefort country in 1988 we ate Roquefort tart, Roquefort flan, salad with Roquefort, and just plain Roquefort.

But we didn't encounter this pingy/scrumptuous Poulet au Roquefort, a recipe by Mapie de Toulouse-Lautrec which we had been served by friends in Paris some years earlier and which we offer here in a healthier form than the over-rich, however enticing, original in which liver pâté was thought by its calorie-defying author to be an essential element.

Well, as the old saying goes, let them eat foie gras.

Interestingly enough, this dish has a Russian country cousin, chicken with raisin stuffing. I like to imagine it was served one evening in the Ukraine in 1882 after a particularly fraught carriage ride near the Davydov estate. In the coach were the composer Tchaikovsky, his mercurial (read flaky) niece Tanya, and Tanya's boyfriend my cousin Stanislav Blumenfeld.

The prim composer, his biographer Poznansky reports, was shocked when he suddenly "not only felt but saw" the play of Stan and Tanya's legs beneath a rug Tanya had spread over her knees and those of my wicked cousin the music tutor. Soon this troublesome and enchanting pair produced a son, and Tanya, like a character in a Tchaikovsky opera, dropped dead aged twenty-five at a ball: morphine had been her undoing. Stan wisely retreated to Kiev where he taught proper young ladies their scales.

Stanislav had at least four siblings who were musicians; the most celebrated was Felix Blumenfeld who must have been the Lennie Bernstein of old St. Petersburg: pianist, conductor, composer, pal of Rimsky-Korsakoff, early champion of Stravinsky, ultimately the teacher of Vladimir Horowitz. He too had a taste for pretty girls.

What snacks must have been set out when Felix visited his sister Olga Neuhaus in Elizavetgrad and played Wagner's *Ring* well into the night for the benefit of her son Heinrich — who, after a thankfully botched suicide attempt in Florence (Artur Rubinstein and Karol Szymanowski would rush down on the train to bring "Harry" home) would become the teacher of one Sviatoslav Richter.

- Pour boiling water over 2 or 3 heaping tablespoons of **yellow raisins** and let them stand for 5 minutes, then drain. Now, playing with the ingredients like pastry dough, use your hands to moosh together a manageable mound of "stuffing" consisting of perhaps 1/6 of a pound of **Roquefort or other good quality blue cheese**, two thirds of the raisins and some **breadcrumbs** soaked in **milk** and squeezed almost dry.
- Using thumb and forefinger, loosen the skin on the top of **chicken breasts** and slip the stuffing underneath, prodding each morsel into an even layer, then conceal your surgery. Next, brown the breasts lightly without fat, drain off the accumulated fat, deglaze the pan with a little **brandy**, add 1/2 cup of **dry vermouth** and simmer slowly, mostly covered, for 25 or 30 minutes.
- A little before the breasts are done add a short 1/4 cup of **cream** and the rest of the raisins: some of course will have fallen out of the chicken with the inevitable tearing of skin as the pieces were turned in the pan. Serve Mapie's chicken with plain rice, or one of those mixes of white, brown and wild.

PAELLA "HOME BISTRO"

(The usual 2 servings, which you may well want to multiply)

When a team of kitchen helpers volunteers for service, prepare paella, the ultimate risotto. It is, of course, a dish like Choucroute Garnie which you never want to eat without a crowd; intimacy is simply not in sync with its grand orchestration. I associate paella with the beamed and bustling Alejandro's in San Francisco's Richmond district, long gone alas. Here we were served by an exuberant waitperson from New Mexico who offered us free of charge a learned little lecture on the differences in Spanish as spoken here and there below the border — "The Costa Ricans, they cut their words in half (swift motion of hand in the direction of our table) . . . ooh, the Bolivians (a big smile of amazement here), they talk so *smooooth* and suave." Berlitz was never like this.

I also associate the adjacent recipe with a fiery Russo-Swedish friend, unfortunately no longer with us, who was forever seeking an excuse to call in friends — she had a lot of 'em, including Igor Stravinsky — and serve a big platter of paella. It was, I'm sure, her metaphor for bonding.

> In a small skillet brown enough **chorizo-type sausage** to provide 5 or 6 thick slices per serving, then drain and slice.
>
> Meanwhile in a large skillet brown **chicken thighs** vigorously without fat; reserve them, pouring off the accumulated unhealthy goop, then in the same pan, the heat reduced, cook 1/2 a large minced **onion** and several medium-width strips of **sweet red and green pepper** in a bit of **olive oil** until soft — note that the peppers will take a couple of minutes longer than the onion and should be inserted ahead of their mates.
>
> Return the chicken to the big skillet and add the sausage from our first paragraph before showering in 1/2 cup of **rice** next to the meat. Stir the rice over quite high heat for 1-1/2 minutes, until opaque, then combine all the elements under your careful supervision, apply a generous dusting of **saffron** and pour in a cup of **chicken broth.** And note here that if you're doubling this recipe you shouldn't quite double the amount of chicken broth.
>
> Now cover and simmer all for at least 30 minutes, until the rice is no longer chewy. Then it's time to add 1/4 pound of **cooked mussels**, **clams** to taste and 4 raw and peeled **jumbo prawns** (for these, bring money!). Cover the skillet again and warm your nearly complete paella for 2 or 3 minutes. Finally, add some thawed, briefly heated **frozen peas**, sprinkle with minced **parsley** and serve.
>
> NOTE: Demi-paellas are possible, for instance a Risotto of Sausage, Peas and Shrimp.

POLLO TRENTINA

An agrodolcean sleeper, adapted from an excellent English tome of forty years ago, the *Encyclopedia of European Cooking* edited by Musia Soper and published by Paul Hamlyn. In this unprepossessing green volume you'll find — I select at random — Piperies Yemistes (Balkan stuffed green peppers), Westfalisches Gaenschenschwarzsauer (giblets as done in Westphalia), Marinated Swedish Sprats, Swiss Apple Sponge, German Marble Cake, Escudella Catalana (a thick soup of bacon, cabbage, turnips, pasta and saffron) etc. etc. In short, a Eurailpass through NATO's kitchens and then some.

I wonder if there are any apple sponges or Gaenschen-thingamies in my past, my diary does have a way of turning up such data, for instance the amazing fact that I was munching pretzels at the Nuernburg station on February 8, 1971, waiting for a train to Regensburg. I don't particularly like pretzels.

Reading further I see that once our express out of East Germany arrived on the safe side of no-man's-land the lady stationmaster like a walk-on providing atmosphere in a Graham Greene novel was busy polishing the door-handles of her trackside fortress.

It's a wonder they let me out of the mysterious East: when those stern female officials came down the aisle wearing passport-stamping (or not stamping) tables across their chests, rather in the fashion of oldtime cigarette girls with their frontal trays of Luckies and Camels, I had an irresistible urge to leave a toe planted outside our compartment door. That was a Nein, Nein, and it was only a spousal "come on now, these folks are serious" that kept this U.S. citizen from possible extradition to a hoosegow where, I suppose, they guillotined the little pinkies of overly witty Westerners.

Marinate your **chicken** pieces and 1 **chicken liver** per serving for an hour or so in:

    1 cup of **red wine**

    1/2 cup of **golden raisins**

    1/2 teaspoon of **sugar**

    several juliennes of **lemon** peel

    1 turn of the **nutmeg** mill

    a pinch of **thyme**

Then brown the chicken briskly with the livers, without added fat. Drain off the accumulated fat, deglaze the pan with a little red wine, add the marinade and a bit of **chicken broth** and simmer for 20 minutes: the sauce should have body without being the least bit thick.

Green pasta with some butter and grated cheese is the ideal companion for Pollo Trentina. But another interesting option is warm poached pears. Or forego the nouvelle touch and open a tin of whole water-packed chestnuts from the Faugier plant in the Ardèche: they're fully cooked and will warm in your sauce at the last minute . . . and you'll have more than enough left over for a good risotto with pancetta.

COQ AU VIN

I cringe at the memory of serving this dish to a famous friend without the texture-defining beurre manié, and with croutons so hard they went CCCRNCH! when attacked innocently by our politely silent guests. It's a wonder those croutons didn't fly across the room, in which case we would have witnessed an aerial battle of the sourdough brigade firing on its own people.

Ah, the coqs au vin in my life, I remember them like milestones. The first was at Alouette, Polk near Sutter in San Francisco, circa 1952. Alouette with its arabesqueing Moroccan headwaiter and bulging repertoire of dark, seductive sauces was the first restaurant I knew that seemed totally French rather than the local graft, however admirable, of

American chop house and nice French bistro. Alouette also served an addictive veal chop in an oniony marchand de vin and called it *Côte de Veau Chez Soi*, a title as svelte and brunette (yes, words can be in color) as that memorable chop.

Two tips about this recipe: the better the wine the better the coq, and forgetting to drain off the bacon fat may only help. Also, should your mate suddenly remember a 7 p.m. lecture bearing down on dinner like a mad locomotive, it is possible to quick-stir bacon-coq-mushrooms-onions all together.

... And 1952, it's just coming back to me, that was the year Fedora Barbieri the great mezzo soprano — oh rapture! — touched my twenty-one-year-old arm as I was interviewing her for the old *San Francisco Call Bulletin*.

> The official Coq au Vin recipe begins: Soften a good dozen **brown mushrooms**, washed and de-stemmed, in a tablespoon of **butter**; reserve.
>
> Then in a large pot fry a dozen oblongs of **thick cut or slab bacon**, adding as some fat develops 6 to 10 small **white onions** (peeled, of course) for light browning: you'll want to toss them with the bacon for a bit. Reserve the bacon and onions with the mushrooms and drain off unwanted fat.
>
> Now in the same pot brown **chicken thighs** without added fat (and remember: more time and flame the skin side than the reverse); then pour off the accumulated fat and deglaze the pot with a little **brandy**.
>
> Next, reduce the heat somewhat, add 1-1/2 or 2 cups of good **red wine**, **pepper**, a **bouquet garni** (thyme, torn bay leaf and retrievable parsley sprigs) and 1 or 2 pressed **garlic** cloves. Return the bacon and onions, plus the mushrooms, to your pot and simmer all, partly covered, for 30 to 40 minutes.
>
> Now reduce the sauce a little if necessary, add a little **sugar** and bind your meat-etc.-and-liquid with a beurre manié (2 tablespoons of **butter** blended with 1 of **flour**), stirring well: the sauce should be neither thick nor thin — which, of course, is the case with most sauces.
>
> Sprinkle your Coq au Vin with minced **parsley** and serve over toasted slices of **French bread**.

AND NOW: For a variation see the next recipe.

OEUFS AU VIN BONNE FEMME

This is Coq-less Coq au Vin.

> With moderate crispness your objective, fry a dozen oblongs of **thick cut or slab bacon** in a large and rather hot skillet. As some fat develops add a dozen small **white onions**, whole or halved, for light browning (be sure to peel them before you start the bacon), and shortly thereafter find room in the pan for a fistful of washed and mostly de-stemmed **mushrooms** to sauté for several minutes with their companions.
>
> Then season all with a little pressed **garlic** and **thyme**, add a cup of **red wine** and a good pinch of **sugar** and simmer your odorous mélange, covered, for 15 or 20 minutes.

Just before serving, stir in 1/4 cup or more of thawed and briefly heated **frozen peas** and, crucial this, a beurre manié (2 tablespoons of **butter** blended with 1 of **flour**). More or less at the same time poach 1 **egg** per serving to be placed on **French bread** toasts in soup bowls with the above ragoût spooned over egg-and-toast.

And there is also my . . .

VIRTUALLY VIN-LESS COQ AU VIN

By some curious circuitous route I've arrived at a satisfying synthesis of the authentically crisp Chicken Contadina served in San Francisco's Classic New York Italian restaurants (Little Italy, the Jackson Fillmore) and good old Sam Chamberlain's Poulet en Cocotte.

Simply follow the Coq au Vin of the previous page, reducing the vinous content to 1/3 cup of **white wine**, chucking out the beurre manié and adding to the pot about 15 minutes before the dish is done a small heap of boiled **potato** chunks. Be sure to sprinkle all with **parsley**, having stirred the contents of your pot nicely.

Interlude: Mozart by Moonlight — or: What Did They Eat?

Suppose you were a cellist, and a peripatetic violinist friend decided to pop in with his pianist for an aggressively nocturnal (read 4 a.m.) chamber music session, well, such marvelous slaving would require refreshments, but what? . . .

I'm not making up the circumstances — some years ago Willy van den Burg, late of the Philadelphia Orchestra, gave me a copy of a letter he received in 1942 from Yehudi Menuhin, on stationery of the Blackstone Hotel in Chicago, reading as follows:

"We are passing through Los Angeles on Saturday, we arrive about 2 a.m. L.A. Airport and leave at 7 a.m. on the S.F. plane. If you are willing, notwithstanding your strenuous work, to sacrifice a night's sleep, we could meet you at the Roosevelt in Hollywood about 2:30 a.m. and have some trio music until about six.

"If this meets with your approval . . ."

COLD CHICKEN ELIZABETH DAVID WITH RICE VINAIGRETTE

One of the happiest moments of my professional life came when I opened a little envelope from London and found that Elizabeth David was enthusiastic about a book I'd written. I trust she'll forgive me for virtually lifting her "Véronique" salad from the Mediterranean cookbook John Lehmann published in 1950. It made its debut in our house on June 7, 1975 and has been our most elegant party-lunch "special" ever since.

A close cousin in the cold chicken department was the centerpiece when, about that time, a Sussex inn packed us a three-star hamper to take to the famous opera at Glyndebourne. The procedure here on a summer evening for followers of a stiff dress code is this: 1) drink in attentively the first two acts of the Verdi or Mozart on offer, 2) lay a blanket on the pristine green outside the theater, Constable cows watching discreetly from the distance, and, like Manet loungers caught in a Cartier-Bresson lens, devour an elegant picnic complete with copious Chardonnay, whereupon, 3) wrestle during the final act an unstoppable urge to dream.

In the mid-70s it was still possible at Glyndebourne to spot an oldtimer like Desmond Shawe-Taylor, the dashing pink cheeked music critic of the *Sunday Times*, who had known Virginia Woolf, Frances Partridge and other "Bloomsburys" quite well and was just a few seats away the evening we took in *Falstaff*. He was, by the way, as sensitive a critic as he was a gentlemanly one. I at the time was a compulsive aficionado of old Bloomsbury: heavens, perhaps the nonagenarian Duncan Grant (bisexual lover of Clive Bell's wife and Roger Fry's lover Vanessa Bell — they were all pals) was a few seats away, over for the opera from Charleston, the Sussex Charleston of course.

. . . And for the name of that Sussex inn, Shelley's as I recall, I'm indebted to the enchanting Calvin Simmons, conductor and wit, whose life was tragically cut short.

> Chop 1 tablespoon each of **onion** and **carrot** and cook them in 2 inches of water; when the water has reached a good boil add **chicken breasts** for that magic 13 minutes of boiling, with the cover on (but be aware that extra-large breasts might take somewhat longer).
>
> Then in a skillet over low heat melt 1 tablespoon of **butter**, pour in a small glass of good **dry sherry** and place the chicken in the butter/sherry liquid. Meanwhile have ready 1 beaten **egg yolk** mixed well with 1/2 cup of **cream**: pour this combination over the chicken, stir until it's slightly thickened and top all with slivers of **lemon** peel.
>
> Transfer your sauced chicken to a serving platter (unless you've prepared the dish in one suitable for use over heat) and cool it. The sauce, which will look very enticing, sort of curry colored, cradling the chicken pieces positioned neatly therein, will thicken somewhat, not too much, during an hour or more of cooling.
>
> Serve Mrs. David's delight with boiled, cooled **rice** dressed in a generous irrigation of **tarragon**-and-**almond**-dotted mustard vinaigrette (1 part **red wine vinegar** stirred into a dab of **Dijon mustard** before 2 parts **olive oil** are added).

CHICKEN CATELLI, VARIATION ON A GEYSERVILLE THEME

This is our interpretation of the probably Marsala'd Chicken Sauté Sec at Catelli's The Rex in Geyserville, heart of Alexander Valley, served by Kitty, seventy-eight and usually humming in her inimitable ostinato of dee-dee, dee-dee-dee.

Here are some vintage Kittyisms: In response to our saying we needed a little more time to decide on a main course, she told us, "That's all right, I work by the hour. You just flag me down." When we asked which she preferred, the ravioli or the tortellini, she announced, "The tortellini are supposed to have ham in them, but I've never found it. Take the ravioli."

It would not, I think, be a violation of chicken sauté traditions in the Bay Area to add some artichoke hearts to the recipe at the right; I'm sure Kitty would approve . . .

and now my mother's innocently seductive chicken in Marsala is coming into focus . . . it appeared in my life at the same time Howard Hanson's soaring *Romantic* Symphony with its sonic peach fuzz was giving me a teenage testosteronic high. Sibelius' First was not far behind. I was, of course, much too young for seduction, but it's a good thing I hadn't heard Hanson's brassily juicy love music from his opera *Merry Mount*, the orgasmic aural technicolor is so alive here the music strides on full-sperm-ahead.

> In a skillet soften 8 or 10 not too thinly sliced **mushrooms** in 1 or 2 tablespoons of **butter**, then turn up the heat, add **chicken** pieces and brown all together: don't worry if the mushrooms crisp a bit. Deglaze the pan (after removing the inevitable pool of fat) with some good **dry Marsala**, lower the heat, add 3/4 cup more Marsala, a large pressed **garlic** clove, a little **lemon** juice and a sprinkling of **thyme** and **rosemary**. Simmer, mostly uncovered, for 15 or 20 minutes — if the sauce threatens to reduce too much add more Marsala.
>
> Shortly before serving, stir in 3 tablespoons of **cream** and shower the chicken-and-mushrooms with minced **parsley**. Chicken Catelli is especially good draped over plain rice, and a little chutney (page 130) makes a nice grace note.

OLD SCHOOL CHICKEN WITH PROSCIUTTO, FONTINA AND SAGE

In the old days there was simply food. Now we're caught between retro and nouvelle, battling it out for diners' dollars, francs and lire — and sometimes nouvelle is really retro in disguise, a lightweight pot-au-feu, for instance. This Valdostanan chicken with its prosciutto and cheese is, I suppose, as retro-rich as you can get, but its lovely wine sauce is scarcely reduced. Moral of this page: eat first, and categorize later, if at all.

> In a skillet brown **chicken** pieces, then remove them to a casserole, draining off excess fat, and deglaze the skillet with a generous splash of **white wine** — leftover Chardonnay will do the trick. Now place 1 slice of **prosciutto** (domestic permitted) and another of **Italian fontina** on each chicken piece and pour over them the saucy brown bits from the skillet and a cup of white wine into which you've stirred 1 teaspoon of **tomato paste** along with a mini-heap of **sage**.
>
> Bake all for about 30 minutes in a moderate oven, basting occasionally, and before serving run the casserole under the broiler for a minute or so. Mashed potatoes advised!

POLLO CISTERNA

A dish with a view: over the Tuscan countryside in this case, from the mellow La Cisterna in San Gimignano.

E.M. Forster probably ate here — and we did, too, in 1966. In fact, we spent the night in one of the Cisterna's cozy rooms and I remember setting a mental timer so I'd wake up around three in the morning: I wanted to look out over the vineyards in the utter peace of night, a stray light or two in the distance. There were more lights another year when I spied the Blue Train gliding relaxedly by Les Roches-de-Condrieu in the wee hours, lit like a great nocturnal yardstick along its plush/dowdy corridors. I couldn't help fantasizing for this famous Paris-Nice overnighter a manifest of duchesses and spies.

And speaking of 3 a.m., I love to look out the window from a cozy sleeper as ten blue cars are steered through the otherworld of Dark. Small town stops are especially magical with their stage-sets peopled by lone cyclists tooling off into limbo while faithful single taxis wait dutifully for their apparently accustomed phantasmal fares — add in the case of Thebes, Greece, a pair of sauntering nocturnal cats, our friend Juliana experienced that.

Lunch at La Cisterna puts me in mind of romantic meals: another was buffet breakfast on the ferry carrying our night express across the sound between Sweden and Copenhagen. Seagulls worthy of a Benjamin Britten orchestration (or Carl Nielsen's Fifth!) squawked atmospherically outside the portholes as we dug into an array of cheeses, breads and superior strawberry jam.

Then we went out on deck to watch the ice crack like the top of a spoon-pummelled crème brûlée.

- In a roomy skillet patiently soften in a tablespoon of **olive oil**: 1 smallish diced **onion**, 1 diced **celery** stalk and 1 **carrot** chopped as fine as you can comfortably manage; reserve.
- In the same pan with increased heat brown **chicken** pieces without added fat, then drain off the disagreeable pool of fat that will surely accumulate. Deglaze the pan with a little **white wine or dry vermouth**, lower the flame and add to the chicken and the vegetables of our first paragraph a good cup of white wine or dry vermouth mixed with 1-1/2 tablespoons of **tomato paste**. Simmer covered, or almost so, for 15 or 20 minutes, basting along the way.
- There is only one authentic accompaniment for this winy/carroty Pollo Cisterna with its Italianate ochre cast: mashed potatoes.

—24-hour—
BOUILLABAISSE DE POULET WITH SAFFRON MAYONNAISE TOASTS

Eat the broth with a spoon, use fork and knife for the chicken and mayonnaised toasts, and there are the vegetables to be dealt with as you please — all in one bowl.

This is definitely a company dish, unusual, quietly spectacular, and not too much effort. It's a Lyon recipe, actually, adapted from Patricia Wells, but they must eat it down in Marseille, bouillabaisse's home base. Well, we could have asked those yacht harbor types neatly positioned by the stage manager of my memories just by the subway exit as we emerged at the tip of the Vieux Port, that index finger of water jutting so picturesquely into Marseille's downtown.

Our two bejeaned Pagnolians were in full accord with the *oo's* and *ah's* of the metro passengers from San Francisco suddenly finding Mrs. Fisher's considerable town thrust upon them, boat sails as far as the eye could see and *N.D.-de-la-Garde* up on its hill as if playing inspiration for San Francisco's Coit Tower seen from a pier reaching for the Golden Gate. Naturally the fellows posed for pictures, and snapped us in turn.

Then we checked right into the Beauvau (Chopin and Ms. Sand slept here), eyed the olive markets, ate an exemplary bouillabaisse at Loury, and listened to the little Saturday night Renaults humming by our window till dawn.

Sequel: A few months later we were debating whether to cross the threshold of an oldtime "family style" Italo-American restaurant in a sagging hamlet west of Cotati, California — there'd be hearty minestrone, lasagna, lots of tomatoey stuff — when out sauntered the red-neckiest sort of fellow, middle-aged, beer-bellied, a sort of Marlboro Man put out to pasture, so to speak, and he strode toward a mammoth, ancient Cad convertible. Well, we got talkin', and it wasn't long before he was extolling the gastronomical virtues of a certain fish restaurant down in central California.

"They've got the best darned Boshbash around!" And who were we to disagree with the Marlboro Man?

One day before your scheduled Bouillabaisse dinner combine in a large casserole:

2 chopped **tomatoes**

1 large **onion**, in quarters or eighths

1 **fennel** bulb, trimmed and chopped

2 pressed **garlic** cloves

2 tablespoons of **olive oil**

as much **saffron** as you dare

thyme, **bayleaf** and **pepper**

Stir all these ingredients together well, then add **chicken breasts** and cover and refrigerate overnight (or at least eight hours), having made sure the breasts are nicely vegetable-coated. One hour before serving, remove the casserole from the fridge and stew the marinated chicken, still covered, for 30 minutes over medium heat; stir it some. Now add 2 diced **red potatoes** and 1-1/2 cups of **chicken broth** and simmer all an additional 30 minutes, cover off the last 10 minutes, until the potatoes are soft. Your end result will be chicken pieces sitting in a kind of chowder. Serve this Bouillabaisse over **French bread** toasts on which you've spread **saffron mayonnaise** (page 59).

CHICKEN AND POLENTA À LA CHESTER

This recipe is drawn from memories of Chester's in San Francisco's Cow Hollow, circa 1950. Chester sat two customers facing a chopping board with a mound of chicken and polenta in the center, to be attacked from both sides — it was a little like playing chess.

(Don't forget that leftover cold polenta is excellent sliced and fried in a little olive oil, then topped with wafers of fried pancetta.)

The problem, home chefs, is this:

If you need 25 or 30 minutes in which to brown and simmer 2 **chicken breasts** in the usual Bloomfieldian manner with no added fat and more time and flame for the browning of the meat's topside . . .

Do you have the 8 or 10 concurrent minutes it would take to slice 1 **onion**, soften it in a little **olive oil** and add to it a 28-ounce can of **tomatoes** with 1 large pressed **garlic** clove, a splash of **dry sherry** and several pinches of **sugar**, all this to get a house tomato sauce going?

. . . And do you have the 5 to 7 minutes it would take to slice and sauté in a little butter the 5 or 6 good quality **mushrooms** which will go into your tomato sauce?

. . . And do you have time to pour 3/4 cup of **polenta** with a liberal amount of **salt** into the 2 cups of **water** and 1 of **chicken broth** which you set to boil just as you threw the mushrooms a little frantically into an adjacent pan, so that now you can begin 8 or 9 minutes of almost constant stirring over very low heat and produce the world's fastest soft polenta, into which at the last minute you stir a short cup of grated fresh **mozzarella**, using the grater's large holes?

The answer is: Yes, just!

P.S.: At the table pass **dry jack or parmesan cheese** *and* the grater.

CHICKEN SAUTÉ WITH GREEN OLIVES, ANCHOVIES AND RED WINE VINEGAR

This is a variation on an old Tuesday "special" at Little Joe's, an ebullient cheaperia in San Francisco's North Beach.

When the now-expanded Little Joe's was truly little, back in the 60s, one would wait for counter stools an inch or two, it seemed, behind busy Giuseppian gastronomes lapping up wonderful fish stew, the world's only three-star Veal Parmigiana, heaping ovals of sausages and veg, gooey baked apples resembling fat little timpani, spring strawberries bathing with admirable immoderation in cheap but good red wine. One knew what to order by seeing what was on the plate of the gent or lady taking up *your* space just in front of your impatiently tapping feet.

It was at the present and larger Little Joe's that I overheard a chef in a backward-aimed baseball cap yell to the waitress, "Which one medium-well? The hamburger or the cheese?"

And I remember a shorter counter in another neighborhood at which I usually sat in position A and ate a bowl of good soup while a spinsterish type habitually perched in position F, always eating with the greatest concentration and delight a hamburger with cheese, and since there were rarely customers in between it was easy to see we were the bookends of this restaurant. Over a period of five years (perhaps a thousand lunches) this burger-involved lady never seemed to notice she had company holding up those invisible tomes.

In a skillet brown **chicken drumsticks-and-thighs** without fat; drain off the accumulated fat and deglaze the pan with a little **red wine vinegar**.

Sprinkle the chicken with **flour**, adding **rosemary** and 1 pressed **garlic** clove, then simmer it with 1/2 cup of **red wine vinegar** and 2/3 cup of water for 30 minutes, the skillet cover partly off: your goal is a thinnish tangy gravy.

Ten minutes before serving, stir in several drained, chopped **anchovy** filets and 2 or 3 tablespoons of pitted, sliced **green olives** of good quality — Greek are especially good. Serve this chicken with plain rice, or polenta (see previous recipe).

Another option — the chicken in this case in not too large pieces — is over our basic risotto (page 65). For this notion, a variation on a quail-and-olive risotto, I'm indebted to a congenial trattoria near San Francisco's Museum of Modern Art named Pazzia. Pazzia means madness, and if such capacious risotti be madness, cook on, I say.

BONUS: Leftover anchovy-olive sauce would work spooned over open-faced toasted mozzarella sandwiches.

SPEAKING OF POLENTA: It never tastes better than when you stir in some baked & mashed butternut squash before serving.

FIVE SPICE CHICKEN WITH CRISPY THINGS BALSAMICO

We offer here a crunchy mélange, a sort of camouflage-sur-plat inspired by an appetizer at Bruno's, a big-boothed San Francisco restaurant with an Ike Age "continental" décor and a very un-50s cuisine fusing upscale French bistro and California East/West cooking: Bruno's really should be called Benoit Mandarine . . . And having written this particular note in 1998 I must report that by 2000 James Ormsby that *enfant terrible de cuisine* had transferred his fusionizing to a restaurant called Red Herring where he was serving chicken salad with apples, pecans and (fanfare, please) sweet & tangy blackberries. But is this more daring than oldtime duck and cherries?

In the center of rather large white or near-white plates place a pile of **mixed boutique greens**; **cilantro**; tinned, briefly baked (on a cookie sheet) **French fried onions**; and halved **dried apricots** poached 10 minutes in a little water, drained and somewhat cooled. Around this pile apply a light dusting of **Chinese Five Spice Powder** (fennel, pepper, star anise, cinnamon and cloves) which, in hip San Francisco at least, is available in supermarkets as well as health food stores and Asian groceries.

Meanwhile in a fat-free skillet fry **chicken legs-and-thighs** coated with 1/4 teaspoon of Five Spice each, along with a few oblongs of **bacon** which will need to be taken out of your pan well before the chicken is cooked through. Finally, deposit chicken and bacon atop each pile of greens-etc. and dress lightly with 3 parts **olive oil** to 1 of **balsamic vinegar**.

POULET BASQUAISE RUE WEBSTER

And as I was waiting for a light in a publisher's eye I invented . . .

While vigorously browning **chicken** pieces in a skillet to your left, in another to your right sauté in a tablespoon of **olive oil** 1 **sweet red pepper** cut in fat juliennes and

2 or 3 roughly chopped **scallions,** adding after a couple of minutes 2/3 of a 28 oz. can of **tomatoes**, 1 large pressed **garlic** clove, a splash of **sherry**, a tiny dusting of **cumin**, a pinch of **sugar**, 2 tablespoons of **pine nuts** and **boutique pitted olives** to taste. Simmer for about 10 minutes.

When the chicken is brown, deglaze its skillet with a little **lemon** juice and simmer for something like 15 minutes, cover partly off, along with the tomatoes-peppers-etc., adding part way en route 1 chopped hard boiled **egg**.

CHESTNUT PURÉE

(to serve with Roast Turkey or Pork Chops and cress)

Quite a long time ago chestnut purée became a given on our Thanksgiving turkey-and-trimmings menu. Earlier than that, back in my Orléans days, it accompanied wild boar or venison when several culinarily deprived GIs trooped to the stately salle of the Hôtel Ste-Catherine for a festive meal.

Another delicious escape from Headquarters Co. 7805 was dinner at a little upstairs place called Au Père Jean where course 2 out of 5 was always escargots and the gastronomic needle tended to get stuck in a groove at this point as we ordered seconds of the good father's amply-garlicked snails.

Put 12 to 20 **chestnuts** in a pot with cold water up to 1 inch above them, bring the water to a boil and simmer the chestnuts exactly 30 minutes. Keep the chestnuts covered in the water as you remove them one at a time, cutting each nut in two and pushing the inside out.

Now put all the peeled nuts in a pot with water to cover and boil them until they're very soft, about 30 minutes. Purée the nuts in a blender or food processor a little at a time, along with some cooking liquid, until they're the consistency of mashed potatoes.

Finally, add **butter** to taste (don't stint if you want a silky texture) and reheat the purée in a double boiler.

ALTERNATIVE: Serve your turkey or pork with the croquettes below.

GIGI'S SWEET POTATO CROQUETTES

A crunchy childhood souvenir, also associated with Thanksgiving. My childhood, in fact, was filled with dark brown zeppelins rolled out by my mother or Hoi our in-house *gratiné* expert: minced salmon croquettes, veal croquettes, rice croquettes with a shaking crown of currant jelly on top. I loved them all — and am now a little wary of such potentially gummy yummies. Meanwhile we confront the renaissance of the fritter!

And old Thanksgivings come into focus, the wartime one for instance when a lonely serviceman was sent out to our house by the USO and Mummy choked on his unseemly anti-FDR spiel.

Peel and boil 1 **sweet potato** per serving until they're soft but not mushy; then mash the potatoes until they're free of lumps, adding lots of **butter**, a little **orange** juice and some grated orange rind.

Now add enough **milk and cream** to achieve the consistency of stiff mashed potatoes; when the mashing is done refrigerate your "dough" for several hours. Shape the potatoes into patties, dip them in fine **breadcrumbs**, beaten **egg**, and crumbs again, then fry them in hot **vegetable oil** and drain afterwards on paper towels.

The color of these croquettes should be dark brown, like crusted oldtime filet of sole when it was done properly.

Manhattan Postscript I:

I've been listening to Michael Tilson Thomas playing the steamy, throbbing, superlyrical, quintessentially Manhattanite Second Rhapsody of George Gershwin and it reminded me of my first visit to New York, an eighteen-year-old hayseed from San Francisco about to taste his first Supreme of Chicken 'neath the memorabilia at Sardi's, with *South Pacific* playing approximately across the street ("Who can explain eet?" sang the dapper Ezio Pinza, "who can tell you whyeee?"), the orchestra conducted by a Broadway maestro wearing, much to my distaste, a gray tux rather than the black or white jacket that would have been suitable.

The chicken at Sardi's was true to its period (1949) and very tasty: the capacious sauce, probably a cream/egg yolk thing, was the color of a Van Gogh haystack and had the texture of a good country gravy, the concept of which had been imported from plantation to asphalt jungle. But I wasn't exactly in the jungle. In an effort, I suppose, to preserve a lone traveler's virginity, my father had booked me in with a family he knew that happened to live in a safely Onassian precinct, Fifth Avenue across from the Met museum. I had what I suspect was the room for maid no. 2. Striding into lotus land from 1010 in my Brooks Bros. seersucker suit, I observed that Manhattan in August was 1) tropical, 2) elegant: virtually the entire air-conditioned population seemed to be clotheshorses, hurried dudes in tattersall vests and such, 3) not as blessed with airspace as my beloved hometown.

I prowled around panelled basement emporiettes specializing in imported classical records, toured the lobbies of proper midtown hotels with my trust-fund aunt who loved to travel from one palm or fountain-attended banquette to the next, watching people and managing her widowhood, and I continued to eat, mostly well: some sort of "sous cloche" fowl in a spiffy sour cream sauce at a boîte on East 53rd called Michel's, and a reasonably good Châteaubriand bouquetière at a big brasserie of a place down in Chelsea called Cavanaugh's — "Opinion of all regulars is that no better food and drinks could be imagined," reports the urbane Lawton Mackall in his *Knife and Fork in New York*.

Meanwhile the humidity was wilting my seersucker, no matter how Brooks Brothery, into something like Ethiopian *injera*. But onward! There were more shows to see, *Kiss Me, Kate* with Cole Porter's delightful petty thievery from Schumann's Kreisleriana, *Guys and Dolls* with the original pin-striped cast, and a wunderbar lost revue named *Lend an Ear*. When I ran out of shows I headed out of peacock city on the New York Central's *Cornelius Vanderbilt*, observing that the biscuits in the diner were tougher than they should have been on an "extra fare" train. Heavens, I was morphing into a restaurant critic.

Manhattan Postscript II:

My father's first cousin Ernie Bloomfield Zeisler, Chicago physician, mathematician, friend of Einstein, Renaissance man, resident of a Lakeshore Drive apartment but an advocate of socialized medicine (and he was, of course, a friend of my as-yet-unfound-wife's uncle Ted at the Cliff Dwellers literary club that met upstairs at Orchestra Hall), this Ernie, whom I would have loved to have known, was also a foodie, and his granddaughter Laura has shared with me the comments in his address book on the New York restaurants he frequented, embraced, and cast aside in a good old Bloomfieldian righteous huff.

After reading accounts of Ernie's starred and ill-starred eateries in Lawton Mackall's bible-ette for gourmets (the copy I inherited is cryptically inscribed to my father as "For the Rifton Récamier from the Old Mountain Pine," this being some arcane message out of old summers in Vermont — and I might note that Lawton looked more like an economics professor than a boulevardier), I think my taste and my fascinating cousin's coincide.

On Ernie's NO list was Voisin, and I shudder reading friend Mackall's account: "Elegance couldn't be quieter than you find it in this Sloane-decorated room in the basement of Park Avenue's haughtiest apartment fortress . . . [the owners feel] that their public knows the way to the door, and anybody else might be unprepared for their prices." But Chateaubriand, an Ernie favorite, "is hosted by beaming-countenanced, sly-humored Alex Hounie . . . this comfortably upholstered room boasts a continuous frieze of distinguished wine bottles autographed with the names of notables who enjoyed emptying them. Water is considered a commodity suitable only for washing the hands."

Ernie also favored Charles à la Pomme Soufflée. "Could [the owner] tempt you with some of his leetle, leetle shrimps? He does, and they're whoppers, exceeded only by his blimp-like spuds, devoured by the hot basketful."

I leave it to millennial New Yorkers to figure where Ernie would have hung his gourmet's hat today . . . and I wonder how he'd feel about the dress code at the Pump Room around the corner from his Chicago apartment!

—MEATS—

LAMB SHANKS CHEZ NOUS

How nice to see lamb shanks with their heady, homey bursts of flavor enter the culinary mainstream in this country. This state of affairs is due in part, I'm sure, to the decrease in "continental" restaurants with their ubiquitous racks of cute pink lamb, and the concurrent rise of the bistro or café favoring socially, and anatomically, lower cuts of meat. (To put it indelicately, eating below the knee is à la mode.) Heading toward oblivion are black-tied navigators of rolling carts with pockets full of matches for setting off tableside two-alarmers. In their place behold servers in shirtsleeves toting simple grills, perky little salsas, wholesome, earthy ragoûts, the food of the people — well, the food of the middle- and upper-income foodie.

I
Our first version is more or less Italo/New American:

> Roll your **lamb shanks** in a marinade of **olive oil**, pressed **garlic** and crinkled **rosemary** needles: the more the jollier. Then brown the shanks vigorously in a large pot without added fat, turning them at least once, pour off the unwanted accumulated fat and deglaze the pot with a good splash of **balsamic vinegar**.
>
> In a 350° oven simmer the shanks, covered, for at least 1-1/2 hours with a little more vinegar, 2/3 of a 14-ounce can of **beef broth** and 1 small chopped **tomato**. Serve (after skimming off some of the remaining fat) with parsleyed mashed potatoes or green pasta with butter and grated cheese, or risotto verde (page 66).

II
This variation was inspired by a meal at Maykadeh, a jolly Persian restaurant in San Francisco's North Beach:

> In the simmering stage add 1 peeled and diced **eggplant** and some **saffron** and **currants** to taste in addition to the previously given ingredients; serve with plain rice and you could pass a dish of yogurt. For the tomato element you could consider a medley of baby specimens in yellow, orange, green and red.

NOTE: An excellent pasta dish may be had by halving the amount of lamb shanks in this recipe, cutting the meat into bite-sized pieces and combining it and the eggplant/etc. with fettuccine or lasagne.

LAMB ST-PAUL-DE-VENCE
—five items on plate—

This one is obviously for company, a classic and attractive harmonization, souvenir of a lunch in Provence in 1969. The vignette that sticks in my mind from a very wet and wintry March day is a waiter with umbrella treading gingerly across the garden outside our window and fetching cheese from a recess in an outdoor grill where it was cleverly stashed, on call for an appearance on our table just below room temperature. No self-respecting Frenchman, of course, would indulge in that ugly habit of holding a good Brie hostage in the fridge.

The adjacent misto I would term a close cousin of a presentation for which I reserve the softest spot, a plank of sliced steak and veg served to Anne and me with a flourish on our wedding night. The place was Pietro's 311, in San Francisco's long-gone produce district. To reach Pietro's after dark one tread lightly along Washington Street past stray turnips, abandoned romaine and supplementary tomatoes dented like tins.

Now in this location we enjoy the mightily attractive Embarcadero Center with its terraced gentrification, but there's much to be said for the no-nonense orange-crate ambience of the old district, an independent state almost, with its heady carnival of the vegetables.

Before embarking on a five-ring circus of a cooking spree, make a Béchamel sauce: melt 1 tablespoon of **butter**, stir into it 1 tablespoon of **flour** and slowly add 1 cup of **milk**, stirring constantly until the sauce — to which you've added a pinch of **nutmeg** — begins to thicken. Reserve, keeping warm, and proceed to:
1. Bake **tomato** halves topped with **olive oil**, pressed **garlic** and **oregano, dill weed or tarragon** for about 20 minutes in a moderate oven.
2. Boil scrubbed **new potatoes**, whole or halved, applying a little melted **butter** when they're done.
3. Steam **Blue Lake string beans** and sauté them briefly in **butter** before serving.
4. Boil **fennel** bulbs, each cut in two and mostly de-stemmed, then remove them to a baking dish, top with the Béchamel and run under the broiler with a sprinkle of grated **dry jack or parmesan cheese** on top.
5. Fry **lamb chops** brushed with a little **olive oil** and pressed **garlic**, observing the usual rule of more time and flame for the first side than the second.

Arrange at least the chops, beans and tomatoes on a platter, put the potatoes in a serving dish if they won't fit on the platter, and serve the fennel from its baking dish.

P.S.: For an emergency mini St-Paul, abandon fennel and beans, mash the potatoes with lots of milk and butter and grit the tomato topping with a nice crumb base.

SONOMA LAMB PARFAIT

We were introduced to this savory parfait/napoleon/sundae at the East Side Oyster Bar and Grill in Sonoma. It's tricky but spectacular, a gastronomic house of cards whose quick and inevitable collapse is not to be considered a demerit: it's the taste that counts, not the engineering. I think this dish's composition is intricate-&-elegant enough perhaps it should have been deconstructed and reassembled in the assonant acrobatics of a John Updike paragraph. Updike is one of the better music and art critics, I wish he'd take on food as well. Meanwhile don't tell anyone we left out the hash brown potatoes.

And lest you voyage to Sonoma and its adobes–boutiques–bike trails–wineries–cheesemongers in anticipation of this parfait-or-whatever, I have to inform you its creator vanished into Florida a year or two ago and the Eastside venue a few doors from the town square is currently, I think, a straightforward Italian bistro, parfait-less.

Your object is to serve a pagoda of the following, reading from the bottom up:

- Mashed **parsnips, sweet and red potatoes** combined
- Sautéed **sweet potato** discs 1/4 inch thick
- **Lamb medallions** (ideally, boneless lamb but chops are entirely viable)
- Caramelized baked **red onion** rings
- Matchstick **leeks**, "deep fried"
- "Au jus" sauce to pour over all

For the mash: simply boil and mash the vegetables as one normally would.

For the discs: save some of the sweet potato from the mixed mash ingredients, slice it, boil it, then sauté it in a little **butter** until somewhat brown.

For the lamb: simply cook the meat until it's done to the home chef's taste.

For the onion rings: remove the rough outer skins of the onions, slice them thick, coat them with a little butter and bake at 375° until they're soft but not mushy (figure on at least 30 to 40 minutes); be sure to salvage some of the accumulated caramelized sugar from the baking.

For the leeks: wash them and cut them into very thin strands about 2 inches long, then toss in some **olive oil** in a skillet (the oil need not be really deep) until they're crispy.

For the jus, rather thin: stir some **meat broth** into the lamb drippings.

TENERUMI D'AGNELLO SAMUELE

This capacious stew comes from the Marche, a mountainous and lovely area of Italy between Umbria and the Adriatic. Here one leaves the big-name towns behind and sinks into an enfolding countryside not much visited by our fellow countrymen. I have especially fond memories of Ostra, a tiny hill town a little north of Ancona where I had the feeling, to quote the purplish tones of my 1978 diary, "of being suspended in a great pastoral meditation tank." The intense quiet, the purity of air, the Tiepolo sky, the Adriatic sitting in the distance: all contributed to our overflowing cup of five-star deurbanization.

It was, in short, a place to listen to rain pattering lyrically on the window, cuddle in the afternoon and have a saucer of macaroons by the side of the bed.

At the Albergo Cantinella a waiter who looked like Arturo Toscanini served us breakfast while the Signora ordered the groceries. At the Trattoria La Vittoria a padrone who said he was related to the great composer Rossini served us, on checkered tablecloths right out of an MGM musical, to the tune of Italian Rock, not Rossini — well, that unearthly pastoral pianissimo couldn't go on forever — an admirable dinner of risotto with wild mushrooms, rabbit sauté and zabaglione. If this was being Ostra-cized it was obviously the way to go.

And it was all totally NEW, we had never encountered a photograph of Ostra among those engagement-calendar scenes one studies every first of the year and hopes one day to step into, in the flesh, as we did in fact when we crossed the Piazza del Popolo in Rome, strolled the Galleria in Milan, turned a corner and found, in Ascoli Piceno, that enchantingly cloistered market place, the sort of market place where a Capulet and a Montague might have bought their peas and carrots.

And did you know that cats in Italy dine on leftover pasta? We spotted some happy lunchers going at it in the alley behind our Ostra inn. Tagliarini, I guess, is the genuinely edible equivalent of a ball of string.

> In a pot brown 4 to 6 **lamb** ribs or 2 large shoulder chops without added fat, adding in due course 1 chopped **onion** to be softened in a little **olive oil** at the side of your skillet. If the onions start to blacken, park them on top of the chops.
> Now add most of 1 28-ounce can of **tomatoes** (you'll want to mash them down some), 2 pressed **garlic** cloves and a little **oregano**, lower the heat and simmer the lot for 20 to 25 minutes, covered (chops will take less time than ribs); then stir into the pot 3 previously steamed **carrots** cut into finger-length juliennes plus about 1 cup of thawed **frozen peas** and simmer all for 10 or so minutes more, uncovered, over somewhat higher heat, until your sauce has some body to it.
> Shower your Tenerumi generously with minced **parsley** and serve in soup bowls or cupped plates with mashed potatoes. Decorating note: you could lean the chops or ribs against a central mound of potatoes.

LAMB CACCIATORA WITH ANCHOVIES

Herewith a true Italian "cacciatora," tart and aromatic, without the tomatoes-and-sweet peppers blanket done to death in oldtime Italo-American restaurants, especially when they were delivering to bulging booth or checked tablecloth (with candle-wax slipping crustily down a Chianti flask) a red-&-green chicken confection barely indistinguishable from Poulet Basquaise.

I am not knocking this sort of restaurant: where in the early 50s was I to find Bolognese sauced spaghetti (erring perhaps just a bit too far in the direction of "red sauce") when such a staple of the American way of life was, curiously enough, not in my mother's large repertoire of dinner specials?

It was also at a stalactitical cave of a place on San Francisco's Bay Street called Veneto, doubtless seated near a mural of the Bridge of Sighs — and there may have been a live gondola somewhere on the premises — that I first experienced that addictive salad, not Italian actually, composed with romaine leaves, anchovies, raw egg, grated cheese and big crunchy croutons.

Now, almost five decades on, I've come virtually full circle: not long ago, in the mood for San Francisco's coziest restaurant, we chose faithful Caesar's, mere yards from the long-gone Veneto, and revelled in Marsala-soused scallopini out of my youth and a tangy mixed greens bathed incorrectly in a short gallon of good wine vinegar, enjoying meanwhile the contagious vibrations of neighboring tables filled with convivial diners from outside the millennial yuppie loop.

The mustachioed host, pure Hollywood Figaro vintage Kelly-Astaire-Caron, was so nice he could have sold us a plate of nuts and bolts in marinara sauce and we would have said *yes, yes.*

And enter here more nostalgia for those much maligned 50s: the ever-sweatered Mort Sahl was monologuing at the Hungry I, white-maned Leopold Stokowski was massaging the air Dr. Miracle-like in front of the Symphony, towering, pre-Nancy Oakesian salads were standard fare at the Palace.

And a pale, petit William Kapell could be seen rushing like a force of nature to a ballroom piano in the St. Francis hotel where he joined the Blinder brothers' ensemble in Schumann's E flat quintet. Down at Carmel's cute Bach Festival an afternoon organ recital ending with a bittersweet chorale prelude would set me weeping beneath dewy cypresses.

- In a skillet over high heat brown a pound or a little less of **boneless lamb stew** cut in rather large pieces; as usual, don't add fat. Comprehensive browning achieved, stir in 1 pressed **garlic** clove and **rosemary** to taste (don't be stingy). Next, sprinkle the meat with **flour**, pressing it in well with a wooden spoon; then add 1/2 cup each of **red wine vinegar** and water, mixing all together while scraping the good bits from the bottom of the pan.
- Lower the flame considerably and simmer your flavored lamb, covered, until the meat is virtually done, about 40 minutes; you will almost certainly need to add water as the cooking proceeds.
- A minute or more before serving, add a half tin of generic supermarket **anchovy** filets, or better, Sicilian salt-packed, trim- and wash-requiring anchovies not previously edited anatomically: chop them, mix with a little water and stir them into your stew with care. Serve Lamb Cacciatora over or next to plain rice and offer a dish of mint or currant jelly.

PILAF ANNA WITH MARY KELLEY'S CHUTNEY

"Spanish rice" here, rosy-cheeked as a *commedia dell'arte* damsel.

And as for the chutney from Mary Kelley, well, it deserves a twenty-one Champagne pops salute. My culinary activities would grind to something close to a halt without the annual infusions of curry powder, chutney, etc. etc. from Mary's workshop. Egged on by husband Tom, she turns out wonderful things from the hotel kitchen in their comfortable Edwardian house overlooking — from said kitchen — the Golden Gate Bridge and Mount Tamalpais.

The Kelleys' annual Christmas party is always marked by good cheer, Tom's yard-long necktie, and a large table of stellar buffet items, the crown of the lot being Smithfield ham which you tuck neatly as you can inside baby Parker House rolls just like the ones my mother used to serve a short mile away, c. 1938.

The attendant cream-colored *au jus* preparation is addictive, and a state secret unknown to me or the CIA, either one of them. Mary, in short, doesn't let that mountain distract her from the sauce. Or the chutney! In a world where too many people are afraid of embarking on kitchen adventures, I hold her up as a role model first class.

- To one side of a large hot skillet brown 3/4 pound of diced **lamb** (either boned stew meat or chops) without added fat; after 3-plus minutes add 1 finely chopped **onion** on the other side and, heat reduced, soften it in a little **olive oil** with 1 pressed **garlic** clove, gradually stirring onion into lamb.
- Next, add 1/2 or more cup of **rice** and stir it over rather high heat along with the meat-and-onion for 1-1/2 to 2 minutes, until opaque; then add a 14-ounce can of **"ready cut" tomatoes** and 2/3 cup of slightly diluted **beef broth**, cover and simmer all, the fire lowered again, for 25 minutes, stirring fairly often and adding the remaining 1/3 cup of broth as liquid is absorbed.
- Serve this pilaf with a pot of chutney. Especially recommended is Mary Kelley's:
- Peel and slice 3 or 4 large **mangoes** and put them in a bowl with 2-1/2 cups of **white sugar** and 1 cup of firmly-packed **brown sugar**. Stir well and let stand overnight: the sugar will not dissolve completely.
- Next day: drain the mangoes into a cooking pot. Add to the syrup:

    1 cup of **cider vinegar**

    2 tablespoons of finely chopped **garlic**

    4 tablespoons of **ginger** chopped fine

    1-1/2 teaspoons of **salt**

    1-1/2 small diced **chili peppers**, seeded and cut into tiny strips

    1-1/2 teaspoons of whole **cloves** (in a tea bag to be removed later)
- Simmer all for 30 minutes, remove the cloves, add the mangoes and 1/2 cup of **raisins**. Cook another 20 to 30 minutes, pour into clean jars and seal them.

ALI'S ASIAN CHOPS
—with a Black Bean Purée or other garnishes—

The origin of this recipe which I got from my daughter and tinkered with is a complete mystery. Suffice to say it's haunting, half-hot, a little like an uncloying barbecue sauce, with a slight hint of teriyaki. It seems to have been born for lamb but I think it would work well with beef too. The chili garlic sauce is available at Asian food stores and chef-friendly supermarkets.

Well, Ali has come some distance in the catholicity of her taste (the men in her life have helped!) since her days as a nine-year-old connoisseur of plain old Amurrican meat and potatoes. When she and her sister were still half-fare flyers we whisked them and their more expensive brother off to France for a grand tour of Compiègne-Ambonnay-Sancerre-Amboise-Aubusson-Salers-Conques-Cordes-&-Auch, plus Paris of course, and Ali's range at that time didn't extend far beyond the "pum sheep" (potato chips, that is) featured at our Amboise auberge and the waffles dispensed in the Luxembourg Gardens.

Still, though, we were as five Michelin men in our quest for the flakiest croissant, the freshest baguette (a good pre-picnic loaf was christened every 11 a.m. in our rented Peugeot 504), and any hotel serving homemade confiture in a crock instead of that packaged stuff in containers about as easy to open as present-day CDs with their twelve-step programs for inept fingers were given A-plus in our reports.

There were, in sum, enough starry croissants, castles and cathedrals to stage an encore trip two years later: L'Isle Adam, Les Andelys, Rouen, Bayeux, La Haye de Puits (A.J. Liebling's army called that one Hooey de Pooey), St-Jean-le-Thomas . . .

Let **lamb chops** sit for an hour in a marinade of:

    2 tablespoons of **canola oil**

    3 tablespoons of **orange juice**

    1/8 teaspoon of **soy sauce**

    1 teaspoon of Vietnamese **chili garlic sauce** (*Tuong Ot Toi*)

Then fry the chops in a very hot skillet, without fat, longer on the first side than the second and with much less flame on the second side. Be sure to pour the full marinade into the pan with the chops — which, by the way, you want to trim of jutting coastlines of fat.

Serve these chops with a black bean purée (soak 3/4 cup of **black beans** overnight in water to cover, then cook them for about 1-1/2 hours with plenty of water, a little **salt** and **chili powder**, a rather generous amount of **lemon** juice and lots of pressed **garlic**, before puréeing them in batches in a blender or food processor) . . . or serve them with plain, lightly buttered rice and pour the pan juices over chops and rice.

Yet another accompaniment would be leftover red-cooked eggplant you've brought home from dinner in a Hunanese restaurant.

I like to follow these chops-etc. with greens dressed with olive oil, raspberry vinegar and lemon juice in a proportion of about 4 to 1 to 1.

MOROCCAN LAMB STEW

Not as romantic a dish as Bastilla with its pastry, pigeon and cinnamon, but quite an impressive one just the same. It speaks to me in a rather dark and earthy voice, in the viola register more than the violin's. For heaven's sake don't spoon up any preliminary samples during the first twenty or twenty-five minutes of simmering, you'll only taste water and oil and you'll almost die of acute kitchen fright. Have patience, because eventually the rather Indian flavors creep out from the primordial scum, like colors in an old painting being restored: first the olives, then the lamb, the saffron . . .

Now the approved choreography for consuming a Moroccan meal is to arrange yourself on a cushion around a table a couple of feet below continental height, dip three fingers in perfumed water and go at the food with your hands: abandon utensils all who enter here! Highly amusing to be sure at a good Moroccan restaurant, where entertainment by an estimable belly dancer may be thrown in for good measure, but we are not insisting you participate in what could be an orthopedically taxing ritual.

Tear 2 **shoulder lamb chops** in half and brown them without fat, longer on the first side and over higher heat. Meanwhile, combine in a mixing bowl:

- 1 cup of water
- 1/4 cup of **olive oil**
- 1/8 teaspoon of **ground ginger**
- 1/4 teaspoon of **saffron**
- 1/4 teaspoon of **ground coriander**
- 1 pressed **garlic** clove
- 1/4 cup of chopped **onion**
- at least 6 good quality **green olives**

Pour this mixture into the skillet with the lamb and simmer all, uncovered, for 40 minutes. Serve your Moroccan stew on and around plain rice and follow it with a simple salad or a little asparagus in a parsley mustard vinaigrette.

BEHIND THE SCENES: Mrs. B., my chief consultant: "There's not quite enough sauce for my rice, how about some butter?" . . . Mr. B, author of this tome: "What are you trying to do, make me look silly, the Moroccans wouldn't put butter on their rice, at least I think not, where's that *World Atlas of Cuisine*?" . . .

"Well, I just would like a little butter, you know, like the king in the Milne poem who wanted a little butter on his bread when the alderney was pushing marmalade instead" . . . "I've got it, how about some of Mary Kelley's chutney, from two pages back, it will be very tasty with this dish, and it will seem correct too . . . "

YUGOSLAVIAN BAKED LAMB GARNI

Our children adored this when they were growing up, it's such a great meat (and veg) fix. And the exuberant mingling of red, white, green, orange and a good deep brown ought to please the most jaded of painters, Picasso-type or Sunday variety. Pile your components in a nice sculptural heap, a grand little chaos, and you won't take a bite until you've admired your artistry worthy of a full-page picture in *Larousse Gastronomique*.

This lamb garni appears to be an unintended primeval version of architectural, or "tall," food — as in a Caesar salad I was served recently that arrived with upright leaves verticalized into something like a chef's toque, complete with a belt of zucchini wrapped around the lot, and just try to eat this incipient *Nutcracker* Christmas tree of a salad without finding a way to untie that confounded zuc. If those old waiters at Balzar in Paris were asked to serve such a mad thing as this millennial San Francisco Caesar they would, I'm sure, throw in their aprons pronto.

In a heavy roasting pan place:

> 2 **red potatoes** cut in eighths (and a little pre-boiled)
>
> 2 **carrots** cut into 2-inch juliennes
>
> 1 **onion**, cut into sixths
>
> . . . and above these items the following:
>
> 1 **sweet green pepper**, in fat strips
>
> 1 **tomato**, quartered
>
> . . . and above these the following:
>
> 2 **shoulder lamb chops**, torn in two, or lamb ribs

Bake all at 350° for 60 to 65 minutes, until the veg are no longer chewy — the potatoes can be the most stubborn holdouts — and serve with mint or currant jelly. If doubling or tripling this recipe, use two pans so no veg are too far from heat-conducting metal.

MOUSSAKA CHEZ NOUS

Moussaka, like Paella, is a good dinner choice when you have a "staff" available for kitchen duty. Actually, though, it's rather a lot of fun to cook solo, but if the meat sauce looks like it needs a left-handed stir while your right arm is heavily engaged by the Béchamel on a neighboring burner you will be turned into the kitchen equivalent of a screwball comedy city editor talking into two telephones at once, one to stop the presses and the other to soothe his ruffled lady love, a star columnist, of course.

Now moussaka may be the headliner, so to speak, of Greek menus, but don't forget the cumin-flavored meatballs and deep fried smelts which are more than walk-ons. A slight shove and the Yugoslavian Lamb of just above might tip right across the border and into the Hellenic kitchen.

And speaking of screwball scribes such as Cary Grant and Rosalind Russell, have you noticed when renting oldtime flicks that more often than not in a 30s Hollywood movie the dining is done in a posh and spacious night club, all powder and pearls, with penguined headwaiters who sound as if they have an Oxford degree in what my dad's old friend New York restaurant critic Lawton Mackall termed "hoverage."

Alas, there is seldom wine on the table, more likely cocktails, or even, Jeez, coffee with the main course. Prohibition, of course, had swept the taste for the antecedents of Chardonnay well into the closet. And addled politicians in Washington continue the war on wine as I write, while savvy Languedocians improve their product for the delectation of screwballers' grandkids in the good ol' USA.

Slice a small **eggplant**, skin on, into rounds no thicker than 1/4 inch. Salt them and reserve them for 30 minutes, then drain on paper towels. After that they're ready for browning in more **olive oil** than you probably think prudent for man, woman or child to be associated with.

During that 30 minutes the eggplant was taking its salt bath (or earlier) make a "Greek Bolognese" meat sauce: soften 1 small chopped **onion** with a small pressed **garlic** clove in a little **olive oil**; add 1/2 pound of **ground lamb** and brown it over high heat, stirring well, until the look of rawness disappears; then drain the lamb along with the attendant onions on paper towels and return these ingredients to your skillet, adding 1 14-ounce can of **tomatoes**, a good pinch of **sugar**, a small shower of **cinnamon**, a little **pepper** and some **dill weed**; simmer for at least 20 minutes, mostly uncovered, stirring occasionally, and re-warm later if necessary.

And make (or commission a helper to make) a Béchamel sauce: melt 1/8 cup of **butter** in a saucepan, stir in 1/8 cup of **flour** and cook the combination gently for a minute; slowly add 3/4 cup of **milk** and bring the mixture to a boil, stirring constantly; let the sauce bubble briefly, then before "paperhangers' paste" sets in remove it from the heat and stir in a little **nutmeg**, **pepper** and a good tablespoon or more of grated **dry jack or parmesan cheese**.

Now, sauces made and eggplant sautéed, place your components in an ovenproof dish in the following order, from the bottom up:

> a layer of eggplant
>
> half the meat sauce
>
> a layer of eggplant
>
> half the meat sauce
>
> a layer of eggplant
>
> the Béchamel with a beaten **egg** and more grated cheese

Bake at 350° for about 45 minutes, then run your elegant production under the broiler until the top crisps a bit.

(En passant: Lost in a dusty attic of my mind is a lamb stew whipped up with peanut butter: it was, I believe, in that old SAS cookbook, long out of print and absent without leave from my cookbook corner. But, sigh, that's just as well, I still have a love-hate thing with peanut butter: adore the taste, regret the fattening hold it had on me as I fed every afternoon a recalcitrant adolescence.)

AUSHAK (Afghan Ravioli)

In this recipe the "Greek Bolognese" sauce of our Moussaka moves east to Afghanistan. I've just been informed by our friend Juliana Duncan that some time ago she and our daughters were in the habit of cooking Middle Eastern dishes like Aushak and, while Mom and Dad were off in Europe collecting data for books like this one, would serve them in a "tent" strung up in the dining room with the help of sheets, large tablecloths and suchlike. They sat, of course, on pillows, like a pack of caravaning Vita Sackville-Wests; this was dining in style, not camping. Feel free to follow their example.

Wash, trim, chop and soften 2 **leeks** in a little **olive oil** with a demi-smidgen of **cayenne**. Next, spoon some chopped leek onto the middle of a **won ton wrapper**, run a watery finger around the edge, place a second wrapper on top and seal; repeat the process until you have the needed number of ravioli. Then boil the completed packets for no more than 4 minutes (in batches if they stick together in the water).

Now sandwich your ravioli with a **mint**-dotted, generously **garlic**-flavored **yogurt** sauce (use at least 2/3 cup of yogurt, and press the garlic) and top with the "Greek Bolognese" of the Moussaka recipe just preceding this one. To reduce runniness in the yogurt drain it — in the fridge — in a colander lined with paper towels for 2 hours, then carefully scoop it out without tearing the towels.

NOTE: Pasta of whatever shape you desire is wonderful Turkish-style with the above two sauces, one atop the other or side by side. Inevitably, of course, they'll come together in a saucy conjugality made in heaven — punctuated by subtle antiphonies of cinnamon and mint. Bake the lot and you'll have a proper Pasticcio.

OSSO BUCO DELLA CASA

A little guided tour of veal shank recipes from North to South yields the following (bear in mind that white wine, tomato and broth are constants): in Normandy, where the title would still be Jarrets de Veau, you might find the meat cooked in vegetable oil and served with whole carrot pieces, while down in Provence garlic appears and, in a version by Mapie de Toulouse-Lautrec, lemon juice is added before serving . . .

Cross the border into Osso Buco territory and rosemary replaces a bouquet garni and olive oil has taken over from its gentler sibling (although just to confuse matters, in Venice they might use butter, and scrap the garlic too). Fairly common at this latitude is a final *gremolada* sprinkle of garlic, parsley and grated lemon zest which, however, is condemned by Marcella Hazan as indecently pungent. Shame, Marcella! That's like taking the seventh out of a climactic dominant chord in a Beethoven symphony.

. . . Meanwhile in Trieste they add anchovies, and some New American chefs serve Osso Buco in broth, which may be very tasty but seems a tad effete. Our recipe is centrist undiluted Lombardian, and we'll stand by it, come Satan or a highly incensed Marcella.

P.S.: After writing this essay I've experienced Tony Gulisano's Osso Buco sprinkled with rough bread crumbs and a few toasted pine nuts. Very interesting!

In a large pot without added fat sauté lustily your butcher-cracked **osso buco** pieces, turning them with tongs so all sides are nicely browned. Then stand them up with the bone vertical, sprinkle on a little **flour** and add 1 grated **carrot**, 1 chopped **onion** and **pepper**, **rosemary** and **sage** in moderate but not unduly timid amounts. Cover the pot and simmer for about 10 minutes.

Now blend 1 heaping tablespoon of **tomato paste** with a cup or more of **dry vermouth** and stir this combination into the juices in the pot; add 1/2 cup or more of **chicken or vegetable broth**, cover and continue simmering for about an hour.

Just before serving, sprinkle over the meat-etc. a gremolada, the grated rind of 1 very large **lemon** combined with minced **parsley** and 2 cloves of pressed **garlic**: the finished mixture should weigh in at about a half cup. (If you're taking the Trieste route, add several minced anchovy filets to the gremolada.)

Serve your osso buco with mashed potatoes topped with grated dry jack or parmesan cheese and run briefly under the broiler for last-minute crisping, or green pasta with butter and grated cheese, or with risotto verde (page ???).

ESCALOPE MILANESE

I daydream about this attractively gritty soul-satisfier quite often. It should be cooked with great attention to the timing and some abandon in the employment of butter. I also recommend the nice rough texture that comes with copious crumbing — remember that if your gratiné seems a shade crumb-bare after putting the chops in the pan you can always sprinkle more on even as the veal begins to sizzle lightly.

I've not had much luck in restaurants finding the Milanese/schnitzel texture I prefer. But perfection was achieved some years ago in a zanily convivial East German diner on the Munich-Berlin express. I remember the chop, and I remember the train diddled through the lovely Thuringian countryside, hurrying up whenever a tempting off-limits city like Jena or Halle had to be erased with Hitchcockian zest. That Mitropa schnitzel I would rate as one of the best things I ever ate at 30-40-50 mph.

The closest competition might be the earthily wonderful apple pie pressed on me recently by a jolly Amtrak waiter as we rounded the famous horseshoe curve near San Luis Obispo.

Dining cars! I've loved 'em ever since, in short pants, I heard the friendly rattle of breakfast cutlery on the old SP *Lark*, a Pullman dowager cruising through the orange groves toward Los Angeles' Union Station. 'Twasn't a bad era when you could watch the scenery zip while enjoying Queen Olives (25 cents), Veal Cutlet, Chili Sauce (80), Jelly Omelette (65), French Sardines (60), Cream Toast (45) — I'm quoting from the menu of a Louisville-New Orleans express.

And I remember my father coming home from wartime meetings in Washington extolling the juicy trout the UP's famous steward Bill Kurthy had so magically hooked for his *City of San Francisco* clientele.

Roll large **veal chops** in a beaten **egg**, then somersault them several times through a good sandpile of **breadcrumbs**: the egg and crumbs should await the chops on separate plates, and be sure to add fresh crumbs for the second chop.

Now cook the chops in a skillet over low/medium heat in a liberal amount of **butter**, about 11 to 12 minutes on the first side if the chops are thickish — for me a Milanese doesn't have to be pounded to be "authentic" — and 5 or 6 on the second. A little scattered blackening will not come amiss.

Like corn on the cob or a wide-angle steak these impressive sauceless objects are not especially hospitable to plate-mates. I find I'm totally occupied with uncovering pearls of veal beneath that equally fascinating breading, but if you insist on an accompaniment in addition to the essential wedges of **lemon** (large ones!) make it spinach boiled just until limp and sautéed with olive oil, lemon, pepper and a touch of red wine vinegar, or broccoli in a little lemony vinaigrette.

. . . Another possibility is a succotash derivative, thinly sliced steamed zucchini tossed in olive oil with a little frozen corn until brown; or go for bracing egg salad — chopped hard-boiled egg and minced parsley in profusion, somewhat less minced onion, a few crinkled capers and a subdued, not very wet Dijon mustard vinaigrette.

CÔTE DE VEAU À LA CRÈME
—*two ways*—

Nothing could be more French than this "forbidden pleasure." I associate it with the plain but comfortable Le Risle in Pont-Audemer, a Norman market town with ten charcuteries on the main street — that, I guess, is the equivalent of six or eight upscale delicatessens in your nearest metropolitan shopping mall. Now what else did they serve at Le Risle, spring of '77? You're right: roast chicken and trout meunière, blessed staples of the French kitchen.

. . . And then we passed through a little crossroads named Vouilly with an eleventh century church, its tower off to one side of its peaked roof "like a fighter's head tucked in behind his shoulder." The quote, of course, is from the immortal Mr. Liebling, and as we almost flew by Vouilly I cried out "Stop, isn't this where A.J. Liebling was billeted during the '44 invasion? Remember how he came back in 1955 to find that majestic woman Madame Hamel, his host during the war. Oh dear, I don't suppose he made her up, she certainly seemed much larger than life, such a jolly, radiant matriarch."

Well, there was a way to find out, as old as time itself, the churchyard being close at hand . . . and yes, a minute later I was weeping at the grave of "M. Hamel 1880–1968."

I

In a rather large skillet brown **veal chops** vigorously in a tablespoon or so of **butter**, taking care not to brown the butter excessively. Add after a few minutes a heap of sliced good quality **mushrooms** for simultaneous sautéing.

When the veal-and-mushrooms are nicely browned pour off the accumulated fat, deglaze the pan with a splash of **dry sherry or Calvados** and add a good 1/2 cup of **cream or crème fraîche**, stirring it in well by scraping up the good brown bits on the bottom of the pan. Shower with minced **parsley** and serve.

II

The same recipe, with the addition of poached sliced **apples** (page 162) which you tuck beneath the veal-and-mushrooms shortly before serving. For added excitement serve all over shredded cabbage bathed in boiling water for 5 minutes and stir-fried in a little bacon fat until limp but not brown.

AND: Version II could be done with chicken instead of veal, giving you the Fricassée de Poulet Normande we had at the good old Lion d'Or in Bayeux, a favorite of Monsieur Liebling mentioned in the adjacent chatter. Allow, of course, more time for cooking the chicken — and consider also sautéing sliced onions with the mushrooms.

MUSTARD-COATED ROAST VEAL WITH PLUM CATSUP KELLEY

Even upscale butchers in the U.S. tend to hide their veal roasts in the back fridge, but they're not to be kept a secret.

Back in the 30s Hoi, our white-jacketed chef/waiter/bottle washer, hushed but charming, and taught his way up Mrs. Rombauer's culinary ladder by my mother, would cook the family an excellent roast veal, not mustard-coated but juicy enough for Curnonsky himself, and glide into our dining room with his masterpiece at his usual tranquil but purposeful soft-shoe tempo. This veal was a favorite cog in the endless cycles of roasts-chops-filets of sole that appeared on our table with the regularity of *wagons-lits* found in another sort of Cook's Timetable.

Between meals Hoi would patiently listen to my sister Anne's accounts of her teenage love life, and he taught her a few Chinese characters too. When he left to work for a much wealthier household — and he made enough money at Big Sur to buy a grocery store in San Francisco — he gave my parents a lovely pair of vases. They sit in our dining room where I'm writing these words.

Meanwhile my Glasgow-born nanny, having failed to teach me to intone an ancient Scotch ditty, married a lawn-bowling baker and manned the counter of their mom/pop confectionery, dispensing admirable butterhorns and applesauce cakes. What a joy to have a bakery almost in the family.

For years I've worried that Hoi, with his family back in China, led an unduly cloistered life in the small bedroom behind our kitchen. But I realize now that his late-night trips to Chinatown, ostensibly for gambling, must have led him, after serving us ice cream and cake, to some back alley pleasure dome.

> Cream together a generous amount of soft **butter** and your basic **Dijon mustard** (in a proportion of about 60 pct. mustard to 40 butter) and spread the mixture all over a **boned, rolled veal roast**. Roast the meat at 300° for 27 to 30 minutes per pound, basting it some and repeating, at least on the top, the mustard-butter application halfway through the cooking.
>
> When it's done put the roast on a platter and dilute the pan juices with a little **chicken broth**, scraping up the good brown bits. And while a helper carves thickish slices from the roast, employ the enhanced juices in the role of "a nice, dark gravy," thin and aromatic.
>
> Serve your au jus veal with watercress, mashed potatoes with a little grated dry jack or

parmesan cheese stirred in (run the potatoes under the broiler briefly before serving) and, to cap the misto, plum catsup Kelley, a good supply of which is made as follows: Scald all together for 45 minutes:

> 25 **plums**
>
> 2/3 pint of **vinegar**
>
> 1 teaspoon of **pepper**
>
> 1 teaspoon of **allspice**
>
> 2 cups of **sugar**
>
> 1 teaspoon of **cinnamon**
>
> 1 teaspoon of **ground cloves**
>
> 1 teaspoon of **salt**

Put the catsup in clean jars and seal.

—48-hour—
VITELLO TONNATO À LA DON

(multiple servings)

This is the cream of luncheon party dishes, from the Frediani file. Don has put his own spin on the classic, browning roast and veg at the start to produce a more robust than usual result. I have a fantasy that Don should have made his tonnato for the count and countess — I mean the posh but low-key old couple we had lunch with once in Florence because a Nob Hill friend in San Francisco insisted, "well, if you're going to be in Florence you must dine with my friends."

So there we were, trudging nervously along a nondescript street by the goods depot at the railway station. Just across the way, behind one of those poetic Finzi-Continian garden walls the Italians specialize in, we found the "Park Avenue" digs of our pressed-into-action hosts.

"We tried to get Muti to join us," announced the starchy/twinkly countess — but obviously the maestro had better things to do. He was about to become conductor of the Philadelphia Orchestra, serving up his elegant and whiz-bang interpretations of Rossini, Beethoven, Britten.

The lunch though, very pure and simple, was delicious: green gnocchi followed by roast farm chicken and potatoes, served by a retainer in a white glove out of a fairy tale — but such an article of apparel is standard issue on the palazzo circuit. The conversation miraculously stayed afloat, in I forget what combination of tongues real and pidgin, and, it was fun to learn, the countess' great uncle was the dedicatee of Puccini's *La Bohème*.

Now I'm sure tonnato was on for tomorrow.

> Chop 2 **carrots** and a rib of **celery** rather fine and reserve for the moment. Next, in a large skillet brown a **boneless veal leg** quite vigorously, turning it often. After 7 or

8 minutes reduce the heat a little, add the carrots-and-celery around the edges of the meat and toss them gently for 2 or 3 minutes.

Now transfer the meat to a roasting pan and pour over your veal torpedo a cup of **dry vermouth** along with the attendant veg and the chopped contents of a 6-ounce can of **solid pack tuna** and a standard tin of **anchovy filets** (or the equivalent in salt-packed Sicilian anchovies with the salt topping scraped away).

Bake all at 300° for about 27 to 30 minutes a pound — try not to overcook that delicate zeppelin.

With the veal-etc. cooked you have a nice warm roast for your dinner, so treat yourselves to some thick slices along with, say, a few dabs of horseradish mustard. Then — to the tonnato!

Refrigerate roast-and-trimmings overnight and next day purée the carrot-celery-tuna-anchovy element in a blender or food processor with dry vermouth (perhaps 1/4 cup), **lemon juice** (1 or 1-1/2 lemons' worth) and a few tablespoons of **mayonnaise**. You want a "hummus" consistency.

Finally, slice the veal quite thin and assemble tonnato layers as follows: veal, the fishy "hummus", **large capers** on top. Let the finished product chill for another day (under plastic wrap held up tent-like with toothpicks), then take it out and serve with watercress or as part of an antipasto misto. P.S.: you can stuff hard boiled eggs with leftover tonnato purée.

VEAL CHOPS POITOU, WITH SQUASHES

A venerable recipe, I'm sure. Although I found it in Samuel Chamberlain, Alexandre Dumas doubtless knew it — then Curnonsky, Monet, Saint-Saëns, and Alice B. Toklas of course, ace memoirist of the vagaries of fine dining in France during the Occupation. Compare it with M. Dumas' veal shanks larded with thick bacon, cooked in bouillon with scallions and parsley and finished with egg yolk and verjus: green grape juice and a few drops of vinegar.

Fry a dozen small dice of **thick cut or slab bacon**, longer and with more flame on the first side than the second. After several minutes add a minced **shallot** for softening. Then reserve the bacon and shallot, pouring off most of the accumulated fat. In the same skillet brown **veal chops**. Return the bacon and shallot to the pan and simmer all for 10 minutes in 1/2 cup of **chicken broth** and a good splash of **dry vermouth**. Just before serving, stir in an **egg** yolk mixed with a little sauce from the pan and a few drops at least of **red wine vinegar**. Sprinkle some minced **parsley** over your Poitevin chops and serve them with sliced, steamed and **buttered summer and crookneck squash.**

VEAL SAUTÉ WITH SAUSAGE AND ARTICHOKES

Artichoke heart juliennes and sliced onion intertwine felicitously in this peppy stew, a textbook case of home cooking as practiced in Tuscany, Sonoma or Brooklyn's furthest reaches. Or think Del Pezzo, that gracious old bistro upstairs in a Manhattan brownstone on West 47th near Sixth: it was a cut above "mom and pop" and Caruso ate there, and doubtless many other pre-Pavarottans as well — I wonder if Gigli and Schipa ever sang for their scallopini.

A good choice, this stew, when you have a little cream and chicken broth in the larder, along with that extra artichoke. Mound each serving of your stew between two halves of crookneck squash or hillocks of rice.

- In a large pot boil 3 smallish **artichokes** in water to cover along with a squeeze of **lemon**: this may take 45 or 50 minutes. Forty minutes along, brown in a commodious skillet 3/4 of a pound of lightly floured **veal stew meat** and two fork-pricked, thickly sliced **Italian sausages** in a dab of **butter**.
- As the meat darkens and crisps add 1 sliced **onion**, 5 or 6 rather large sliced **brown mushrooms**, 1 pressed **garlic** clove, and toss all for 3 or 4 minutes. Then deglaze the pan with a little **dry vermouth**.
- Now lower the heat and stir in 1-1/2 cups of dry vermouth and 1/2 cup of **chicken broth** mixed with a good tablespoon of **tomato paste** and a bit of **sage** plus the sliced inner leaves and bottoms of your newly boiled artichokes. Simmer mostly uncovered for 30 or 35 minutes, stir in 1/6 cup of **cream** and serve topped with minced **parsley**.
- The outer artichoke leaves? Nibble 'em as you finish cooking, or serve them with vinaigrette.

CALF'S LIVER À L'ORANGE WITH TOASTED ALMONDS

Half unctuous, half crisp. The cream, orange and almonds are borrowed from a trout dish we had at the rather elegant Hôtel France in Montmorillon, east of Poitiers. That's where we splurged on foie gras rolled in black pepper, which *almost* cut the richness, and there was a lovely chicken with liqueur-soaked prunes to keep us amused. Terrified teenage apprentices in white jackets hovered about our table, little soldiers in the perennial campaign to preserve the hotel's Michelin rosette.

Alas, they did not convince the dreaded inspector who must have arrived soon after we left.

- Pat 3/4 of a pound of **calf's liver** with a paper towel, **flour** it and sear it in a very hot skillet in a little **butter**: it won't take more than 2-1/2 or 3 minutes the first side and a minute on the second unless it's unusually thick.
- Remove the liver to a serving plate and keep it warm while you stir into the pan juices — over somewhat reduced heat — about 1 tablespoon of **Dijon mustard** blended with 4 tablespoons of **cream** (or crème fraîche) and the juice of an **orange**. Pour the sauce over the liver and sprinkle all with diced or slivered **almonds** toasted briefly in a small skillet.
- Serve this liver with almost any kind of potatoes you can think of, or perhaps a little pasta with butter and grated cheese. And it's good cold the next day with cilantro.

Interlude on Track 10

I'm still thinking about the *Lark*, that crack overnighter to L.A. I used to ride to boarding school in a stew of conflicting emotions, fear of group living (and being tossed in the pool) jostling with the thrill of Taking the Sleeper. Normal bedtime — before The Great Gildersleeve roared out of the radio into my darkened room — was waived on travel nights. And off we'd drive to Third and Townsend station, skirting the jaywalking winos behind the Palace Hotel.

Step 1, check in at a table manned by elderly gents in many-buttoned black uniforms with stiff, trim caps like the streetcar motormen wore. Next, down the platform hoping a massive, rumbling train two feet from one's ear would not emit from its metallic udders a sudden and deafening hiss of steam. Then up the child-challenging steps, around the corner and into our compartment, gleaming, organized, cozy with its lower berth standing so to speak horizontally at attention, fuzzy blankets with the SP logo pulled taut over the sheets. Mom, of course, took the upper.

The diner up a car was lit and serving Tenderloin Tips Southern Pacific and maybe the line's celebrated Omelet Eclair, but for this little connoisseur, already fed his chop at home, it was time for bed. Then the long cat-like engine standing maybe grumpily in the dark, 4-3-7-6 or some such number, carried me away.

VEAL AND EGGPLANT NAPOLEON

In a moment we graduate, if that's the word, from veal to beef and I can't leave veal behind without a little salute to Lucien and Gaby who used to serve me the simplest veal chops with pan juices and boiled potatoes, preceded by old-time *crudités* and followed by a farewell shot of Marc, every Wednesday noon.

It was 1954, I was serving my not altogether unhappy term with the U.S. Army in France and somehow a buddy and I had fallen into the habit of escaping the mess hall and its tin trays "tous les mercredis." Our objective was the chill but beckoning little dining room of Lucien and Gaby's seemingly unoccupied auberge, five miles west of Orléans on the south bank road to Blois. Lucien, bent but happy in his classic blues and beret, was quite deaf, and Gaby, shuffling about in her house dress and apron, talked a blue streak — which made, I think, for a fair balance of disabilities.

Gaby cooked our lunch, always the same unless perhaps there was an entrecôte, and served it cooing away in a quavery soprano. Déjeuner completed, hovering Lucien poured the Marc before waving us off in my little sportscar which he thought (I didn't!) was a candidate for entry in that grueling road race at Le Mans.

Oh dear, that old directive "You can't go home again" was never more charged than when I returned to the auberge three years on with Anne and was told that Lucien and Gaby had retired and were living in the next town. We couldn't bear to stay, my little pair of entertainers no longer on tap, and lunch would have to be taken elsewhere.

Yet all was not lost, near our old caserne I saw through a window that Papa Nicaud was still polishing wine glasses in Le Petit Bar (*La Petite*, we GIs called it) where we'd devoured cheese omelettes every night at 9 because, three hours earlier, we had only toyed disconsolately with the contents of those abysmal tin trays, and downtown, at the République, the genial waiter who resembled the English actor Jack Hawkins was still in his apron, toting aperitifs; and the Joan of Arc statue still stood . . .

The Orléans memories roar back: misreading a tiny roadsign driving the N20 from Paris at midnight in an open car and ending up in a wheat field; shining our Honor Guard finery, we Eisenhower serfs who chose parading in front of Ambassador Dillon to the tune of a wheezy band rather than appear on the dread rosters signalling KP (kitchen police) assignments; and Major M. of course, the grumpy Maryland Napoleon (not a food!) under whom we labored, who wanted everything done "Tout Goddam Suite" . . .

Perhaps it's not surprising that the more bookish and urban of the 7805ers chose the Guard, buffing boots into some kind of Shinola infinity being somehow a more aesthetic endeavor than the endless peeling of potatoes not to be consigned to a Bocusian gratin. It was also in the Guard that young X appeared, an impish and beautiful young man who caused half us straights to fall in love, or some such emotion. We were, at any rate, teetering at the edges of our androgynity. The fellow I call X later married a lovely, somewhat older Frenchwoman, and enjoyed calling her by the masculine version of her name.

. . . And there were excursions, to Beaugency for quenelles, to Chambord to sip wine outside the great château, to Sully-sur Loire for a picnic, to Fontevrault to see the tombs of the Plantaganets who, to Virginia Woolf, looked straight and narrow as Edith Sitwell.

> More skyscraper cuisine here: to the recipe for Eggplant Parmigiana (page 33) add, between the eggplant and the mozzarella, browned **veal chops**, and add a thimble or two of **cream** to the tomato sauce.

BOLLITO MISTO WITH WHITE BEANS AND THREE SAUCES

A big production, but worth the trouble with so many good things to eat involved. A *Gran Piatto Bolliti Misti* is hard to find in U.S. restaurants, and even in Italy (only the North would consider it) it's a bit special. For some reason it's often offered only at lunch — are Italians really less hungry in the evening?

In restaurants the components are generally wheeled to your table on a great chariot if not up the aisle in a kind of kettledrum holding gustatory rather than auditory rewards. The home chef's alternative is a very large platter and several sauceboats. I love the romance of multiple sauces — the ones proposed on this page are our favorites.

Some cookbooks suggest horseradish sauce but that seems a little harsh for the relatively delicate chicken and too competitive with the flavor-detonating cotechino. At Fini in Modena we were served rock salt and a little ragoût of sweet peppers as well as the indispensable mostarda di frutta and salsa verde. (Fini, alas, was the only restaurant in our many years of Euro travel that was too busy with tubs of bollito and such to answer a San Franciscan's request for a copy of an old menu to take 6000 miles home as a souvenir of a wonderful dining experience — I'm not really the vindictive type, but I'm still annoyed at that maitre-d': well, there are lots of epithets out of Verdi I might fling in his direction . . .).

We make a somewhat less dense salsa verde than most recipes propose because the mostarda is rather bulky. A great game is deciding which sauce to eat with which meat. Inevitably, of course, they run together, but no problem, they're as cozy as lovers.

In a large covered pot in 2 inches of water boil: a **cotechino sausage** for about an hour; suitable-for-boiling **beef** for an intermediate amount of time within that hour (the timing depends, of course, on the cut and size) and **chicken** for the established 13 minutes.

And in a large covered saucepan boil 1 cup of soaked and drained **cannellini or Great Northern beans** in several cups of water with a little **olive oil**, **sage**, pressed **garlic** and **tomato** diced very small — figure on 1-1/2 to 2 hours for cooking these (plus the soaking hour).

Serve the meats and beans with:
1. **Mostarda di frutta**, cut up fine.
2. Salsa Verde: 2 parts **olive oil** to 1 of **red wine vinegar** with lots of minced **parsley**, a little minced **onion** and chopped **capers** and **anchovy** filets to taste. This can be puréed — in which case, slowly add the olive oil (minimum 1/2 cup) to the other ingredients already in motion in a blender or food processor.
3. Tomato mustard sauce: a little **Dijon mustard** stirred into our house **tomato sauce** (page 69).

AND there is this alternative sauce, especially good with boiled beef, *salsa alle olive*: in a smallish skillet soften 1 chopped **onion** in a little **olive oil**, add 1 small tin of chopped **black olives**, 1 chopped **tomato**, minced **parsley**, pressed **garlic**, **pepper** and a pinch of **sugar** and cook all gently for about 10 minutes, the cover of the skillet almost on.

SECOND DAY BOLLITO
—*based on Tante Marie's Boeuf au Gratin*—

A rare and interesting dish, an ancient hashy ancestor of today's "layered cuisine" presentations.

Tante Marie was, at least to an earlier-day book jacket designer, a slightly stout Mom-Irma-Julia sporting a jaunty white bow above a kindly good-housekeeper's face. Years of worthwhile bourgeois kitchen experience spill off this welcoming visage as Tante stirs what appears to be a lovely lobster bisque, or perhaps it's a navarin of lamb. A thousand recipes are promised, 500 menus, ideas for leftovers.

And, as the impish Mr. Liebling would have fondly translated her opening statement, "this book of cuisine addresses itself to modest Interiors where one is obliged to take into consideration the time and the money."

In a skillet fry a dozen or more **slab bacon or pancetta** oblongs, drain them on paper towels and place them on the bottom of a casserole.

On top of this meat place 1/2 of the following mixture:

chopped **onion**, a generous amount

chopped **mushrooms**, a bit less

minced **parsley**

pressed **garlic**

pepper

a raw **egg** blended with **breadcrumbs**

On top of all this place strips of boiled **beef** spread rather liberally with **Dijon mustard**, then top the beef with the other half of the onion/mushroom mixture.

Bake this mélange at 350° for 25 minutes, then run it under the broiler briefly for light crisping. Serve it with additional mustard which you may want to stir through the hash.

AFTERTHOUGHT: Add a little chopped spinach to the onion/mushroom mixture and you'd have a distant cousin to what San Franciscans — old ones, that is — know as a Joe's Special.

GRILLADE DES MARINIERS DU RHÔNE
—Round Steak with Caper Vinaigrette—

Reading Elizabeth David's thousands of recipes you sometimes wish for nine lives so you could cook and eat the whole *oeuvre*, so to speak. This one, slightly altered, is a great favorite, its rather murky contents not for every day but certainly very amusing two or three times a year. It is, she says, Very Old French — but life, of course, is cyclical and beef vinaigrette seems trendy as can be as the millennium arrives.

The valley of this recipe's title! It summons me down a ladder of lovely francophilic memories, meridional rung by rung — and forgive me for missing the exact spot at which ace aesthete Cyril Connolly proclaims the seductive South begins. I see the Pagnol types playing cards in a little bar in Les Roches-de-Condrieu, their all-day-sucker cigarettes puffed toward some nicotinal nirvana. There was, of course, our creamy lunch at La Pyramide, sacred place! And I'm feeling again the serenity of an elegant lunch at Avignon's silvery Hiély on a very cold winter's day, twenty hours after running my Austin-Healy (no relation!) into a snowbank and having to spend a night in St-Etienne, an improbable second-rate city with clanky trams suitable for a creepy Expressionistic film and the quenelles at dinner were tough, too.

More recently I've enjoyed zooming down the valley toward the Mediterranean in the arms of a whooshing *TGV*, which is rather like being shot through a pneumatic tube with wonderful picture windows.

In a casserole tuck 3/4 of a pound of **round steak** between blankets of chopped **onion** — 2 medium-sized onions should be sufficient — and dot all with several little beurre manié balls: the math here works out to about 2 tablespoons of **butter** blended with 1 tablespoon of **flour**.

Cover and bake this concoction at 300° for 1-3/4 hours, after which you should drain off a good half of the broth if the pot looks quite liquid, as it doubtless will.

Pour over the meat/onions/juice a simple salsa verde made of about 4 tablespoons **olive oil** to 2 or more of **red wine vinegar** along with lots of minced **parsley** and some **large capers**, then bake another 45 minutes.

Serve this "grillade" (well, it's really a piquanted pot roast such as you might eat at Pierre's Beaujolais Diner) over mashed potatoes or long-simmered white beans. If you can find those large Greek limas called gigantes they'll fill the bill admirably.

And bring a pot of mustard to the table.

POLPETTE

These are meatballs with breeding and tang. The moment of their culinary truth is a little elusive, but have patience. It's the lemon zest and nutmeg that particularly distinguish these rounds — something I'd remember if I were the proprietor of a chain of up-market McWhatzits. The ingredients, if not the frying times, are from an old Sam Chamberlain cookbook. I've not encountered this particular combination elsewhere, and that is not, I think, because I live in a city whose population is thirty-four percent Asian and most of my meatball experiences are Chinese — even if they often seem Italian. I think Marco Polo had his hand in the polpette trade.

Offering great competition to the crunchy-zingy balls of the adjacent recipe would be the giant, sensuous, fall-apart objects cooked in a rich "Lion's Head" broth at the Fountain Court on San Francisco's Clement Street. To experience these is to dally in a kind of gastronomical Venusberg, capturing with your chopsticks fluffy morsels as the Big Sphere bobs about in its broth.

I   (LOMBARDIAN)

In a sizeable mixing bowl combine well:

> 1 pound of **ground beef**
>
> the grated zest of a **lemon**
>
> 2 cloves of pressed **garlic**
>
> 2 tablespoons of minced **parsley**
>
> a good pinch of **nutmeg**
>
> **pepper**
>
> 1 teaspoon of **breadcrumbs**
>
> 1 slice of crumbled **white bread** soaked in a little **milk** and squeezed dry
>
> 1 beaten **egg**

Form this mixture into slightly puffed patties about 1/2 inch thick and 1-1/2 inches in diameter, roll them lightly in **flour**, then fry them in 2 or 3 tablespoons of very hot

olive oil for about 4-1/2 minutes on the first side and 1-1/2 on the second, this to produce polpette rather crisp on top and medium rare or a shade less inside and on the bottom.

Drain on paper towels and serve the polpette (there should be three to a serving) with at least half a lemon per person, and mashed potatoes — also, if you wish, a nutless pesto (page 70) made with aggressively de-stemmed watercress instead of basil. A green salad is a nice clean followup to these meatballs with their inevitable ooze of grease.

I also have a fantasy about floating miniature Lombardian polpette in Vichysoisse: I'll let you judge the merits of such a maritime experiment.

II   (NEAPOLITAN)

In this case combine in a mixing bowl:

    3/4 pound of **ground beef**

    1 or 2 tablespoons of minced **parsley**

    salt and **pepper**

    1/4 cup or a little less of **breadcrumbs**

    3 good tablespoons of seedless **raisins** soaked until soft in warm water, drained and coarsely chopped

    a lightly beaten **egg**

Take this mixture, which looks like a marvelous raisin-specked tartare, form it into patties as in the previous recipe, and fry them for the same amounts of time to a side as above, then serve with our house **tomato sauce** (page 69) to which you've added a little **cinnamon**. Ladle the sauce on each plate between triangularly arranged polpette.

LENTIL STEW FREDIANI
—a demi-chili—

Think of all the excellent dishes people *aren't* eating: Don says he's forgotten this recipe. Happily I've rediscovered it and find it a great shortcut to a nice chili experience — which you can pepper up more if you choose. It seems, by the way, to be a second cousin to a Lucca hash called garmugia in which peas and artichoke hearts (taking less cooking time, of course) stand in for the lentils. Ada Boni, the Tante Marie of Italy, suggests serving garmugia on toasts, like a green veg bruschetta, I guess.

In a large skillet sauté gently 1/4 pound of **ground beef** without fat until the look of rawness is gone, then push the meat aside and soften 1 roughly chopped **onion** in a tablespoon or less of **olive oil** in the same pan: in a minute, of course, you'll be mingling beef and onion.

Now add 1 28-ounce can of **tomatoes**, 1 cup of **lentils**, 2 pressed **garlic** cloves, **thyme** to taste and a smidgen of **cayenne**, and 2 or 3 cups of **chicken broth** for starters — you may well need more during at least 1-1/2 hours of simmering with the top off.

Serve this stew dotted with minced **parsley** and offer a pot of chutney, for instance Mary Kelley's (page ???).

HAMBURGER WITH GUACAMOLE SAN MARINO OR OTHER GARNISHES

When Cousin Tom brought us a bursting bag of avocadoes from his San Marino garden we swung into action.

Tom is a globe-trotting lawyer for whom the description *bon vivant* might have been invented: his postcards from the field are crowded with lyrical accounts of operatic and culinary triumphs in New York, London, Santa Fe. An excellent occasional chef — between appearances before assorted Supreme and lesser courts — Tom is much concerned with the proper vinous "irrigation" of a good sauté or stew. There's no one better to share a meal with: in this era of rush and confusion Tom takes his time at table, savoring morsels as if they were lovely phrases of Bellinian *cantilena*.

It was on a visit to Tom that we found the site of the prep school near Pomona where I'd been incarcerated forty years before. Odd sensation: all but one building on campus, the timbered residence of the elegantly monikered yankee headmaster, had just been torn down to make way for a new housing tract, but standing on the rise more or less where my old dorm *should* have been I suddenly knew by some strange vision, a telltale lay of the land, that I was on the spot. I'd cried buckets of homesickness in that dorm; it was in the cool and ivy'd dining hall, with the green Adirondack chairs outside, where I crunched away my sorrows devouring sugar-intense cinnamon rolls crafted by Cal Prep's resident baking genius.

Meeting Hopalong Cassady at Paramount studios was supposed to help — but only Superman would do.

> In a very hot skillet cook thickish **ground beef** patties without fat, longer and with more flame on the first side, this to achieve a crispy top and a medium rare-to-rare interior, a "black and blue" burger as they say at San Francisco's Zuni Café. Serve on **French bread** toasts with:
> 1. Guacamole San Marino
> or
> 2. Orange Mayonnaise
> or
> 3. Remoulade (page 8)

GUACAMOLE

> In a bowl combine 2 pitted, quasi-mashed **avocadoes**, 1 smallish finely diced **tomato**, 2 pressed **garlic** cloves, 1 tablespoon of minced **shallot**, 2 tablespoons of chopped **red onion**, a bit of **chili powder**, some minced **cilantro** and the juice of half a **lime**; cover with a thin layer of **olive oil** and refrigerate for a while if you wish, but there's no need for chilling.
>
> Do, though, let your green glop sit a few minutes for its rather independent-minded elements to harmonize. It's all right to leave some of the avocado in small chunks: this "salsa" of a guacamole could be used in an omelette or with chile rellenos. Or de-tomato it, add minced almonds to taste and serve it over pasta, with grated cheese suggested.

Orange Mayonnaise

>Combine 2 tablespoons of good **mayonnaise** with 1/2 tablespoon of **Dijon mustard**, 1/2 tablespoon of **orange juice**, a short splash of **dry sherry** and a little **tarragon**. By the way, if you twirl leftover orange mayo into an already vinaigretted salad, presto, you have a creditable "ranch dressing." Recommended especially for frisée and beets.

HAMBURGER MARCHAND DE VIN

This cordovan-colored sauce, good enough to drink, is traditionally assigned to steak, but there's no reason it can't be used to dress us a not-so-plebeian burger. The combination on this page I would call a French hamburger (not that the average inhabitant of Limoges or La Rochelle would think of sullying a classic sauce for entrecôte with ground beef) as opposed to the San Francisco Italo-American (hefty patty smunched between top and bottom of a fat, fat slice of baguette) or the upscale All-American Dagwood (patty writhing happily, one hopes, beneath tomato, onion, lettuce and mayonnaise in a wheat toast sandwich arrangement).

The Italo-American burger I got to know many years ago in newspapermen's pubs near the offices of a long-defunct San Francisco daily tolerating my inept services as a back-of-the-city-room reporter aiming for the music critic's cubicle.

Ah but there were a few moments of something close to glory: when, for instance, I subbed on the star-manned rewrite bank and, a four-alarm fire having inconveniently broken out three minutes before the late morning deadline, I had to, shall we say, "embroider" before the leg man at the scene called in with the facts. After living so dangerously, that hamburger on French, plus the de rigeur martini, hit the spot.

By the way, that was the era when reporters on the police beat never took off their hats — well, perhaps in bed . . . And across the alley from the press room in the old Hall of Justice was the Blue Fox where twinkly maestro Pierre Monteux regularly demolished his ration of oysters and Mumm's.

The battered city room I can see as if no time had passed: Jack McDowell the squat, tough but friendly city editor who liked to call roving reporters on his Dick Tracy two-way radio; his gentlemanly sidekick, Gyp Stalker, with a flock of press agent's "handouts" for us cubs to rewrite; the equally courtly obit writer "Duc" Meyer with his little goatee who'd call for a copy boy in the most sonorous howl imaginable; and rumpled, grey flanneled rewrite man Fred Storm who'd covered the White House in FDR days, knew of Woodrow Wilson being naughty in a presidential office — on the desk, yet — and liked between stories to write up the mythical adventures of a Judy Holliday type he'd invented who "shattered the calm of the clink."

>Soften 1 small minced **onion** in a good teaspoon of **butter**, stir in a teaspoon or more of **flour**, add **pepper** and slowly blend in 1 cup or more of a rather full-bodied **red wine**; bring to a boil, reduce the heat to a minimum and simmer uncovered for about 15 or 20 minutes with 1 tablespoon of **tomato paste** and a pressed **garlic**

clove, stirring frequently to achieve a sauce of middleweight consistency — or a shade thicker.

Shower this sauce with minced **parsley** (or perhaps cilantro) and pour it over **ground beef** patties cooked according to our prescription of more time and flame on the first side than the second.

NOTE: Although this winy hamburger is very tasty without accoutrements, eaten perhaps on toasted French bread, it can be turned into a nouvelle *event* by serving it over chard that you've trimmed (but leave some stems), washed, boiled, drained well and — this is the fun part — sautéed quickly in a little olive oil. If you decide on mashed potatoes, pour the sauce over the meat and around the potatoes. The chard can be boiled in advance and reserved, else you may find yourself with more rings to your kitchen circus than you need just before appearing serenely in your dining room, Marchand de Vin in hand.

ANOTHER THOUGHT: Up in the first paragraph of this recipe you could simmer along with everything else the meat scooped out of 4 **veal marrow bones**. Forget the hamburger and serve Marrow Marchand de Vin on toast.

STEAK TARTARE
—two treatments—

Once when I was trying not to expose myself too much to hospital cooking Anne regularly brought to my performing-fool of a bed the adjacent care package (version 1) which requires no warming. The sandwich version I think of as a hamburger on a vegetable — if you're a little squeamish about raw meat the grand warm rounds of aubergine go some distance toward muting any negative gastronomic vibes.

Now my father had some patients whose meals were air-lifted, so to speak, to Stanford Hospital from spiffy old Jack's, Hemingway's favorite San Francisco restaurant, but such delightful frills were not an option for me, I wasn't Louis B. Mayer or Alexander Woollcott.

Mercifully I can't remember any of the official meals-on-a-tray brought to this reclining patient during seven weeks hung up in a traction device designed for sufferers from considerable tibia loss. And, come to think of it, I cannot remember any of the many meals I must have eaten at Stanford University's Stern Hall. Perhaps our resident advisor, name of Bill Rehnquist, could help.

. . . And now the creaking springs of memory bring it back, at the hospital there was an elderly Florence Nightingale who appeared like clockwork by my torture rack every midnight, as if the administrator of her own extracurricular catering service, a sort of sandwich fairy who blessed me regularly with peanut butter and marmalades on whole wheat, as uninstitutional a snack as ever there was. Feverish and literally high-strung, I wondered if this dumpy figure in the shadows of room 317, this Papagena-like angel of gastronomic mercy, was a mirage.

Well, real or dream, she was a faithful one, not to be forgotten.

My only other hospital experience of note took place at Fort Ord, courtesy of the U.S.

Army. Lucklly I had contacted a whopping case of pneumonia just before a terrifying sixteen weeks of Basic Training was scheduled in the duney northern precincts of Monterey peninsula, a short but heartbreaking distance from such charming stopping places as Carmel and Monterey. For two weeks I lay there with a stratospheric fever while my livelier ward-mates engaged in the clattery game of rolling beds up and down the aisle as if they were so many go-cars at Playland at the Beach. But even that was better than Basic!

It wasn't long, amazingly enough, before the good docs were letting me commute from the hospital to San Francisco on weekends.

I (BASIC)

Moosh together and serve on or with **French bread** toasts:

3/4 pound of **ground beef** of unimpeachable quality

5 or 6 tablespoons of chopped **onion**

minced **parsley**

large **capers** to taste

pepper

1 raw **egg**

a good splash of **soy sauce**

II (EGGPLANT SANDWICH VAL SASSINA)

Sauté 1/4-inch slices of **eggplant** in the necessary amount of **olive oil** (it will seem like a gallon); after cooling them, make sandwiches using a thick layer of **tartare** for the filling. You can spoon up the mix with a pie server. Serve if you wish with an herb mayonnaise (3 parts commercial mayonnaise, 1 part Dijon mustard, generous lemon juice, a bit of dry sherry, and dill weed to taste). Accompany with **French bread** toasts.

—24-hour—
TERRINE ARDÈCHE LO PODELLO

(4 servings)

Souvenir of a 1984 lunch at the funky Lo Podello in Antraigues, in an unknown but beautiful part of France, west of the Rhône. A land of mist, woodsmoke, baahing sheep, conical rock gorges, impressive visual symphonies of blossoming arborial phenomena. We ate at a long table next to jars of preserved pickles, peppers and mushrooms, as if in some apothecary's aquarium, our order taken by a *patron* in jeans, vest and gold chain who looked more like a graduate of Haight-Ashbury than Cordon Bleu.

This terrine seems to be related to the Tian de Courgettes of Provence, on the more fashionable side of the Rhône, the Peter Mayle side. When you invert it onto a plate the zucchini suggest roof tiles atop a "house" of meatloaf.

Lo Podello, of course, was not listed in the red Michelin, increasingly obsessed with bathing facilities up to the millennial minute: mile-long 1922 bathtubs are frowned on. I retain a fondness for the hieroglyphical vocabulary of meaningful spoons–forks–cups–rocking chairs–lecterns–garden benches–lithe divers–slashed dogs–crossed tennis rackets–reclining telephones and other figurines of Michelin speech which became for us many years ago a kind of mother tongue, but snobbery has crept into the inspectors' hearts.

> Steam 3 or 4 rather large **zucchini**, refresh them under cold water, pat them dry, halve them lengthwise and place skin side down in one layer on the bottom of a **buttered** round casserole: it may be a slightly tight fit.
>
> Meanwhile, soak 1 cup of torn-to-bits **French bread** in 1/3 cup of **milk** for 10 minutes, then squeeze out the excess milk.
>
> Using a fork, combine the crumbs in a mixing bowl with:
>
>> 1/2 pound of **ground beef**
>>
>> 1/2 pound of **ground veal**
>>
>> 1/2 pound of **ground pork**
>>
>> 2 pressed **garlic** cloves
>>
>> 1/2 teaspoon of **turmeric**
>>
>> 1 cup of minced **parsley**
>>
>> **pepper**
>>
>> **chives**, **dill weed** and/or **thyme**
>
> Spread this mixture in an even layer over the zucchini and bake covered with lightly **canola oiled** waxpaper at 350° for about 25 to 28 minutes — be sure not to overdo.
>
> Let the terrine cool, pour off unwanted fat and refrigerate it, covered, overnight. Then remove the waxpaper, run a knife around the edge and invert a serving plate over the terrine; turn the terrine onto the plate.
>
> Serve Terrine Ardèche at room temperature with our house tomato sauce (page 69) or simply a pot of Dijon mustard. Marcus' Potato Salad (page 48) would make an appropriate accoutrement.

ANNE'S MEAT LOAF

(4 servings)

An American cousin to the previous recipe.

Now I suppose I dined on something like this loaf when I made my lone Atlantic crossing at sea level. No, I did not ride the Aquitania, near-contemporary of the superstar Titanic, which as a small boy I spied steaming into San Francisco during the last good war, a svelte four-stacker translated into troopship grey. Nor was it the Queen Mary, the beached version of which my wife slept on while attending an historians' conference at Long Beach. And surely it wasn't the romantic France, a sheaf of whose anemoned *cartes du jour* my sister Julie brought home to her jealous sibling caught in a miasma between visits to The Continent — the only continent, of course, in those days before the U.S. renounced dark bars for sidewalk cafés.

No, my vessel was the General Warren, another grey one, and I was a lowly draftee in transit. But even huddled like Brueghel peasants at long tables in a cramped mess hall we khaki'd employees of Mr. Ike were eating better than you usually do at 39,000 feet. The food wasn't stylish, but it was good enough to look forward to from one's hammock in the hold, which felt like 39,000 feet down. Well, this trip was my stand-in for the colorful freighter voyage I'd find in an A.J. Liebling omnibus or an M.F.K. Fisher memoir.

Now while we're on the subject of ground meat, let me admonish you: Please, No Ketchup. It's a free country, of course, but I have serious, no, critical reservations about the use of this ubiquitous condiment, those oopsy gushings and squirtings of superfluous red matter issuing from little glass lighthouses in themselves as beautifullly designed as an Eames chair but containing a would-be elixir frequently applied with no more thought than that employed by a smoker tossing his butts into my front plot.

- Cube into a bowl 1/2 cup of crustless **white or brown bread** and add a little **apple juice or leftover red wine** to moisten it. Next, add 1 pound of **ground beef** and 1/3 pound of **ground pork**, mixing it in with your hands and/or a fork, then add 1 large grated **carrot** and 1 grated **onion** (use the small holes), **pepper**, **chervil** and **marjoram** to taste, 1/4 cup of **untoasted wheat germ or oatmeal** and 1 raw **egg**. Keep mixing.
- Now heap the lot into a bread pan and push it down with a fork, slope the edges as if you're crafting a little crowned highway, then bake at 350° for almost an hour, until the loaf is brown but not tough.
- Shortly before the loaf is done pour off the accumulated fat, which may be considerable. Serve — 5 or 10 minutes after removing it from the oven — with our house tomato sauce (page 69) minus the onion, and a small baked potato for each diner.
- LEFTOVERS NOTE: If you have extra meat loaf, serve it at room temperature with greens and warm sliced potatoes in a mustard vinaigrette. It would also be pleasant with caponata (page 32).

GOULASH 88 WITH POLENTA OR SOUR CREAM CORNBREAD

I've had excellent goulash at Paprikás Fono in San Francisco's Ghirardelli Square, but goulash makes me think of Budapest. Even under the Communists, thirty years ago, Budapest — and you reached it after they searched obsessively-compulsively under the train at the grim border, looking, doubtless, for goulash runners — seemed a jolly, vibrant place, peppery like its food. As our friend the conductor János Ferencsik put it over dinner at a restaurant that looked as if it came out of some 30s Hollywood *Shop Around the Corner*, "We are poor, but we know how to live."

Performances at the opera were so tingly with excitement Vienna's famous old Philharmoniker seemed frightfully blasé in comparison, rolling out *Carmen* like a carpet of ermine while Budapest's *Tannhäuser* traveled a much ruggeder, and more fascinating, road. The cymbal player might have awakened Wagner himself!

We ate interestingly in Budapest: that noodles, ricotta and bacon combination, an "almost dessert" you could call it, at Mátyas Pince, bean soup with smoked meats at the Royal Hotel, and crêpes with *two* jams at courtly old Gundel's, where we expected

Joseph Wechsberg to turn up with trout and truffles on his mind . . . Now that cornbread here: not Hungarian at all, of course, but after tasting something similar at the East Side Oyster Bar in Sonoma I couldn't help thinking *goulash, goulash* . . .

P.S.: In the excellent restaurant at the Cologne Opera (between acts of a minimalist production of *Siegfried* piloted by a conductor wearing dark glasses) we delighted in a cold goulash appetizer: it read, you might say, as a carnivore's caponata. Brochette of dragon was not on that night, doubtless too tough. And the audience being native didn't laugh at the innocent Siegfried's line about the reclining heroine he finds on a rock, "*Das ist kein Mann!*"

> To the side of a very well-heated pot brown 8 or 10 little oblongs of **thick cut or slab bacon**, adding after a minute or more 2 roughly chopped **onions** for simultaneous sautéing. Next to all these throw in 1 pound of cubed **beef stew meat** and brown it aggressively, ultimately stirring beef, bacon and onions all together.
>
> Lower the heat, **paprika** the stew LUSTILY, add 1 heaping tablespoon of **tomato paste**, 1 large pressed **garlic** clove, 1 cup of **chicken broth** and another of **water** and simmer all over a minimal flame, cover mostly on, for 40 to 45 minutes — the time it takes to undress, take a rather leisurely shower, dress, and return to the kitchen smelling the Hungarian profumo wafting through your house.
>
> Now taste this maturing goulash as it runs its last lap of simmering and make sure the paprika's blazing.
>
> When the beef is tender for sure and its good brown coating just the right degree of not-quite-thick, serve your stew one of two ways, either in soup bowls over soft polenta (3/4 cup of polenta stirred into 3 cups of salted boiling water, then stirred over low heat for 10 minutes) or on regular plates with a Sour Cream Cornbread. If you opt for polenta, a little chutney to the side won't come amiss.

Train Spotters' Interlude:

The only embarrassing moment I know of in the annals of the French National Railroads occurred a rainy spring day in '71 when our Paris–Milan *rapide* unaccountably got stuck negotiating a rather steep hill in the Jura Mountains. Sitting in the diner we couldn't help noticing the engineer of an express in the opposite direction making the gesture of wiping the sweat off his brow as he passed our hapless string of mortified streamlined coaches . . . And the cream of train jokes: the conductor taps the shoulder of the engineer in the glassed-in cab just ahead of us, points to the sharp Alpine curve ahead and advises, "*Tout droit,*" in other words, "Straight ahead!"

I've been on Amtrak a lot lately and have not witnessed any of the staff achieving such a peak of rail-wit, but I have delighted in how many interesting strangers one meets in the diner. One day four of us even formed a group, complete with name, and had three meals together, professing of course eternal friendships that haven't quite come into play. (I'm told, by the way, on a more intimate note, that fascinating strangers in coffee houses who give their telephone number to captivated souls are apt to be unavailable when further pursued: it's a shipboard situation).

Trying to communicate with a Yorkshireman whose accent was as impenetrable as the glowing Utah menhirs outside our late afternoon window on the *California Zephyr* was a problem not to be solved. But that was an exception to the pervasive rule of conviviality. Once I actually deserted my breakfast biscuit and crossed the aisle to pry two Americans loose from a hopeless linguistic misconception: the German farmer at their table was talking about raising what in his language would be corn but in English sounded like mice . . .

Here is the cornbread recipe:

Sift together:
- 1 cup of whole **wheat flour**
- 4 teaspoons of **baking powder**
- 1/2 teaspoon of **baking soda**
- a half teaspoon of **salt**

and combine with 1 cup of yellow cornmeal.

Beat 2 **eggs**, 1 cup of **sour cream**, 4 tablespoons of melted **butter** and 3 tablespoons of **honey**.

Stir the dry ingredients of the first paragraph into the eggs/sour cream mixture until moistened, then spoon the batter into an 8" by 8" pan and bake at 425° for 20 minutes.

KOREAN BEEF RIBS

Authenticity here: a Korean school chum of our daughters prepared us this haunting meat fix out of the East. And wouldn't you know, it being San Francisco, when I asked the nice butchers at the Cal Mart to cut me some ribs as prescribed on this page they immediately responded, "Oh, you're doing Korean barbecue." When they heard I was writing a cookbook they said they'd be delighted to be in it, and I am happy to oblige, I'm indebted to them for anatomy lessons gladly given when necessary.

Have the butcher cut about 1-1/2 pounds of **beef back ribs** into approximately 2 by 3 inch blocks, then marinate them for an hour or more in 3 or 4 tablespoons of **sesame seed oil**, half as much **soy sauce**, 1 large pressed **garlic** clove, a pinch of **sugar**, some **pepper** and a good teaspoon of toasted **sesame seeds** (tossed briefly in a small skillet). Be sure to turn the meat now and then during its bath.

Then broil the ribs, turning them once, and basting them from time to time with the marinade, for no more than 30 minutes: they're really more exciting with a little "give" to them than too comprehensively crisp. Serve with plain rice, some of the drippings, and, if handy, plum or fig jam. You are strongly urged to heat the jam.

DAUBE PROVENÇALE CHEZ NOUS

(6 servings, or 3 with hefty leftovers)

An excellent party stew, *sub*-Burgundian: for me it's defined by the cinnamon and orange as much as beef, garlic and red wine. I find cooking a daube an excellent way to cope with that accursed tailpiece of a working week, Sunday afternoon. But open the door to garden or deck, lest all that beef-browning steam your kitchen into something resembling a Cunard White Star boiler room at full tilt. Take care, too, about nasty clouds of ginger befogging your formica, and try to avoid standing ankle-deep in errant onion skins.

. . . And meanwhile perhaps you've procrastinated about cleaning the broiler after cooking those Korean ribs one recipe back. Do procrastinate, that flaming sesamean aroma will cling to your kitchen like an ecstasy-inducing elixir, a kind of olfactory sun eager to etch its insinuating way into YOU.

I guess this is the Asian equivalent of that heady bouquet of meat stock wafting up to your auberge window when you're staying in the French countryside — meanwhile one hears the crunch of gravel down in the courtyard as the cross-country baker delivers his baguettes for your cozy breakfast with butter, jam, *tous les trimmings de la table*. Stay alert at that table: in croissant flakes interesting memories might lurk.

In a large pot soften 3/4 cup of diced **thick cut or slab bacon**, then raise the heat significantly, add 3 pounds of good **beef stew meat** cut into approximately 1-inch cubes and brown it with abandon on the first side — you can be more circumspect with the succeeding surfaces. If not all the meat fits in a single layer, use a separate pan for browning the excess.

Now stir in 5 large quartered **onions**, 8 **carrots** cut into 2-inch-long juliennes, and, optional this, 2 julienned **sweet red peppers**. When the vegetables have taken on a little color, add:

> 1 28-ounce can of **tomatoes**
>
> 2 pressed **garlic** cloves
>
> **parsley** sprigs, **bayleaf** and **pepper**
>
> a good pinch of **ground ginger** and another of **ground cloves**
>
> 2 teaspoons of **cinnamon**
>
> the zest of an **orange**, cut into strips
>
> 3 or 4 cups of **red wine**

Bring to a boil, cover the pot and cook your daube over low heat for 2 hours, the cover partly or fully off the last several minutes to facilitate sauce reduction: you want a just slightly thin consistency. Bear in mind that wine may be added more or less at the last minute.

Serve this daube with a pompadour of mashed potatoes topped with grated dry jack or parmesan cheese and run under the broiler for crisping. The warmed-up leftovers, spiked with a little fresh wine, are capital over pasta, white or green, tossed generously with butter and grated cheese. The name of the "sauce" in this daubian incarnation? Bolo-nizza.

BISTECCA FIORENTINA

The Italians' favorite steak, generally washed down with a fizzy uncredentialed Lambrusco, is first experienced by many Americans at Sostanza, that no-nonsense trattoria in Florence that looks like a butcher shop in disguise. My Sostanza debut, in 1957, figures prominently in my book of Steaks to Remember. Funny how a man can call up past meat fixes like a libertine his affairs. My memory bank when jogged delivers:

- 1939, San Diego, an old-fashioned tile-floored grill, the steak thick as a Dickens novel, crunchy-exteriored and very beefy — this was my first steak out in the world! My escort was a lively lady from Kiev, a housemother at my prep school who, bless her, almost filled the maternal void for a lonely eight-year-old.
- 1946, the Isle of Capri, a cutely arcaded trattoria in San Francisco's North Beach, the steak an eminently respectable filet mignon crowning a six-course "family style" dinner after the Big Game between Stanford and Berkeley. Price? Ninety cents. (And the Capri is now, I believe, what sage Beachian Herb Gold would term the newest New Pisa.)
- 1952, Chez Valentin, off Paris' Champs-Élysées, an amiable crone in a tea apron serves me a juicy tournedos crowded onto a plate with frites, Bearnaise and watercress — or was it creamed spinach? — while civil servants at neighbor tables read their *Paris Soirs*.
- 1981, the Elite Café, an Art Deco yuppietorium in San Francisco's Upper Fillmore, the steak is a great New York topped with a pepper-gritty Cajun butter.

And oh yes, summer of '53, a much-needed martini and a handsome echo of that Diegan sizzler one Friday night in Carmel, your carnivore on a weekend pass from Uncle Sam having just completed at nearby Fort Ord Basic Training's most fascinating project, a nocturnal crawl across a field beneath a rat-tat-tat of machine gun fire at dining table height.

Marinate the desired poundage of **Porterhouse or rib steak** in 2 or 3 tablespoons of **olive oil** and **pepper** to taste, fry in a hot skillet without added fat, longer and with more flame on the first side, and serve with **lemon** wedges. A short minute before the steak is done throw a little chopped **garlic** and **parsley** and some sliced **portobello mushroom** into the pan — this may not be Florentine, but don't worry, the authenticity mafia won't harm you.

The best accompaniments for this bistecca are broasted potatoes (sliced, boiled, then slowly sautéed in a little butter) or spinach which you wash, boil and quickly sauté in a hot pan with olive oil, pressed garlic and a dash of red wine vinegar. Or you can serve the steak and lemon as the sole but impressive inhabitants of a pretty dinner plate, with a salad to follow on said plate after a little mopping with French bread. OR: If you opt for pepper steak, deglazed with brandy after frying and bathed in mustard, cream and white wine, accompany this treat with steamed unsliced leeks tossed for 2 minutes over moderate heat with a little olive oil, garlic and tarragon . . . another fun thing is steak with cilantro vinaigrette.

Mrs. Miketta, my Kievian savior, must have been five feet tall, with a puff of white hair. She had come to America, I suspect, following the events of '17. Her sons, a trimly mustached lawyer and a dashing gas station proprietor, seemed to be well established under the pre-smog sun of L.A., the rays of which I can feel as I write in a San Francisco fog.

Ferried up and down the coast on dangerous three-lane highways by Greyhound's throbbing Deco fleet, Mrs. M and I weekended in the big cathedral (I mean mission) towns like Santa Barbara, staying in pleasant first-and-a-half rate hotels with tile-floored lobbies stocked with capacious red leather armchairs, spittoons at the ready nearby, like sleeping dogs; and upstairs, in the compact bathrooms next to the usual fire escape, there were always aromatic little cakes of soap different from what I knew at home and conveying somehow a message of cozyness.

In the morning in the coffee shop downstairs there'd be pancakes and syrup, the birthright of every American child . . .

MANZO DONALDO
—With Vegetables Rondalla—

This is a skinny cousin of Escalope Milanese.

The accompanying colorful ragoût is modeled on a combo of vegetables spooned over carne asada at the inimitable La Rondalla in San Francisco's Mission District. The complex atmosphere of Rondalla, compounded of authority, charm and a certain deadpan zaniness, seems to have sprung full-born from the head of a concept-person who wouldn't know a concept from a confit. Enter from the outside world and the perennial Christmas decorations blink gently, a mellow rhythm issues from the jukebox, chefs glide about the minuscule open kitchen shaking sauté pans and mashing beans with huge, dangerous-looking instruments, red-sweatered waitresses of assorted ages gossip lightly by the counter . . . in short the whole place hums.

Rondalla stays open very late, and I used to turn up there sometimes after reviewing the opera, in black tie if a new production had been unveiled on a "dress up" Tuesday evening. In that uniform I'd stride out to the newspaper's composing room a bit after midnight — these were the days when elderly eye-shaded bronco-busters tickled the ponderous ivories of Mr. Mergenthaler's behemothic Linotype machines, *usually* getting the words in the right order — and, as debonairly as I could, hand over my prose to the copy-cutter, the maitre d' of that wonderful palace of purposeful clatter.

Pound the desired amount of **round steak** quite thin with your weapon of choice, and cut it into 2 or 3 oblong helpings — a portion will stretch across your plate in a kind of horizontal yawn. (Or buy pre-sliced "beef scallopini" from your butcher). Then squeeze on a large pressed **garlic** clove, add the grated zest of a **lemon**, and after letting this seasoning take effect (figure half an hour here) dip the meat in beaten **egg** and, not too heavily, **breadcrumbs**.

Now in a large hot skillet — avoid crowding! — brown the flattened pieces of meat in a tablespoon or more of **olive oil**, observing the rule of less time and heat for browning the second side; the whole process won't take long, perhaps 5 minutes.

Serve Manzo Donaldo (translation: Beef Don-style) with lemon wedges aplenty, and partner it with a mélange of **onion** rings sautéed to a light brown in a little olive oil (use a roomy skillet), **tomato** wedges that you bake for 20 minutes in a moderate oven with a little oil, then semi-smash and briefly sauté, and **potatoes** cut into the shape of fat french fries, boiled and briefly sautéed with their asadan siblings in a little additional olive oil, along with a small splash of **red wine vinegar** and a pinch-ette of **chili powder**.

CARBONNADES FLAMMANDES

Carbonnades one rarely finds in American restaurants, but beef in beer is a characterful alternative to beef in good red wine. Bless those ever-hungry Belgians, occupied so tenaciously with their mussels and frites, they've given us carbonnades, waterzooi, endive . . .

There's a pervasive luxuriance about Belgian cooking that sets statisticians of caloric intake on edge, but the little country's gastronomical zest is not to be despised. Now think of Switzerland, all they have is Emmentaler and Orson Welles' cuckoo clocks.

But it was in Switzerland, the dignified and slightly dowdy dining room of the Hotel du Lac in Interlaken to be exact, where I finally recaptured, not long ago, a lost experience from my "dining out" childhood back in the late 1930s, the era of FDR, Lotte Lehmann and the Lone Ranger. There it was, that warm olfactory buzz, a kind of interior woodsmoke I'd remembered from hotel dining rooms like the lovely one at the Mar Monte in Santa Barbara with its high-backed, button-lined chairs and waitresses in tea aprons.

Who knows what produced it: maybe nothing more than radiator dust and chicken broth. The Mar Monte, I should add, had by the 80s become apartments and claimed among its happy homemakers one Paul and Julia Child.

Lotte Lehmann, come to think of it, spent her last decades not many miles away. Now I can't claim to have met the Lone Ranger at Paramount, and FDR resided well inside the speaker cabinet of our Deco Philco (at a time, by the way, when radio announcers were charmingly mellifluous Kentuckians, ill-tutored network twangers or scarcely believable fops) but I was fortunate to have lunch with the enchanting Lotte — the greatest protagonist ever of that fragile Wagnerian maiden named Sieglinde — when she hit the 80 mark.

She had so many things to do, she bubbled, she wanted to live to be 112. She thought perhaps she should have sung Isolde. She loved her big Cadillac. And she recalled the towering and somewhat irascible conductor, initials O.K., who paid her extracurricular attention when they were young colleagues at the Hamburg Opera, noting:

"When he was wanting, I was not wanting; and when I was, he was not . . ."

In a large pot fry a few little oblongs of **thick cut or slab bacon** until they're almost crisp; meanwhile add 2 small sliced **onions** and brown them. Pour off the accumulated fat and reserve the bacon and onions. In the same pot brown a good pound of lightly floured **beef stew meat**, then deglaze the pan with a little **beer** and return the bacon and onions.

Now combine the beef/bacon/onions with 15 to 18 ounces of **beer**; a dash of **vinegar, either red wine or balsamic**; a small teaspoon of **sugar**; **thyme, bayleaf** and **pepper**; and 1 thin slice of **french bread** per serving, slathered with **Dijon mustard**, dotted with minced **parsley** and tucked under the sauce line so to speak.

Simmer all over low heat, the pot covered, for about 40 minutes and serve in soup bowls, each portion framed with small chunks (Mr. Nabokov would have called them chunklets) of boiled potato.

PASTEL DE CHOCLO
—A Chilean casserole—

Representing the deepest culinary South, this agrodolcean third cousin to a goulash is a souvenir of the lamented Curanto's (excepting, of course, its Rorschachian carpet!) across from The Cannery on San Francisco's north waterfront. A potentially diffuse dish, this: your job and mine is to translate a tumble of ricocheting ingredients into a poised *pas-de-six* of gastronomical fluidity. The novelist confronted with syllabic crumbs on his thesaurial chopping board sets out, of course, on a similar mission in finesse.

In a well-heated skillet brown until nice and crispy 1 pound of cubed, **paprika**-seasoned **round steak** without added fat, stirring in, midway along, 2 chopped **onions**. Then lower the heat and simmer all, the skillet covered, for 10 or more minutes, stirring occasionally, until your meat is tender. Meanwhile, warm 1-1/2 cups of **frozen corn** in a little **butter** with 2 or 3 good pinches of **sugar**, stirring constantly; reserve.

Now in a lightly buttered casserole arrange over the beef and onions 4 or 5 tablespoons each of **raisins** and pitted, chopped **black olives** (Greek, of course, are best), plus a quartered hard boiled **egg**, and cover all with the corn.

Lastly, top the lot with an **egg** beaten with a little water, sprinkle sugar lightly over all, and bake your Pastel de Choclo at 400° for 25 minutes, or until the top is golden. Serve with a dish of **yogurt** and pass the paprika.

CHICKEN APPLE SAUSAGES WITH BLACK BEAN PURÉE, AVOCADO VINAIGRETTE AND SOUR CREAM

Modern California chefs love this kind of harmonization, a far cry from the meat-potato-and-veg of olden times standing their ground in separate areas of a crowded plate. The point here is that everything mooshes together nicely in an embrace of vinaigrette, cream and purée.

> Simple fry **chicken apple sausages** (or Italian sausages if they're more readily available) for about 15 minutes without added fat, then drain them; purée **black beans** (see page 131); and make a vinaigrette of 2 parts **olive oil** to 1 of **red wine vinegar** along with quite a bit of diced **avocado**. Then arrange the sausages on the beans, spoon vinaigrette over all and top with **sour cream or yogurt**.

ITALIAN SAUSAGE WITH WHITE BEANS AND SALSA VERDE

A crash course here in Modern California bistro cookery: you have it all, the beans, the salsa, the layering of ingredients.

I can hear it being described by a sonorous host in one of our upscale modern beaneries peopled by the multi-media brigade, and that reminds me of the tweedy orator, now stilled alas, who worked the room at a lamented candelit bistro, complete with masseuse of the Steinway ivories, in San Francisco's gritty yet gracious SOMA. Virtually unrivalled in mellifluity on the dining circuit, Reid Gilmore could tell you *"we have a lovely sautéed sweetbreads tonight, in a Normandy sauce finished with Calvados"* and it would almost sound as if he were making love.

> Put a cup of **cannellini or Great Northern beans** in a saucepan with water to cover, bring to a boil, cook for a minute, remove from the fire and soak for an hour with a light sprinkle of **thyme**; then simmer them, covered, for a good hour or more until they're no longer chewy. You may need to add water along the way.
>
> (And since writing the above I've discovered tinned, cooked "butter beans" imported from Italy — they only need to be warmed up. So much for changing recipe horses in the middle of this book's stream).
>
> During the final lap of that simmering fry 2 good quality **Italian sausages** per serving for 12 to 15 minutes, having pricked them with a fork before cooking and turning them frequently for even browning — they should lose all evidence of rawness but not be tough; then drain them.
>
> And make a simple salsa verde with 2 parts **olive oil**, 1 of **red wine vinegar**, lots of minced **parsley** and 4 or 5 **large capers** per serving.
>
> Place the sausages on top of the beans, lined up like good mirror images to left and right, and spoon the salsa over all. Slightly cupped plates (Japanese peasant pottery, for instance) are ideal for this somewhat vertical combination with its lively liquid component.

ALTERNATE VERSION:

Fry the sausages as above, omit the beans and salsa and serve over **poached apples** prepared as follows:

Wash, scrub and quarter the desired number of apples, core and slice them into half moons and put them in a saucepan with a little water; bring to a boil and simmer until soft while the sausages are frying on the next burner.

MINI CASSOULET

As Waverley Root notes in his charming bible, *The Food of France*, arguments grow hot about the "correct" ingredients of a cassoulet. It's as touchy a subject, he says, as the proper construction of a mint julep in certain parts of the American South. But at least everyone agrees that beans are the chief protagonist in this rustic ragoût. After that it's every chef for himself; a composite of method and whim is the norm, as indeed it is in most human endeavors, from cooking cassoulet to conducting Brahms' First for the 432nd time.

Our recipe makes no claim to be complete, it's designed for the fairly harried home chef who wants a cassoulet fix without too much fuss. Not here the pork shoulder, sausage, mutton, bacon and preserved goose gathered together in some cassoulets de Toulouse, just sausage and beans and some flavorings. Root doesn't mention the tomato element, but Elizabeth David and Alma Lach do. Heaven knows where I got the idea of adding cream, no cookbook I know mentions such a schismatic component. But I think you'll find this little cassoulet very tasty just the same.

And Toulouse, cassoulet hq.? A vibrant, gritty university town with, as late as 1999, an element of Haight Ashbury East.

Soak and boil a cup or more of **cannellini or Great Northern beans** as in the recipe for **Italian Sausage** and Beans on the previous page and brown some Italian sausages and drain them.

Then in a skillet soften 1 small minced **onion** and a pressed **garlic** clove in a little **olive oil**, stir in a tablespoon of **tomato paste**, a small chopped **tomato**, 1/3 cup or more of undiluted **beef broth**, a jigger or more of **cream,** a bit of **sage** and bring all this to a boil; stir in the beans and transfer the lot to a baking dish.

Arrange the ingredients in this dish as follows: beans and sauce on the bottom, sausages next, then **breadcrumbs** with a little grated **dry jack or parmesan cheese**, and a little melted **butter** on top. Then bake your mini cassoulet uncovered at 350° for 45 minutes, and run it under the broiler briefly before serving. It will actually be bubbling!

TRANSPORTING THE BISTRO: Since this cassoulet keeps warm nicely in its casserole, it's a good dish to take to a shut-in laid up with an orthopedic disorder and unable to cook. For this purpose I can also recommend our Chicken Onslow-Ford (page 97), substituting for the pasta Marcus' Potato Salad (page 48).

CHOUCROUTE GARNIE

(4 servings)

Spectacular, the ultimate carnivore's delight, and it saves a trip to a Paris brasserie where it's not always quite as good as when Anne Bloomfield does this recipe. If there's any secret to her success it is, I'd say, tipping the bottle of dry vermouth or white wine into the choucroute pot at a slightly more rakish angle than that adopted by the timid chef. Was it Mae West who said nothing succeeds like excess? Well, choucroute garnie is not an inelegant dish, but it's all about heartiness and should be prepared with a certain abandon, especially in regard to the lubrication which makes that cabbage sing.

Meanwhile I must admit I'm intrigued by the notion of an Asian chef in San Francisco who leavens his version of good ol' C.G. with a neighborly helping of poached apples or pears. That, I strongly suspect, is not an idea that would have been embraced at Hardtke, the Tadich Grill of West Berlin, where we had an estimable choucroute lunch, a Schlachtplatte, some years ago.

That was a big day, climaxed by an act and a half of *Lohengrin* at the Deutsche Oper followed by a healthy fraction of a Philharmonic concert across town. The taxi driver who shepherded us from Wagnerian procession to Bartók concerto took our concert-hopping in stride, quickly dialing his FM to a Beethoven sonata.

Traveling to East Berlin for the Komische Oper during the days of divided Berlin was less congenial: at one S-Bahn station you had to drop your passport into slot A, a veritable operatic Lion's Mouth, and pray it would emerge, after an agonizing *luftpause*, from slot B, and without a flunking grade from some Grand Inquisitor lurking in a baggy suit between A and B.

- In a heavy pot with a cover soften 1 very thick slice of **slab bacon or pancetta** per serving, then reserve, leaving the bacon fat in the pot and soften therein 1 giant chopped **onion**.
- Now take an approximately 30-ounce can of good quality **sauerkraut** (Libby's, for instance, with no ingredients other than cabbage, salt and water), put the contents into a strainer, rinse liberally in cold running water and squeeze out the liquid thoroughly.
- Combine the nearly dry sauerkraut with the onion along with 1-1/2 cups of **dry vermouth or white wine**, 1/3 cup of **red wine vinegar**, 20 **juniper berries**, 10 **whole peppercorns** and 2 tablespoons of **caraway seed**; bring all to a boil and cook over the lowest possible heat for 30 minutes. More wine may be needed along the way.
- Next, bury in the sauerkraut 1 thin **smoked pork chop** per serving and the reserved bacon, plus some **cloves**, and simmer covered for about 30 minutes.
- Then bury in the kraut 1 good quality extra-long **frankfurter** per serving (second choice would be a small peeled garlic sausage) and cover and simmer another 30 minutes. All the liquid should be absorbed; if, five minutes before serving, that is not the case, adjust the flame.

To serve: separate the meats from the kraut, trying not to let the bacon get tangled (it could be cooked separately), then arrange separate piles of meats & kraut, or one around the other, adding to your display a supporting chorus of 1 whole boiled **potato** per serving. Be sure to pass a pot of **Dijon mustard** at the table.

Twenty-seven years after that S-Bahn Suspense, "East" Germany welcomed us: we were on a Roots trip, finding the village churches (or partial updates thereof) in Saxony where Anne's Lutheran forebears four and five generations ago were pastors. An Iowa or Missouri, this, with umulauts. And inn breakfasts groaning with sausages, good dark breads and yogurts of many shades. At nestled-in-the-countryside Etzdorf a volunteer brass band was assembling in the chuchyard — not for we Amerikaners, though, their job was to play, with touching solemnity, for a couple's fiftieth wedding anniversary. Very moving indeed.

And now I see by my atlas we were not very many kilometers from the Odyssyean route of Third Reich diarist Victor Klemperer's surreal escape from bombed-out Dresden in '45, the tissue of forged papers and other deceptions necessitated thereby suggesting to the much-harrassed professor (who was, by the way, the first cousin of Lotte Lehmann's *almost* lover in old Hamburg) a tale out of Sherlock Holmes, with his good wife the "tour manager."

Well, we were traveling in a land that had experienced a kind of ideological strip tease, shedding one big veil of Naziism, another of Communism, and in 1998, to an outsider, even after no dividing line truly presented itself outside the windows of the Paris-Frankfurt-Dresden express, it remained exotic somehow, and certainly fragile when one beheld Dresden's intermittent ruins, the little Orangerie, for instance, standing near downtown looking sweet as well as broken. But perhaps it was merely because I knew the history that I had to pinch myself in the city's teeming old hauptbahnhof, discount its just-possibly Hitchcockian atmosphere up there on the high platform awaiting the Vienna train and remind myself, you're not in the Eastern zone anymore.

RED CABBAGE WITH GARLIC SAUSAGES LANDAIS

Another homage to Elizabeth David, whose name even appears in Jonathan Raban novels. Multiply this recipe and you have a company dish most guests will not have experienced before — the agrodolcean aroma at your door will mesmerize them into thinking you're the proprietor of a French country inn . . .

It was near the piney Landes of this recipe that I glimpsed a shadowed hillside from the window of a crowded *rapide* and had this exquisite sense of déjà vu, a poetic, indeed almost erotic response to a dark yet verdant slice of landscape that seemed to beckon me to that Other Dimension we read about in a Nabokov novel, say, and sometimes feel on the brink of actually entering, if only we could. Is it death? Is it the womb? Don't laugh.

Two years later I had an answer. Visiting the excavated site of the southern California prep school to which I'd been banished forty years earlier I was amazed to see, to the south of campus, a shadowed hillside that must, with its almost cradling curve, have comforted a homesick eight-year-old unaccustomed to the sweet-scented tropics and pimply sadistic roommates (not to mention chipped beef) and planted in the deepest recesses of his soul a memory.

What did I come to love in southern Cal? Riding the thundering "big red cars" of the Pacific Electric interurbans, eating High Sin chocolate cake at the Farmers' Market way out Wilshire Boulevard, lunching off a rickety tray attached to Dr. Mason's Buick at one of those new-fangled drive-ins such as we didn't have in dowdy old San Francisco.

But to the cabbage . . .

Quarter, core and slice rather thin — you may have to do some shredding too — 1 medium **red cabbage** as well as 2 **apples**; also slice 2 **red onions** and julienne 2 **sweet red peppers**. Put these items, carefully avoiding military stacking, in a large pot and season with:

>3 good tablespoons of **brown sugar**
>
>1 pressed **garlic** clove
>
>**chervil**, **mace** and **ground cloves**, a virtual 1/4 teaspoon each
>
>thin strips of the peel of 1/2 a small **orange**

Now moisten all with a near-cup of **red wine** and a bit less **red wine vinegar**, cover and cook over quite a low flame, for about 1-1/2 hours. The first 70 minutes or so can be done somewhat ahead, allowing you quality time in your favorite coffee house where, in San Francisco at least, your neighbors are likely to be speaking French, Japanese and Turkish.

Twenty minutes before serving, add 1 sliced **garlic sausage** per portion. At this point you should take the cover off and reduce somewhat the liquid element beneath the apple-cabbage-onion forest in your pot. You do want your stew moist (it should glisten), but not the texture of vegetables in soup. When the stew is ready serve it with a pot of **Dijon mustard** — I love to stir some through all the meat/fruit/veg.

CARMEL HAM AND PEACHES ANNA WITH SWEET POTATO BISCUITS

(multiple servings)

This aggressively retro combination is firmly associated in my mind with dinners in roomy rented houses on the north side of Ocean Avenue in Carmel-by-the-Sea, the sun still up, the sound of the surf in the distance, diners exhilarated by tennis and laughing off sunburn — the same sunburn that attacked me in my beloved Carmel when I was a chubby little gourmet-to-be sixty years ago.

My first "dining out" experiences, age of three, were in Carmel, especially at that snow white Andalusian hostelry La Ribera, now Doris Day's Cypress Inn, at the corner of Lincoln and Seventh. I remember so well the copiously syruped griddle cakes served at breakfast in the beamed, almost ecclesiastical dining room (last table on the left, by the window, near the fireplace, pretty tiles all about).

Then, a few seasons later, there was roast turkey with a giblety gravy smooshed into the crater of a mashed potato Etna at cozy upstairs Sade's, powdery light brown biscuits along with unremembered meat-and-veg at the very tea-roomy Normandy Inn, and *rice griddle cakes* in the exotic recesses of the San Carlos coffee shop over the hill in Monterey, not to mention the chowder and dark, crusty filet of sole at Pop Ernt's.

And those picnics on the beach, my Victorian father in Fitzgerald-era knickers, floppy tennis hat and consulting-room necktie. The fare was always the same: steak on buns, in which baby teeth were often lost, and corn on the cob in bulk. Heaven, in short — except for the anxiety attending dental distress.

And sand, of course, crept into those buns.

Bake a 12-serving **pre-cooked bone-in ham** for about 30 minutes; meanwhile, in a separate pan, make a paste of:

1/2 cup of **brown sugar**

2 tablespoons of **dry sherry**

1/2 teaspoon or more of **Dijon mustard**

1/2 teaspoon each of **curry powder**, **allspice** and **nutmeg**

Take the meat from the oven, score the fatty parts on top into diamond shapes, spread the paste over the diamonds, and on top of the paste arrange halved peeled **peaches** cut side down (by the way, canned are entirely acceptable) before returning the meat to the oven for another 30 minutes. You may need to toothpick them down.

Use the pan juices to make a light gravy and serve your ham-and-peaches with sweet potato biscuits:

Mix 3/4 cup of mashed **sweet potatoes**, 2/3 cup of **milk** and 4 tablespoons of melted **butter**. Sift together 1-1/4 cups of **flour**, 4 teaspoons of **baking powder**, 1 tablespoon of **sugar** and 1/2 teaspoon of **salt** and add this mixture to the sweet potato combo. Drop the dough in greased muffin pans and bake at 450° for 15 minutes.

BISCUITS, MY PASSION! Powdery light brown specimens surfaced in my life again recently on Amtrak — while the big rigs purred by in the Nevada dawn, lit up like pinball machines.

PORK CHOPS COURLANDAISE AND SQUASH FRITTERS GIGI

This duo makes for rather a period piece meal, the chops coated with an old-fashioned gravy and my mother's fritters cooked in a steady flow of oil. But the gravy takes on a special lightness and zing with the infusion of lemon, and the fritters are comfort food extraordinaire. I like the way the puffy discs of light brown black-specked squash nestle against the dark bulk of the chops — go for it, you plate arrangers.

I'm sure my mother served these fritters from one of the many little kitchens she was at war with during those old Carmel summers in rented board-and-batten houses near the sea. Perhaps just after the long drive from San Francisco, down through Silicon Valley, which was prune groves then (and there was fresh juice at the Nipa Hut), past

Gilroy (where, one year, a truckload of GIs just ahead of us smiled meaningfully at my older sisters), and on to Salinas (grilled cheese sandwiches at the Santa Lucia Inn, a comfy Mission Revival post house). Finally, at the top of Carmel Hill (trumpets, please!) there was a view of the ocean pretty for the others in our Chevy and ecstasy for me.

And at the house of the year, a vintage one we hoped, woodsmoke in the air and carillons of plinging coathangers waiting in musty little closets where we'd stow our sneakers.

A bittersweet memory: in August '41 we took a house in Carmel for a shorter period than usual, further away from the beach than was our custom, and something seemed not quite right. It was as if, like an animal sensing through its own brand of sensations an imminent earthquake, I could feel Pearl Harbor ahead . . .

> Dip **pork chops** in a little beaten **egg** and brown them in **butter**, very briskly on the first side and with less flame on the second, then cover the pan and simmer them for at least 10 to 12 minutes.
>
> Stir 2 tablespoons of **flour** into the drippings, moisten with a good 3/4 cup of slightly diluted **beef broth** (I prefer a brand proclaiming "rich" broth), simmer about 2 minutes, and just before serving stir in 4 or 5 tablespoons of **lemon** juice, lots of minced **parsley** and a good teaspoon of **dry vermouth**, reducing your sauce to taste.
>
> Serve these chops over stir-fried cabbage (which you bathe in boiling water first) or, a little more racy, squash fritters made as follows:
>
> Cut several unpeeled **summer squash** into very thin rounds, dip them in **egg** with a little **milk**, then **flour** them and shake off the excess.
>
> In a skillet sauté the rounds in hot **olive oil** over a medium flame until they're lightly browned on each side: you'll doubtless have to sauté in batches, so keep the first-made fritters warm in the oven, on paper towels, while you finish cooking the later batches.
>
> NOTE: Gigi's fritters would make a fascinating starter with sweet, gingery "Asian Tamarind Sauce" for a dip. A comprehensively stocked deli or supermarket should have it . . . and on the subject of pork chops: they're always good finished with a healthy stir-in of 2 or 3 tablespoons of Dijon mustard and a short cup of dry vermouth or leftover white wine, plus some dill weed. About 4 minutes' near-constant rotary action on your part during your chops' home stretch of simmering should produce a creamy cream-less sauce.

PORK CHOPS AL LATTE WITH GRAPES

And here a more contemporary offering in the pork chop department.

Now I experimented with a beet purée as a good prim foil for such cholesterolic stuff, but I couldn't make it taste like anything a truly sane person would want to eat. I do rather like beets — best of all sliced, chilled and parsleyed atop a pyre of room-temperature garlic mashed potatoes — but as Laurie Colwin reassures us, "A life without beets or lima beans is a fine, full life."

Actually, in 2002 I think beets are picking up speed on my list of favored foods. Meanwhile I see that a Silicon Valley restaurant is serving coq au vin incorporating a certain unconsulted red veg. At the risk of sounding like a culinary right winger I must, wherever I stand on beets, and very solemnly in Mrs. David's name, on a stack of tattered old *Joy of Cookings*, cry No, no, no.

> Coat and brown pork chops as in the previous recipe, deglaze the pan with a little **dry sherry** and season with **rosemary** to taste.
>
> After the chops have simmered for 10 minutes stir in a very small amount of **flour**, pour over them a cup of **milk** and continue cooking them with the pan uncovered, stirring the sauce as it thickens: the consistency you want is that of a very light cream sauce and this will take at least 5 minutes.
>
> Just before serving, stir in at least half a cup of **seedless red grapes**, regular or baby size, a splash more of sherry and serve the chops-grapes-and-sauce with, or over, plain rice.

—6-hour minimum—
ROAST PORK OR DUCK WITH GLAZED DRIED FRUITS OLD SUNSET

(4 servings)

These dried fruits are an addictive preparation, poised nicely between sweet and sour. Traditionally we've mated them with pork for a Christmas feast, but duck — rather as they used to combine it with fruits at the excellent Warszawa restaurant in Berkeley — makes a great partner.

So now you know, this is a Polish dish!

> Cook your festival roast to taste, adding in the last half hour a coating of 1/4 cup of **brown sugar**, 1/4 teaspoon of **ginger** and a tablespoon of **vinegar**. Serve with glazed dried fruits prepared as follows: Add to 1 package of **mixed dried fruits** 1 sliced **lemon** and pour boiling water over all; soak 6 to 8 hours. Then drain and reserve the liquid for use in gravy. Melt 1-1/2 tablespoons of **butter** with 2 tablespoons of brown sugar and a little **cinnamon**, stir well until the sugar is dissolved, than add the drained fruits-and-lemon and heat, stirring lightly, until the fruit is warm and coated.

RETRO PORK SHOULDER POT ROAST WITH CIDER

A "Gigi" recipe, this, and a good one, a near-sauerbraten with a velvety camel's hair sauce to blanket crumbly slices of tender pork.

But I don't remember my mother ever cooking it. (Have I told you "Gigi" was our three-year-old son's name for his grandmother?) Finding in my files a pristine copy of these directions in her majestic hand was like locating a long lost Furtwängler recording in the outer reaches of one's record collection. Note that since this pork scarcely requires a knife to unlock its meaty delights it works eminently well for a plate-on-lap dinner — if you must eat that way . . .

Another pork dish, which I shall only mention in passing, I have a very soft spot for, because it was one of the staples of our happy home before I took over most of the cooking from a busy mother/volunteer/political activist/Preservation expert.

Enter here thick chops fried with cumbersome brown-sugared apple halves on their backs and bathed in sour cream. Well, it's much too heavy a package to feature in this book, much too dated, it seems now the culinary equivalent of one of those baggy leopard-skin one-piece bathing suits you see in the window of a store featuring period clothing to be worn by curvaceous damsels of our G-stringed era as a joke.

- Buy about 2 pounds of fresh **pork shoulder butts**, cut away any excess fat and **flour** it and roll it in **vegetable oil** with **pepper**, **thyme**, **oregano** and **fennel seed**.
- In a large pot brown the meat on all sides, then drain off the accumulated fat; now add 1/2 cup of **chicken broth**, 1 cup of **apple cider**, 2 pressed **garlic** cloves and a small sprinkle of **nutmeg**, cover the pot tightly and simmer all for close to 2 hours, turning the meat once or twice. You may need to add a bit more cider before the meat is done.
- When it is done make a gravy by stirring 2 teaspoons of **flour** mixed with water into the drippings, cooking it very briefly and adding 1/2 cup of **yogurt** along with sufficient cider to keep this volatile sauce from thickening into a grumous paste. After a brief final stir serve your meat-and-gravy with mashed potatoes or puréed celery root (boiled and diced first, of course) combined with a little mashed potato.
- NOTE: This pork is delicious cold, with a not too complex mayonnaise. And nice puffy rolls of the Parker House type seem to me natural support staff here — rolls like the ones I devoured in Fort Ord hospital where, under post-pneumonia observation, this dutiful GI spent weekdays in bed on Ward C before signing out on weekend pass and driving up to San Francisco Saturday mornings, only to return Sunday nights for five more days in a more-or-less-horizontal position, waiting for the next batch of delectables from that talented baker, before the next weekend on the town eating at Alouette, Veneto and the other favorites of the day.

CONFIT DE CANARD AND DORDOGNIAN TRIMMINGS

If someone had told me in, say, 1964 that confit de canard with lentils, apples, potatoes or what have you was going to be the rage of American restaurants — well, American restaurants in New York, San Francisco, Los Angeles and other gastronomic meccas — I probably would have told that someone he or she was indulging in wishful thinking based on undue expectations of the extent to which French country cooking, southwest variety, might conquer the world of hamburgers, hot dogs and ham with pineapple slices.

Now the home chef is honor bound to produce at least a halfway decent imitation of what he can find so readily at his neighborhood bistro. Yes, we've come a far distance since my expatriate Wisconsin cousin R.D. Blumenfeld, editor of the *London Express* in the reign of his good friend George V, proclaimed: "The Americans, they are fine people, but their wives won't cook, and most of them, nourished on pie and flapjacks and Susan B. Anthony's exhortations, have indigestion."

I'm afraid, though, I still mount my pulpit now and then to suggest that one or five items on a plate may be preferable to the ancient trinity of meat-potato-veg. And at the risk of sounding like an awful snob I must admit being somewhat disconcerted one recent nippy night in California's Gold Country — not quite so gastronomically hip as Carmel, Yountville and Mendocino — to find at the far edge of my copious plate of excellent and more-or-less up-to-date pasta a portion of broccoli and Hollandaise sauce that seemed to have been delivered by decade-vaulting lateral pass from, say, 1965.

Ah, Comfort Food in the shadow of those gorgeous foothills.

. . . And after homey Victorian Nevada City we dipped to the Central Valley, California's nuts-and-bolts valley, past those buttes set down by inspired mistake near Highway 5 (there's a sister bunch south of Padua in Italy), then uphill again, skirting Clear Lake, and down a woodsy corkscrew into the *paradiso* of Napa Valley, a New World Dordogne crafted by the creator when He or She was in an especially good mood. The shock of urban Cool lunching among the yuppies at Tra Vigne in St. Helena after our brush with some of California's true bits of "Middle America" was . . . well, as the French say, *quelque chose*.

The Michelin inspectors coming to this valley will have to bring rosettes, lots of 'em.

Cheat here and use the contents of a Petrossian jar of Confit de Canard from a "gourmet" food shop . . .

Remove the contents of a 12-ounce jar, separating the **goose fat** from the pieces of **duck breast**, then sauté the duck in a skillet, skinside down, until crispy. Now turn the pieces over, reduce the heat and simmer for 10 minutes.

Serve your quick confit with poached apples (page 162) or potatoes fried with garlic in the above goose fat.

WURST WITH WARM POTATO SALAD AND SIMPLE GREENS OR BAKED KALE

Baked kale, our alternative green, is a strange one: it emerges from the oven its leaves like miniature trees pressed flat by some exuberant aggressor in a canine cartoon. It even rustles like foliage in a breeze when you pick it up to eat. By the way, try a hamburger topped with baked kale and yogurt: this is creamy crunchiness extraordinaire.

Boil **sausages** of your choice and serve them with warm boiled sliced **potatoes** and **salad greens** in a **mustard vinaigrette**. Or substitute for those greens baked kale, prepared as follows:

Wash, dry and trim 1 bunch of **kale** and toss the leaves in a mixing bowl with 1 or 2 tablespoons of **olive oil** and up to 3 or 4 (!) pressed **garlic** cloves.

Spread the leaves flat on a cookie sheet and bake them at 400° for 10 minutes, then turn them and bake another 10 minutes. Serve immediately thereafter.

OXTAIL STEW WITH TURNIPS AND FENNEL

Oxtail stew reminds me of Roman trattorie like Galeassi with its attractive terrace opening onto the slightly scruffy piazza of Santa Maria in Trastevere. The grissini in a glass or sweet-dough rolls carefully positioned by your napkin, the pitchers of tangy, grassy Frascati, the warmth in the air even in March: it all rushes back to the front of one's consciousness thirty years on.

And how can I talk about Rome without mentioning Piperno and its roast kid, the fritto misto of zucchini, mozzarella and risotto, the famous oil-fried artichokes served with their stems in the air, like proud menhirs looming in a miniature Monument Valley.

In a large pot brown 2 pounds of **oxtails** without fat over moderately high heat, then lower the heat some, push them aside and soften a chopped **onion** in a little **olive oil**, adding 1 pressed **garlic** clove after the onion colors — this won't take long; now drain off the accumulated fat.

Cover your oxtails-and-onions with 14 ounces of **beef broth** and some water, add a little **oregano** and **rosemary** and a fistful of **fennel** sliced into rings, and simmer all for 2 hours with the top on. You will doubtless need more water along the way, several cups in fact.

Then stir in a cup of peeled and diced **turnips** along with a heaping tablespoon of **tomato paste** and continue the simmering for another 20 minutes, cover partly off. Finally, just before serving, garnish the stew with minced **parsley**. Mashed potatoes would make an appropriate sponge for its aromatic sauce.

SAVOIE SUPPER

For a "letting down the hair" meal, good in the city but maybe better by the fire in a mountain cabin.

Matter of fact, it would have been just right the evening of my U.S. Army career when a group of us headquarters company nerds, pressed momentarily into driving elephantine trucks through the French countryside on some comic opera maneuvers, ended up taking dinner at the boondocks social club of a Polish auxiliary corps, displaced persons, I believe, serving as night watchmen as a first step on their road to American citizenship.

Saarland beer flowed, a Beethoven quartet came over the radio, and here we were, Americans in romantic-looking field jackets out of Hemingway breaking bread among Poles smack in the middle of Touraine. Unfortunately I've forgotten what we ate, but I do know this was the first, and last, time in my life I felt I was inhabiting a remote paragraph in some exotic novel of war and peace.

Next day we were off again, lumbering through the garden of France, the naughtier drivers among us perversely allowing their two-and-a-half-tonners to backfire, scaring the livestock out of their Courbet calm.

A month later we were on the road again, but with all romanticism withheld: this time we slaves in drab fatigues had to camp like strewn baggage in our trucks for several days near the tiniest of Sologne hamlets, a place named Ennordes, I think, an identification as mournful as that attached to Mr. Milne's ever-drooping Eeyore; and there was nothing to eat but C rations (hence my aversion to tinned pineapple to this day) along with the French bread, very good actually, which the more imaginative of us found by knocking on the unmarked village door out of which local babushkas, living in the Middle Ages not many kilometers east of Route Nationale Numero 20, were detected exiting with warm loaves under their arms.

> In a large skillet fry thinly sliced **red potatoes** in **bacon fat**, turning them often, and don't be afraid to add more fat if it's needed.
> In another pan fry some **link sausages** without added fat and drain on paper towels. And a few minutes before supper time fry 1 or 2 **eggs** per serving in a non-stick pan without fat.
> Serve the potatoes topped with egg or eggs and bordered by the links, dare one say it, "links und rechts." And pass a pot of mustard.

OR: If you happen to have doggy-bagged some smoked ham from a first-class Hunan restaurant, substitute this lively item for the links, depositing pieces of ham over your eggs.

DINNER AT ALEX'S

In 1986 we discovered Templeton, a short rise out of Paso Robles on U.S. 101, sleepy, oak-lined, a cross between artistic and hick, with Dianne Garth's charming inn (whimpering closet doors, croaking loo, magnificent breakfasts, the sound at night of long freight trains rumbling clumsily down from the Cuesta Pass) and a down-home restaurant, Alex's BBQ, where we ate our California "ranch" dinners, specialty of the region with their celery, olives and crackers, creamy croutonned salad and a main course of grilled meat, potatoes of choice, beans, salsa, garlic bread and, if baked potatoes were ordered, sour cream as well.

I always ordered french fries, and borrowed Anne's sour cream for *them*, applying the all-purpose salsa to sweetbreads or chops. Alex's, alas, no longer graces Templeton, and to recreate a feed in the spirit, at least, of this engaging eatery I propose the adjacent Easy Ranch Dinner . . .

The sequel to the above is that as this book headed toward the press we lunched at the original Alex's, a mother church as it were of Santa Maria style barbecue at Shell Beach. This is a small resort south of San Luis Obispo with tawny hills bearing down on it like the landscape equivalents of mother hens — and it's the neighbor, by the way, of the town whose name inspired W.C. Fields to add to his two-legged menagerie Mr. A. Pismo Clam.

Not only were the beef ribs absolutely *comme il faut* but our sweet-as-apple-pie waitress also served us an excellent deep fried calamari steak, surf schnitzel in other words, breaded to the nines but not overbearingly so and accompanied by an uncloying tartar sauce any city-slicker chef would have been proud of. Well, I intoned, this is one of the three best restaurants between Silicon Valley and Santa Barbara along 101 and our waitress had to agree.

But hold the ketchup — that "barbarous adjunct" as the impish Miss Toklas would say.

1. Fry some good **lamb chops** that you've marinated in a little **olive oil**.
2. Boil until nearly done some sliced **potatoes**, then sauté them slowly in a large pan with a little **butter**, turning them often to achieve an even browning — these are, in other words, our "broasted potatoes."
3. Buy some good quality bottled **salsa** for the chops, **sour cream** for the potatoes, and warm a can of upscale **kidney or black beans**.

Postscript by the Sea:

On the high-speed boat from Nice to Corsica — the name of the line, amazingly enough, is *Ferryterranée* — you stand at the stern and watch the fast boil of the ferry's wake. Spray and a meridional hypnosis are your portion in this Mediterranean surround. Thanks to the curvature of the earth the boat seems to be scratching an incision down the middle of a great blue egg laid flat as a Dutch landscape. The sky, of course, has become a dome; the French coast is disappearing.

We traveled to Corsica to visit Henri Blumenfeld, *Monsieur l'Inspecteur* I call him, because he looks like a seasoned Maigret. Henri had the good sense to buy a vacation home overlooking the elegant bay of Calvi, a pristine crescent that reminds me of Carmel-by-the-Sea only there's a fortress at its head instead of Point Lobos, and the mountains surveying the scene, with a toy train rattling by down near Lumio plage, are considerably more heroic than any hillside the Monterey Peninsula can muster. No highway in sight is wider than two lanes: this is a time-warp isle, a mystery even to savvy travel agents.

Henri also had the good sense to marry Marie Jącqueline who's a keen chef as well as the superb designer and custodian of a bougainvillaea and cactus-stuffed *jardin*. Thanks to her I can tell you about a symphony of gastronomic browns providing a footnote to our Daube recipe several pages back.

Marie Jacqueline dished up a daube featuring sanglier, that's wild boar, marinating it in red wine, garlic, shallots and local herbs, and cooking it long and well, without tomatoes you should note. M.J.'s harmonizations for this aromatic stew were the biggest cannellini beans I've seen yet, surpassing, I believe, their Oakland Greek counterparts, and chestnuts simply taken from the tin and boiled to perfection.

The warm, gently humid air on Henri's terrace was superb, the company, including son Alexis, a marine biologist of a lyrical turn, excellent, the sunset a gorgeous rose, the Paris plane landed neatly in the distance, a ferry eyed its dock across the bay, the toy train mumble-rumbled by on schedule near crisp-cut little houses straight out of Cézanne, and, as Henri observed of it all, "C'est presque trop parfait." But only *almost* too perfect!

. . . Then it was back to Nice, the crossing too rough for a passenger to conjure metaphors, and home to San Francisco where, at ebullient Plouf, I was seduced by an upwardly mobile but not too chi-chi Salade Niçoise, perhaps the most elegant in my experience while retaining bistro status. To "duplicate" it you could begin with our salade on page 3, but for the tuna element employ seared ahi slices, for the olive component tapenade toasts with their caper-accented spread, and weave through the lot strands of poached fennel. And where is the book on *100 Salades Niçoises*?

In Corsica I asked Henri (as I had other of the several European cousins I know on the Jewish side of my much-researched family tree — I seem, by the way, as what you might call an "artistic type" to identify much more with my Jewish half, although I was very close to my mother), at any rate I asked Henri how his immediate family had survived the Second World War in Paris, and he told me he and his siblings were distributed among several Catholic schools where, more or less as in a Louis Malle film, they sank into the Aryan woodwork.

Matthias my Berlin Blumenfeld cousin told me "a good German" *saved* his grandfather back in the 30s and Matthias' uncle went on to be a distinguished diplomat in Willy Brandt's post-war government.

In Holland my cousin Rob, the grandson of Freud's larger-than-life colleague and eventual "victim" Viktor Tausk (they had a disagreement and Viktor committed suicide) told me his Viennese father, working in Holland when the Nazis arrived, had to produce his pedigree, and when Marius Tausk's lawyer back in Vienna tallied it up as extremely damning from the Nazis' point of view, Marius wired his lawyer, "That cookie recipe you sent me is not quite to my taste, would you send me another?"

But we've gotten a long way from Corsica . . .

Sidewalk Postscript:

Now I'm on the way to my favorite coffee house/sidewalk café in my neighborhood — not one of the big chain coffee houses! — because I have my usual afternoon date to scribble on paper napkins.

Yes, the cocoa is lovely, those Moroccan fellows make the best this side of Cazenave in Bayonne; and you can order it in English, French or Arabic. But it's this inscribing on napkins that matters: a book has to be conceived somehow. Well, the regulars are at the next tables, maintaining their privacy and observing mine. It's study hall, of course, with medical and dental schools not far off; I suppose I might learn some anatomy if I listened carefully. But the confessions of lovers are more interesting.

Then there's the distinguished looking woman who works so assiduously on Greek. When she has fellow students of Plato at her side I call her group the Spanakopita Brigade.

Meanwhile, on the high street, everything is as yesterday or tomorrow: one's likely to run into Fred the Mahler-loving bookseller with the marvelous muscles, macho

Dino the Greek will be eyeing the girls outside his pizzeria, the pleasant beggar will be saying "Greetings!" in a bright C major. I will cringe at the dental school security officer armed like a Task Force for an invasion by Buck Rogers and his Naughty Martians bent on stealing a drill or two, and I will pity the distracted lady at another coffee house who spends her day bumming cigarettes.

But I'll rejoice in meeting sassy Mrs. Dewson who sells fedoras to the Mayor, I'll discuss the state of the world with Phil the mellow maestro of pots-pans-nuts-bolts as he waters the plants outside his hardware store, I'll happily line up at the French bakery (shades of *Chocolat*) that magnetizes to its door every French-speaking person in the next nine counties, seems to enlarge its repertoire of tarts-croissants-brioches-baguettes-batards every day and even makes a gâteau Basque . . .

And I'll kibbitz with the jolly butcher from Puglia who sells me sausages and lamb and seems to have sprung from a 1935 Hollywood musical and doesn't mind my flamboyant fractured Italian; and I might run into an elegant friend with a zesty poodle who announces in quietly imperial tones, "I'm taking you to lunch at Galette."

I will, in short, enjoy my Upper Fillmore.

—DESSERTS—

MINI MACÉDOINE

This is your simplest everyday non-festive dinner finale, the merest tip of the big berg of desserts to follow in less modest garb . . .

Fill pretty bowls with sliced **orange**, **banana** and **pear,** or whatever fruits are in the market, adding **sugar** and **lemon** juice (but Curaçao is better!), both in rather liberal amounts, and serve with cookies, for instance the hazelnut-and-chocolate zeppelinettes on page 193.

COTTAGE PUDDING WITH CHOCOLATE SAUCE

(4 to 6 servings)

Now we're getting into something a little richer, homey dessert-fix material guaranteed to soothe the man who's tired of macédoine six nights running. The adjacent recipe is a variation on vintage Mrs. Rombauer, page 724 of our old *Joy of Cooking* which has been consulted so much in forty years, and decorated so much with flour, baking powder and improperly aimed egg, that it's almost totally illegible. But buy a new and trendy edition, with neither Cottage nor that other dessert-time security blanket, Chocolate Cake Pudding? Never. As they say in the opera, *Infamia*!

Well, sensing revolution, Joy's publishers have followed their cockily post-classical tome with a reissue of Mrs. Rombauer's original cookbook: here the gastronomical pillars of our nursery years are safe and sound, free from the wrecker's ball.

Whisk together 2 tablespoons of **butter** (at room temperature) and 2 tablespoons of a neutral **oil**; then whisk into the butter/oil 1/2 cup of **sugar** until the mixture is fluffy.

Now whisk in 1 **egg**, a teaspoon of **vanilla** and 1/2 teaspoon of **almond extract**, with fluffiness your continued objective.

Next, whisk in one third of 1/2 cup of **milk** and one third of 1-1/2 cups of **flour** sifted with 2 teaspoons of **baking powder** and repeat the process twice. (A musician would call this operating in ABABAB form).

Now heap the batter into a greased pan 8" by 8" by 2" and bake at 400° for no more than 25 minutes: this pudding is most enticing when a little pale, on the border of undercooked.

And the sauce: gently melt 1/2 square of **Baker's Baking Chocolate** in 3 tablespoons of **milk** and stir until it's smooth, then add 1/3 cup of **sugar** and boil until the brew is the desired consistency; cool it slightly, add a teaspoon of **vanilla** and serve the sauce warm.

ALTERNATIVE! Pour the batter over a layer of marmalade, bake as above and invert before serving; now the sauce is optional.

PEAR BREAD PUDDING WITH AN APRICOT JAM SAUCE

(4 servings)

Bread puddings, like crisps, can be made with just about any fruit, so be advised that the winter treat that follows could easily be adjusted for another season. This culinary genre, great cobbler bowls of soggy fruit-specked goodness, takes me back to the hushed and stately country dining of special-lunches-out in my California youth, to grand salles, say, like the Pebble Beach Lodge Dining Room where Salvador Dali sat solo in the corner, his surreal waxed mustache tickling his Vichysoisse.

Not being a golf type, or in a very high income bracket, I haven't tackled the stately corners of that particular lodge in the years of my maturity, but something of the same *calme-et-luxe* has been savored at the rather less inhibiting Benbow Inn up in the Eel River country. Here, just like in my cherub years, earnest college-kid waitpeople tote aristocratic salads, sandwiches and puddings to neatly dressed trippers to the tune of tinkling ice in tall tea glasses.

And is that a flute playing Debussy in the background?

I like to think bread pudding was served at the monthly salon my great aunt Fannie the pianist used to stage with uncle Sigmund on Division Street, later South Woodlawn, in Chicago. I know sandwiches and Milwaukee beer were part of the ritual; there must have been a grand sweet on the sideboard as well. No clues, alas, in the guest book, a time machine is required.

As an enterprising decade-scaling fly on the wall I see the guests in passionate conversation as they negotiate designer ham on rye, a good foamy substance and the not yet decoded sweet in one or another of those memorabilia-lined houses: Dr. Richard Strauss of Berlin, Ignace Paderewski of "Poland," Mischa Elman of Arkwright Road, London, Myra Hess, Moriz Rosenthal, Xavier Scharwenka, Ernestine Schumann-Heink, Teresa Carreño, Edith Mason Polacco . . .

Listen to the "Brrrs" in several accents as the snow-dusted guests hand their furs and galoshes to the maid, diminutive Fannie darting about in the background.

Cut dry **bread** into enough cube-like pieces to make 5 cups; place half in the bottom of an 8" ovenproof dish and slice 1 large **pear** over the bread. Sprinkle 1/4 cup of **raisins** over the pears and top with the remaining bread; sprinkle another 1/4 cup of **raisins** over this portion of bread.

In a separate bowl beat 2 **eggs**, 2 cups of **milk**, 1/2 cup of **sugar** and 1-1/2 teaspoons of **cinnamon**; pour this mixture over the bread/pear/raisins and soak for 10 minutes. If the bread on top is not completely submerged, press it gently with the back of a spoon so it absorbs the custard.

Now bake the pudding-to-be at 350° for 40 minutes or until it's firm. Serve with a sauce made by heating 1/2 cup of **apricot jam** with 1/4 cup of water.

AND: A caramel sauce is an excellent alternative.

CHOCOLATE BREAD PUDDING WITH CHOCOLATE SAUCE

(4 servings)

Chocolate on chocolate appalls my chief consultant, but tempts me regularly. Obviously there's a market for such indulgence. In New York, for instance, at that rather eccentric Café Nicholson, I've experienced chocolate sauce sinking into the froth of chocolate soufflé, and I'm told that Capsouto Frères down in Tribeca provides the same service for chocomaniacs. The Nicholson goes back many years, perhaps to the time I arrived in New York from Orléans courtesy of Uncle Sam's Federal Express, traveling a circuitous route doubtless thought up by a khaki'd travel agent suffering from at least a mild case of temporary insanity.

First, an admittedly civilized stop for a steak at the old Relais Gastronomique on the mezzanine of Paris' Gare de l'Est (two Michelin rosettes), then an interminable wait for military air transportation at a Frankfurt barracks, next a transatlantic ride via Keflavik, Iceland — and how mortified I am not to be able to impress you with the contents of a snack eaten on Icelandic soil, 'neath the current polar route — which landed us in Springfield, Mass. at 2 a.m., from which exotic point several of us taxied to Manhattan where we saw the January dawn.

I remember a weekend of pastrami sandwiches and a trek to Carnegie Hall for a concert by that soulful young tyrant Guido Cantelli which has just been rescued from Things Past via an historical CD: such elegance and brio, and how delightfully time-out-witting it is to hear in the twenty-first century the exact *sound* of that Sunday afternoon of many years ago, the particular Carnegie acoustic so warm, full and cradling, so sonically aristocratic. And I remember so vividly standing on the steps outside the balcony during intermission, feeling (this is corny, I know) as if those storied walls were about to talk of all the musicians who'd appeared there, Tchaikovsky, Toscanini, Bruno Walter, Cantelli who in rehearsal would exhort the musicians to play with *purity* . . .

Then at Staten Island I found my Austin-Healy which I'd shipped from France and it was decorated with icicles like a Christmas tree.

First off, butter a soufflé pan well.

Now mix 2 heaping teaspoons of **cocoa** with 1 teaspoon of **sugar** and a little of 2 cups of **milk** until a paste is formed; add the rest of the milk and warm the mixture a little to make sure the cocoa is dissolved.

Remove the crusts from 10 thin slices of stale **bread**, cut each slice into 2 or 3 pieces, and **butter** each one. Make two layers in the prepared pan, buttered side up.

Beat 2 **eggs** lightly and add 2 good teaspoons of **sugar**, mixing until the sugar is dissolved. Slowly add the cocoa milk mixture from this recipe's second paragraph, stirring constantly. Add 1/2 teaspoon of **vanilla** and pour your eggs/sugar/milk over the bread mixture and soak the incipient bread pudding for an hour.

Finally, bake it at 325° for an hour, or until a knife inserted in the center comes out clean. For the **chocolate sauce**, see page 177.

AN OPTION: Replace the chocolate sauce with marmalade.

ORANGES TERRAZZA, SOUVENIR OF ROMILLY STREET, SOHO

(4 servings)

This is an excellent light party finale, for winter in particular.

La Terrazza was the only restaurant we could find open late one evening in London after arriving from Paris during a railway strike that drastically slowed ferry landing procedures at Dover (our boat actually circled and circled the port, just like a plane waiting for an invitation into rush-hour Kennedy or fog-bound Heathrow) and forced us to take a bus up to town instead of British Rail. The hands of station clocks, tower clocks, all visible timepieces, moved inexorably on as our tummies growled and thoughts of darkened bistros and shut-tight pubs jammed our minds in the stuffy, gear-grinding bus rattling through lovely complacent Kent, with the sun long sunk in the West. Dropped off, finally, in central London, we rummaged through familiar streets with horrifying thoughts of lost omelettes, scallopini-deprivation and never-to-be-eaten chocolate soufflés. Our desperation became less and less quiet. And then, like the tattered inhabitant of a *New Yorker* cartoon desert island, we spotted the lights, yes lights, of La Terrazza. Never was there such a gastronomic port in a storm.

. . . And next morning we cozily tucked into our cold toast and bitter marmalade at the Marazzi's little hotel in Bloomsbury, surrounded by professor-types in from Manchester or Leeds to visit the British Museum. Storming toward the kitchen, the waiter in less than pristine white jacket would sing out our order, *Due boiled eggie*! And that matutinal siren song lured us back year after year.

Attack with a potato peeler 1 medium **navel orange** per serving and cut the resultant peel into juliennes; cover them with water and boil for 10 or 15 minutes.

Drain, rinse and dry the juliennes; then in a bowl almost cover them with **Curaçao** or some other orange liqueur.

Now for a syrup: boil 1 cup of **sugar** and 1/3 cup of water until it spins a thread and pour it over the juliennes.

Remove all the white from your oranges and slice them into cartwheels. In a serving bowl alternate layers of orange slices with the juliennes and their sauce, and chill.

HOT FRUIT SALAD
—Souvenir of Margaret Costa and Bill Lacy's restaurant, London 1971—

Jolly Margaret Costa was *Gourmet*'s London dining critic and responded warmly to correspondence from an unknown San Franciscan. Look for mention of the Costa-Lacy restaurant in Simon Hopkinson's hilarious and enchanting *The Prawn Cocktail Years*, a trip down a Brit's memory lane and arguably the best cookbook of the Late 90s.

Cut up such fruit as **strawberries**, **bananas**, **grapes**, **oranges** and/or **pineapple**, **sugar** them and let them sit while you're eating dinner so they'll develop plenty of juice.

Then, between main course and dessert, stir 1/2 teaspoon of **rum** per serving into the fruits, put them in individual ovenproof dishes (baked egg ramekins, for instance) and broil them as close to the flame as possible, until the tips of some of the fruit are a little brown.

Just before serving, drizzle 1/2 teaspoon of **cream** over each ramekin of fruit.

—8-hour minimum—
RASPBERRY TORTONI "PICKWICK"
WITH A CHOCOLATE COOKIE CRUMB BASE

(6 servings)

It all started when I was trying to recall the contents of a dessert "coupe" at the old Petite Auberge in Marin County, something on the order of vanilla ice cream *mélangé* with crushed almond macaroons and whipped cream. Oh, said Cecily, you're thinking of Biscuit Tortoni, let's look at your *Joy of Cooking*. And there, under Mrs. Rombauer's recipe for Tortoni, was another combining said Tortoni with Raspberry Ice. Ah, I said, that sounds like that wonderful old frozen dessert called Pickwick they used to make at Blum's, the candy store with that great soda fountain where so many young San Franciscans sucked up milk shakes so rich, smooth and foamy — they were precision tooled, I remember, by natty soda jerks straight out of F. Scott Fitzgerald — they've been spoiled for life.

But I digress. Now did that "Pickwick" have a crumb bottom too, underneath the almondy center and shocking red topping? Anne thought yes, I wasn't sure, Cecily wasn't born yet. Well, all this discussion resulted in what would seem to be a quite new confection, a mélange of Rombauer, Blum and Bloomfield. The technical problems have been solved, following a very amusing debut.

. . . And to be totally honest I must report that a week or so after writing this page

I found, *finalmente*, after twenty-five years' searching, a perfect shake at San Francisco's ebullient Fog City Diner. 'Twas agitated lovingly to the optimum stage of light brown bubbledom.

P.S.: This out-of-the-freezer Pickwick would have appealed to a certain chillophilic Scandinavian in a bit of light verse penned by my incurably impish cousin Leonard the linguist of Chicago and Yale — not only did Sigurd Jansen bicycle serenely under gleaming icicles, and have as his pet device sleeping on a bed of ice, he went downtown one day *without his pants on*.

THE RASPBERRY ICE:

Soak 1 teaspoon of **gelatin** in a tablespoon of cold water. Combine 1/2 cup of **sugar** and 1/2 cup of water and boil the mixture for 3 minutes, then dissolve the gelatin in the sugar-water syrup and cool.

Purée 2 10-ounce boxes of **frozen raspberries** and strain them through a fine sieve into the syrup. Add 1 tablespoon of **lemon** juice, taste and adjust the lemon vs. sugar balance if necessary. Now put your bowl of red goodness in the freezer for 30 minutes or until crystals begin to form.

Next, stir your raspberry mixture and transfer it to a 9" springform pan lined with waxed or parchment paper. Freeze the mixture for 4 hours or overnight.

THE BISCUIT TORTONI:

Combine 3/4 cup of crushed **almond macaroons**, 3/4 cup of **whole milk**, 1/4 cup of **powdered sugar** and a pinch of **salt** and refrigerate for an hour.

Then whip 1 cup of **cream** until stiff, fold it into the macaroon mixture with 1 teaspoon of **vanilla** and freeze the lot for 30 minutes or until crystals begin to form.

Now, heap this biscuit tortoni onto the raspberry ice, flattening it carefully, and freeze your creation for 2 hours.

THE CRUMB BASE:

In a blender or food processor crush 1-1/2 cups of **chocolate wafer cookies** and combine them with 1/2 cup of melted **butter**; let the mixture cool, and reserve 1/4 cup.

Cover the raspberry tortoni with your crumb mixture, gently pressing and making a smooth, even layer; freeze for an hour.

Then:

Release the springform pan, invert the crumbed tortoni onto a cake plate and remove the paper. Decorate the top with a sprinkling of the reserved crumbs in a star shape or some other attractive pattern.

SOUFFLÉ IN DISGUISE: WARM CHOCOLATE TARTS

(4 smallish servings or 2 for living dangerously)

This answer to a chocolate-lover's most extravagant fantasy is turning up everywhere, although I doubt it will dethrone tiramisù from its prime spot on the hit parade of millennial desserts. The restaurant identifying it as The Ultimate Gooey-Centered Chocolate

Dessert has my vote for most accurate description of the matter at hand. Note that if your tart pans are larger than four inches in diameter, cooking time, always a thing of high drama when this recipe is hopefully addressed, your oven at the ready like a rumbling and possibly temperamental 747, will be a little less than in the adjacent recipe.

Safe to say this confection's too tricky to serve to the beggar who, in a vignette of my father's, came to the back door asking for a sweet, oiling his request with an earnestly but hastily rendered bible story, the one about "this strong guy Simpson and all those Philadelphians."

- For this recipe use baked egg ramekins or 4" tart or muffin pans; even if they're "non stick," brush them with melted **butter** and coat with **flour**.
- Mix 1-1/2 ounces of chopped **baking chocolate**, 5 tablespoons of **sugar**, 3-1/2 tablespoons of **butter**, cut up, and a tiny pinch of **salt**; carefully melt the mixture and cool it to room temperature.
- Then combine 3 **egg yolks** with 2 tablespoons of **sugar** and beat until they're thick and lemony in color and sugar granules are not, or hardly, visible. Fold in the cooled chocolate mixture.
- In a separate bowl combine 1 **egg white** with 2 teaspoons of **sugar** and beat until soft peaks form — be careful not to overbeat.
- Now carefully fold one third of the beaten white into the chocolate mixture, then lightly fold in the other two thirds and spoon the preparation into your waiting pans, filling them to within 1/2 inch of the top. Bake immediately, or cover with plastic wrap and refrigerate for up to 8 hours.
- Bake 8 minutes if not refrigerated, 9 if refrigerated, at 475°. If your oven refuses as ours sometimes does to ascend beyond 375° you will probably need 12 or 13 minutes.
- Whatever the timing, the tarts should jiggle in their centers when done; the outside should be cakey and the inside a soufflé or sauce-like texture. Well, this is no more difficult than producing asparagus that's a deep healthy green and absolutely unchewy.

CHOCOLATE SOUFFLÉ CARUSO
—Souvenir of Hotel Caruso Belvedere, Ravello—

This slightly piquant soufflé gave Signor Caruso's spectacular view over the Amalfi coast some competition. Never, I think, have we stayed in a city, town or village with such a "position" as Ravello. The only problem was avoiding contact with over-energized Maseratis piloted by deranged boulevardiers down on the Amalfi Drive.

My diary reports: an enraptured 2 a.m. gaze at the silhouette of a hillside tumbling toward the sea in the twinkly night, a zesty cock crow half-heard at 4, the elegant silence of the house as we come up for breakfast, drinking in the "off season" (or is it perennial?) calm. At lunch the soothing white-haired Gino Caruso, suavely twisting his hands, a character almost from a Merchant/Ivory film, informs us that tomorrow he will serve us a *lemon* soufflé.

And what a contrast, all this, to nearby Naples, that misfit of a town, the food indifferent and the traffic frantic, eastbound car traffic in one tunnel, for instance, aimed directly at trams hustling in the opposite direction. But silly old Naples does have its Vesuvius sitting inscrutably in the distance — rather in the same relationship to this vertical town as stately Tamalpais to San Francisco. If these two old Maureen Stapletons could only gossip! Well, I know Mt. Tam sends smoke signals: she does it with wisps of cloud that dangle above its immaculate silhouette in autumn twilight, shaped, of course, like question marks.

Naples was not our only less than ideal experience under all those wonderful Italian suns. Once I guessed wrong reading Signor Michelin and booked us into a small hotel in the Chianti hills, an old country palazzo that made Gloria Swanson's digs in *Sunset Boulevard* look sprightly. The only other clients were a pair of nonagenarians mumbling into a tiddy-widdy consomme, and the Signora presiding over this incipient graveyard looked as unforgiving as the ancient countess in *Queen of Spades*.

Our reward upon escaping was an enchanting stand-up breakfast at a pocket bar just outside Siena, the owner's little grandson manning the coffee machine with an earnest zeal. Then we rushed into Florence like fugitives (well, we had stolen that signboard off the Rome Express three years earlier) and apologized to the desk clerk at the Berchielli for being a day early, but it seemed to him the most natural thing in the world that we'd arrived on his doorstep by the Arno. I didn't know then that this was the hotel my grandparents chose when they visited Florence in 1902!

> Butter a shallow baking pan and arrange on the bottom little islands of **cherry preserves** (that's what Signor Caruso's chef did in 1971) **or marmalade** (that's what we've taken to doing in recent years). Then separate 1-1/2 **eggs** per serving, beat the yolks and add to them 2 tablespoons of **confectioner's sugar** and 1 heaping tablespoon of **powdered chocolate** per serving: this much can be done ahead.
>
> Between courses, or 15 to 20 minutes before serving, give a stir to the yolks-and-chocolate mixture, beat the whites until they're stiff but not dry, fold this "A" and "B" together and gently arrange the combination in the prepared pan. Now bake your soufflé in a moderate oven for about 12 minutes, at which point the the top will — in principle! — be slightly crusty and the center still sauce-like. Sprinkle more powdered sugar on top and serve at once before this delicate dessert, as flighty as a Tennessee Williams heroine, collapses.

PRUNE WHIP CINCINNATI WITH CRÈME ANGLAISE

Comfort food Anne's mother taught her: a prune-flavored Floating Island that sits like a benign Alcatraz in a sea of custard sauce. Apricot would be a viable alternative flavor.

This dish reminds me of a sweet old restaurant in London's Soho called the Moulin d'Or, on its last legs, I suspect, back in the *Mod, Mod* World of 1970. Its category was bistro, or, more accurately I think, "non-pompous continental." French antipasto was followed here by chicken pot pie, and there was applesauce with the roast duck. I remember homely little lamps on the tables, cords showing, celery in pitchers, and the affable Anglo owner or headwaiter gabbing about the old days with an elderly couple in from the suburbs.

This was a restaurant for folks just off the Aquitania, Berengaria or Majestic, not the Astors, just the Smiths — and it was certainly a tonic for us after a performance of Wedekind's *Lulu*, a psycho-roller coaster of a play.

Next day we'd be off on our Bloomsbury archaeological rounds, looking for Lytton and Maynard and Vanessa's digs. It was next to the cigar stand in the lobby of a relatively new hotel in Tavistock Square that we realized we were more or less on the spot marking Leonard and Virginia Woolf's living room in the house they occupied before the Blitz. So here we were trying to connect London to its artistic heritage and scoring a miss: cigars not Lit.

And yet, this postwar lobby shared with the Woolfian rooms of yore a certain unglitzable quality, a midtown dowdyness "Brit" to the core.

> Cook 15 pitted **prunes** in water to cover for about 15 minutes, then purée them in a blender or food processor with enough cooking liquid to produce a smooth result. Next, beat 5 **egg** whites with a tiny bit of **salt** until stiff and add gradually almost 1/2 cup of **sugar** as when making meringues.
>
> Into the sugared whites fold the prune purée along with 1 teaspoon of **lemon** juice; bake in a greased oven dish at 275° for 20 to 30 minutes — it will expand — and cool to room temperature before serving.
>
> And the sauce:
>
> Beat lightly 3 **egg** yolks; add 1/2 cup of **sugar** and a tiny bit of **salt** and mix well; then add 2 cups of **milk**, stirring well.
>
> Cook this preparation over low heat, stirring constantly with a wooden spoon, until it's thick enough to coat the spoon. Cool, and add 1/2 teaspoon of **vanilla**.

CRÊPES BALKAN GRILL

(4 to 6 servings)

In the tiny lobby of the Sacher Hotel in Vienna, thirty years ago, Regina Resnik the reigning Klytemnestra of the operatic stage commanded: "You must go to the Balkan Grill," and off we taxied in the snow to some remote bezirk, had a charming dinner to the tune of a lively "gypsy band," and came away with a dessert which serves us well on occasions requiring, well, nothing less than crêpes with jam and chocolate sauce.

Crêpes with the world's greatest sauce were good in Prague too, another distant year, eating in the dowdy dining room of the not-quite-right Alcron Hotel while a palm court quartet lit into Tchaikovsky. It was in Communist-era Prague, that sleeping sepia beauty Prague, that I lunched divinely on cauliflower soup, carraway rolls and three-star beer in a famous but scantly patronized tavern up by the palace and the waiter asked me, like some character in a thriller, to carry a message to his girl friend (alas, she was not as fond as he thought) who happened to work in the Swedish consulate four blocks from our house in San Francisco, 7,000 miles away.

Coming into Prague from the airport (our plane had stopped with proper Eastern European coyness as far from the terminal as possible, it's a wonder they didn't choose an irrigation ditch) my only mates on a wheezing, coughing, terminally sick bus were two Englishmen straight from Hitchcock's *The Lady Vanishes*, Basil Radford and Naunton Wayne all over again — but this time it was the Oxford boat race on their minds, not some ineffable test match at Manchester.

The city itself was like a stage set, before the cast of characters comes on. A city turning its back on the street. The happiest inhabitants I detected were the musicians tootling away at Rossini's *Barber of Seville* in the romantic obscurity of the orchestra pit at the lean and lovely Tylovo theater where *Don Giovanni* had its world premiere. The pit had become their parlor.

- Gradually add 1 cup of **milk** and 1/2 cup of **water** to 1 cup of **flour**, beating constantly so the batter becomes very smooth. Add 1 **egg**, 1/4 teaspoon of **salt**, 1-1/2 teaspoons of **salad oil**, 1-1/2 teaspoons of **brandy** — or 1 teaspoon of vanilla — and beat until smooth and set aside for 1 or 2 hours.
- Then, heat a large frying pan and oil it slightly. Pour a serving-spoon of batter into the pan and move the pan around until the entire surface is covered: the batter and the resulting crêpe should be very thin. When brown, turn the crêpe with a large spatula and cook the other side.
- Repeat the process, slightly oiling the pan each time, until all the batter is used. As each crêpe is made, spread it with **apricot jam** and roll or stack it on an ovenproof platter. When all the crêpes are cooked, jammed and rolled or stacked, cover the platterful with wax paper and set it aside. All the proceeding can be done ahead.
- Now, 20 minutes before dessert time, heat the crêpes, still papered, in a slow oven. Then remove the paper, dust the crêpes with **powdered sugar** and serve with **chocolate sauce** (page 177).

BLITZ TORTE OLD ST. PAUL
—with assorted additions—

(6 to 10 servings)

The closest thing we have to a Wayne Thiebaud painting.

This unusual meringue-topped cake was Anne's father's birthday cake as a child; I've never had anything quite like it in a restaurant. When we do the ice cream version I like to serve the chocolate sauce from a gravy boat, just as they would in one of those cozy grand hotels like the Strand in Stockholm or the de l' Europe in Amsterdam where you sleep under huge quilts behind panelled double doors giving onto wide silent corridors with potted plants. (And at the Strand even in early spring you could wake up to the sight of ice breaking like crisp toast outside your window and tugs going about their early morning business in a mist worthy of Sherlock Holmes' London).

Naturally that chocolate sauce will taste better than usual poured from a gravy boat

— especially if the ice cream is served in thick aristocratic slices, which does require a little maneuvering, rather than ordinary soda fountain scoops.

> Cream together 1/2 cup each of **butter** and **sugar**, add 4 **egg yolks** and mix. Then to a cup of **flour** add 2 teaspoons of **baking powder** and some **salt**. Sift 1/4 of this flour mixture into the butter mixture and blend well, then add a teaspoon of **vanilla** and 2 tablespoons of **milk**. Add another quarter of the flour mixture, then 2 more tablespoons of milk and repeat these two steps once more, finally adding the last quarter of the flour mixture.
>
> Now, after a breath, spread your batter in 2 greased 8" round pans or 1 9" by 13."
>
> Next step is to make the topping: add to 4 **egg whites** some **salt** and **vanilla** and beat until stiff, then gradually add 1 cup of **sugar**, beating all the while with an electric mixer until no granules of sugar show.
>
> Spread the topping over the batter with a spatula and bake at 350° for 30 minutes. Then serve this blitz torte with **crushed strawberries and whipped cream** or **vanilla ice cream and chocolate sauce** (page 177).
>
> OR: For a super blitz, you could call into action coffee ice cream, crème anglaise (page 184) as well as chocolate sauce, plus a handful of slivered almonds. This extravaganza was hatched after sampling a magnificent multi-color *vacherin* at Bizou, an enchanting bistro near San Francisco's Museum of Modern Art.

SEVEN LAYER (or higher) CAKE À LA GIGI

Soon after my parents were married my father asked my mother to reproduce the birthday cake his late mother, a child of the Austro-Hungarian empire, used to make. There was no recipe, great discussions took place ("No, it wasn't a Doboschtorte"), and only after a number of trial bakes did my mother arrive at the adjacent confection, which was known in the 30s and 40s, probably at the prodding of this writer, to reach ten layers.

Even with seven you'll find your kitchen overrun by cake pans, but any amount of inconvenience is justified in this instance.

I especially remember my father's last birthday, and cake, in 1962. Our son John was only three years old and had been properly packed off to bed long before the grownups would reach the cake stage in their three-course festival meal. Well, you would know, of course, that John materialized from his place of repose at precisely the moment the seven layer wonder appeared in the dining room. And this was not the only time in his early years he managed this proto-Houdinian feat: he was positively telepathic about yummy desserts.

I like to eat these "old country" layers very slowly, to the tune of a Chopin nocturne gliding off a CD by my cake-baking grandmother's first cousin, the magical Moriz Rosenthal.

And speaking of Moriz . . . there he was, tiny and mustachioed, living in a pullman car suite at the Great Northern hotel next to Carnegie Hall, his wife Hedwig teaching piano at one end and Moriz, to a more select batch of students, at the other. Hedwig, I guess, wasn't too much of a cook or was so busy shepherding her charges up and down the keyboard that my teenage cousin Evelyn was commissioned to sizzle up lamb chops on a hot plate. She'd also run to the Automat for Moriz' oysters.

Moriz was known for his devilish wit (you may know his quip about Artur Schnabel failing his Army physical because of "*no fingers*") but Evelyn feels, and I concur, that all this heavy joking was nothing more than an impish acceptance of the fact he was considered a wit. The jokes may have sounded a little mean now and then, but the musicologist Charles Rosen who was a pupil of Moriz says he was an unfailingly sympathetic mentor.

Rather than shouting, "That's not good," to Rosen, Moriz would ask him if perhaps he'd like to try that passage *like this* . . .

Take 7 or more 9" round cake pans, grease them with **vegetable oil or butter**, line them with wax paper and grease them again, then **flour** them.

Make a "1-2-3-4 Cake" (see below) and spread the batter evenly among the pans. Bake at 350–375° for 12 to 15 minutes, then remove the layers from the pans, taking off the wax paper, and replace the layers on the same wax paper to cool. Do not stack. Choose a nice-looking layer for the top, and using the back of a spoon, spread the remaining layers with **currant jelly**. Assemble the cake on a plate one layer at a time, icing each as you proceed with Hungarian Chocolate Frosting (see below) — don't stint! Ice the sides and top, and let the cake stand to harden before serving (unless you absolutely cannot wait!)

1-2-3-4 Cake:

Beat 1 cup of **butter** until soft, add gradually 2 cups of **sugar** and blend until light and creamy, then beat in 4 **egg yolks**, one at a time, and add 1 teaspoon of **vanilla** and 1/2 teaspoon of **almond extract.**

Sift 2-1/2 cups of **flour** with 2 teaspoons of **baking powder** and 1/2 teaspoon of **salt**. Add these sifted ingredients to the butter/sugar/yolks/vanilla in three parts, alternating with thirds of 1 cup of **milk**, beating the batter until smooth after each addition.

Now whip until stiff but not dry 4 **egg whites** with 1/4 teaspoon of **salt**; fold lightly into the batter.

Hungarian Chocolate Frosting:

Melt 6 ounces of **unsweetened baking chocolate** in a double boiler. Using a portable electric beater, gradually add, in this order, some sugar, egg, sugar, egg, sugar, and water as necessary, until you use up about 1 pound of sifted **confectioner's sugar**, 2 whole **eggs** or 3 yolks, and up to 1/2 cup of hot **water**. There will come a point in this process when all seems lost: the mixture suddenly turns solid. Fear not, just add more water and go on beating. Finally, add 6 to 8 tablespoons of **butter**. Quantities should be juggled to achieve the most spreadable texture — "Tinker with it," Gigi used to say. As you spread the frosting, keep it over hot water.

LEMON PIE CHARLESTON

A lemon meringue pie here, but not of that dreadful gelatinous sort encountered by this pie lover in assorted school cafeterias and downscale soda fountains during his youth. As a matter of fact, its interior is rather like a boozeless zabaglione.

In millennial San Francisco I sometimes seek out this sort of confection at Sears', a Middle American restaurant fearlessly lodged in the eye of our storm of cutting-edge gastronomy. No concessions to *nouvelle* here, no panna cotta, no arugula. And the waitresses, kind as nurses in a pediatric ward, have served longer than six-stripe sergeants. When Monday's soup unaccountably appears on Tuesday they'll soothe the habitué ruffled by such a dire logistical snafu.

First, make a **pie crust** (see page 39, but note that you should use a 9" pan), line the pastry with foil, weight it down with dried beans or rice and bake for 15 minutes at 425°. Carefully remove the foil and the weights.

Now separate 4 **eggs** and beat the yolks until they're light. Add 1/2 cup of **sugar** mixed with 1 tablespoon of **flour,** then add the juice and grated rind of 1 **lemon** and cook, stirring constantly. Be warned, the mixture will thicken suddenly: to avoid scorching it must be removed from the fire at once and cooled.

Beat the egg whites until they're very stiff. Slowly add 1/2 cup of **sugar**, beating constantly to make a meringue. Gently fold half the meringue mixture into the lemon mixture, fill the pie crust with the resulting meringue/lemon mix, top with the remaining meringue and bake in a medium oven for 20 minutes.

—24-hour—
GÂTEAU BASQUE LE TRINQUET

(8 to 10 servings)

Once bitten by the Gâteau Basque bug, one is quite helpless to keep this subtly custard-centered confection out of the active recipe file. The road to the finished product is strewn with intricacies worthy of a Raymond Chandler mystery, but persevere. This version is from Monsieur Arcé's restful hotel at St-Etienne-de-Baïgorry — we stopped (literally) at this riverside retreat in 1972.

Fond memories, too, of nearby Sare, up in those poetic Pays Basque foothills with their white-washed illustrators' houses, sheep-dotted meadows and pointy mountains overseeing all the calm. We dressed for dinner — Jambon de Bayonne, Poulet Basquaise, Iroulégy — to the tune of sonorous village bells, distant barking dogs, a friendly swish in the trees, roosters waking their compatriots, one supposes, from an up-country siesta.

. . . And then, traveling to Paris in the lone train delegated to do the work of five during one of those classic rail strikes, we exchanged tranquility for comedy. Our compartment, as if auditioning for the Marx Brothers, played host to a constant eight or unofficial nine, including a man with a large plant and a woman with a very small dog, who resembled her mistress exactly, a mother and sleeping child borrowed from the loaded corridor, and oh yes, two gorgeous Swedes on a honeymoon isle in our midst.

> In a bowl blend 3/4 cup of softened **butter** with 3/4 cup of **sugar** and beat in 2 **eggs**, one at a time, beating well after each addition. Now beat in 1/8 teaspoon of **almond extract** and 1 tablespoon of **rum** and stir in 2-1/4 cups of sifted **flour** to make a smooth, soft dough. Form the dough into a ball, dust it with flour, and chill it, wrapped in plastic, overnight.
>
> You'll also need pastry cream: In the bowl of an electric mixer thoroughly beat 1 **egg yolk** and 1 small whole **egg** and add 3 tablespoons of **sugar** a little at a time, beating the mix until it ribbons when the beater is lifted. Add 2 tablespoons of **flour**, beating, and 3/4 of a cup of **scalded milk** in a stream, still beating.
>
> Transfer the mixture to a heavy saucepan and cook it over moderately low heat, stirring constantly, until it's quite thick. Remove the pastry cream from the fire, whisk it smooth, and whisk in 1 teaspoon of **vanilla**, then let the cream cool, topped with a buttered round of wax paper (to prevent a crust forming) for at least 1 hour.
>
> Roll 2/3 of the dough into an 11-inch round on a well-floured surface, then fit it into a buttered 10-inch tart pan, pressing the edges of the dough against the sides of the pan. Now spread the pastry cream on this dough; roll the remaining dough into a 10-inch round and place it on top of the pastry cream. Press the upper and lower layers of dough together at the sides of the pan and chill for 30 minutes.
>
> Next, brush the top dough, so to speak, with a little **cream**. Then etch the top of your cake-to-be with the blunt side of a knife in a crosshatch pattern. Now you're ready to bake this rather complex confection at 400° for 10 minutes, after that at 350° for 20 to 30 minutes, or until it's lightly browned and puffed. Then let your sure-to-get-attention gâteau stand until cool.

LUCY'S CELEBRATION CAKE

(numerous servings)

When Zachary Bloomfield was christened in Newburyport, Mass., his mother baked this sherried nut-raisin cake which was unlike anything we'd tasted before. Now he's old enough to demand she do it again.

A lot of flavor energy in this cake: it's the edible counterpart of a peppy organ recessional pealing through a cathedral on the heels of a jolly pledging of vows, flower girls giddily tidying up the altar as the music swells amazingly in a glorious accompaniment to their simple task, all this audio/visual counterpoint seemingly concocted by Jean-Pierre Ponnelle or some other visionary stage director, a poet of heart-stopping "moments."

. . . These adjectives-and-adverbs happened one Sunday afternoon at St-Etienne-du-Mont in Paris.

> With a spoon cream together 3/4 pound of **butter** and 4 cups of **sugar** until they're well blended. Next, separate 7 **eggs** and beat the yolks until they're light and lemon-colored, then add them to the butter/sugar mixture, blending thoroughly.

Now sift together 4 cups of **flour**, 2 heaping teaspoons of **baking powder** and 3 teaspoons of **nutmeg** and add this mix to the batter in several portions, alternating with shots of **sherry** adding up to a cup.

Next, add a cup of chopped **pecans** and 1-1/2 pounds of **raisins**. Beat the egg whites until stiff, and fold them into the mixture. Bake in a large well-buttered cake pan for 3 hours at 300°, and cool before serving.

CECILY'S MANGO CAKE

(4 to 6 servings)

The first step here is to go to the market and ogle a basket of mangoes, plump, flushed and freckled, their fetching surfaces orchestrated in lovely shades of green, yellow and red.

Mangoes might have been invented for Cézanne, Zurburán, Chardin, connoisseurs of romantic-looking edibles with great forms to be filled, shifting colors to be caught. But their origin, of course, is East Asian. Mango, reports the *Concise Columbia Encyclopedia*, is an "aromatic, slightly acid fruit, a fleshy drupe [which is] an important food in the tropics." Well, old Columbians, it's an important food in Berkeley, Santa Monica, Manhattan, Boston.

When I was growing up, though, I never heard the word. Obviously such drupey food was considered only fit for Tarzan — and maybe Graham Greene or Evelyn Waugh on some malarial mad-dog safari. Cecily's recipe, a cousin to a cobbler, is zingy all right but no more exotic than a United flight to Hawaii, not to speak of a quick run to your neighborhood super. It needs absolutely no help, but a crème anglaise accompaniment (see page 184) would be a nice frill.

This confection is, by the way, an upside down cake served right side up.

Butter a deep 8" round pan (to avoid leakage of good juices be sure not to use a pan with a removable bottom), then peel and slice 2 large **mangoes**, fairly firm ones, and place them in the pan. Sprinkle them with 2/3 cup of **sugar**, 1/2 teaspoon each of **cinnamon** and **nutmeg** and the grated rind and juice of a **lemon**, then dredge with 1 tablespoon of **flour**.

Now pour 2 tablespoons of melted **butter** over the fruit mixture.

Sift together 1 cup of **flour**, 1/2 cup of **sugar**, 1 teaspoon of **baking powder** and 1/4 teaspoon of **salt**. Beat separately and add to the flour mixture 1 **egg**, 1 tablespoon of melted **butter** and 1/3 cup of **milk**, mixing all until just blended.

Spread your batter over the fruit and bake for 30 minutes at 425°.

ALISON'S HIGH ALTITUDE CAKE

(10 to 12 servings)

Totally American, fudgy and approximately the texture of your favorite teddy bear. Our daughter first made this delightful cake while vacationing in the Sierra. Thin air up there, water boils at a low temperature, and cake recipes must be adapted; the recipe on this page is adjusted for sea level, relatively speaking.

Alison has lately been employed singing Cole Porter to well-heeled Japanese tourists at the ancient but hip Viktoria Jungfrau Hotel in Interlaken, tucked into central Switzerland. And there she is surrounded by all that chocolate, not to mention 1001 five-star mountains, the ultimate in bracing air, and those clocks of course, but for her birthday she asked us to fax her one of Emily Luchetti's to-die-over cake recipes from San Francisco. Chocolate begins at home.

> Using an electric beater in what we call "a big brown bowl," cream together 1/2 cup of **butter** and 2-3/8 cups of **sugar**, then add 3 **egg yolks** and 4 ounces of gently melted **baking chocolate**. Now sift dry ingredients (2 short cups of **flour**, 2-1/8 teaspoons of **baking powder**, 1/4 teaspoon of **salt**) into the chocolate mixture in thirds. Alternate with thirds of 1-1/4 cups of **milk** plus 1 teaspoon of **vanilla**, beating after each addition.
>
> Next, whip 3 **egg whites** until stiff but not dry and fold them into the chocolate mixture, then bake it in 3 previously greased (with vegetable oil) and floured 9" layer pans at 350° for 30 minutes or until done.
>
> Ice this cake with a chocolate icing made as follows:
>
> Over boiling water melt 4 ounces of **unsweetened chocolate**, then remove it from the heat and allow it to cool. Cream together 1/2 cup of soft **butter** and 4-1/2 cups of sifted **powdered sugar**, next add 4-1/2 tablespoons of **cream** and 1-1/2 teaspoons of **vanilla**, stirring until smooth, then blend in the melted chocolate. This is enough to frost three 9" layers.

OUR BRETON "SUNDAE"

I suspect the people of Brittany don't know what a sundae is. But I think of this soda fountain extravaganza as Breton because it was at Ti Couz, a Breton crêperie in San Francisco's Mission District, that I was introduced to *marrons* and chocolate, a harmony of the gods.

> Over **vanilla ice cream** of good quality dollop some sweetened chestnut purée (**Crème de Marrons de l'Ardèche**, available in specialty food stores and some upscale supermarkets) and pour over and around these items our **chocolate sauce** (page 177). Figure 2 tablespoons of purée for each 2 scoops of ice cream.
>
> P.S.: Sandwiching all this between a waffle and a spoonful of whipped cream is something to consider.

Glace Partington:
NICHOLAS ROOSEVELT'S RASPBERRY ICE CREAM

Nicholas Roosevelt, a cousin of the great Teddy, was a cello-playing diplomat and *Herald Tribune* editorial writer who retired to Big Sur and a house suspended so dramatically above the Pacific you saw from certain windows only a great expanse of blue, and had the feeling you were flying at 20,000 feet at least in a 7-something-7.

Only the food was marvelous, because Nick adored to cook and, in fact, wrote a couple of cookbooks, sensible, witty, even feisty little tomes. I didn't agree with every one of this gentle aristocrat's recipes, but I know that his raspberry ice cream — we call it Glace Partington because Nick's house was on the Partington ridge, near Henry Miller's — has been a favorite in our house for many years. Its flavor is delightfully intense, with a "long finish" calling up those tenacious chords at the opening of Jascha Horenstein's recording of Haydn's 104th.

I'm sorry Nick didn't live to see the era of garlicked or pesto-ed mashed potatoes: writing in 1956, he observed with an urbane sigh that potatoes are prepared too often "in a spirit of resignation rather than of gustatory anticipation." Reading on in *Creative Cooking*, faithful disciples can't help pausing to drink in the palpable *richesse* of a Partington staple Nick writes about with something close to passion, a risotto finished with plenty of chicken livers and mushrooms cooked in butter. Add some chopped parsley and there you go . . .

Hello, I've just found in my copy of *Creative Cooking* a publicity picture of Nick surveying his ocean, bushy eyebrows at attention, binoculars at the ready. To the hilly Amalfan north old Highway 1, which must each winter pass through the needle's-eye of terrible storms, looks like a narrow string of Christmas tinsel trying in its sinuous way to encircle a giant slope of green. Listen — you can hear the shooosh of the surf far below.

> Take 1 box of **frozen raspberries**, put the contents in a blender or food processor with a teaspoon of **honey** and blend until smooth. Now add slowly 1/2 pint of **whipping cream** and blend with continued smoothness your objective, then pour the mixture into a freezer tray or serving bowl and freeze. After an hour take the developing ice cream out and stir it, then return it to the freezer until it's solid.

CHOCOLATE-DIPPED HAZELNUT COOKIES MAISON

(about 75 cookies)

The basic recipe here is Old German, from Anne's family. She invented the chocolate ends, which seem nothing less than essential, and I invented the notion of dipping the cookies a little deeper into the chocolate.

Well, I've been obsessed with chocolate for many years and I admit it. There were the chocolate sundaes and malts with my father at beloved Blum's, the famous nominally seven layer cake with its roots in the Vienna of Freud and Schnitzler (friends of my father's family, of course) and there were those Schrafft's honeycomb bars, two to a package, wrapped in excellent chocolate and consumed by this pre-teen and fellow blue-suited brats during intermissions at the San Francisco Symphony's Friday matinees, superbly conducted by cute little Pierre Monteux (Perry MonTUX we called him) before an audience composed in large part of well-gloved ladies in funny hats.

Immediately upon his careful military turn toward the wings after some rapid-fire Beethoven or new-fangled Shostakovich we wiggly ten-year-olds would scurry to the Opera House candy counter, then zoom to the Gents' next to Box Z and devour our treasure while bouncing on air foam sofas.

A few seasons later chocolate was in danger of being at least momentarily upstaged when a little old lady living next to our rented house in Carmel invited me over to hear the then-rare recordings, in tawny heavyweight HMV albums, of the Beethoven sonatas, all of them, played by Artur Schnabel. Mrs. Palache wooed me as well with fabulous Scotch shortbread, bursting with butteryness.

So, while my contemporaries were exhibiting their pecs at the plage, I slunk next door for Beethoven and butter. Perhaps I have that in the wrong order.

- First off, grate finely, in a food processor or grater, 1 pound of **hazelnuts**, skins on. Then in an electric mixer beat 2 **egg** whites until stiff. Gradually add 1/2 pound of **powdered sugar** and continue beating for 10 minutes. Fold in the hazelnuts.
- Form the dough into small oblong shapes about 1-1/2 inches long and the diameter of your little finger (but maybe a little more if you're slim in that area). Bake on ungreased trays for about 10 minutes at 300°, then cool.
- Now in a small double boiler melt 3 ounces of **baking chocolate** and the same amount of **bittersweet chocolate**, stirring them together. Dip one end of each cookie in the chocolate — if you need more chocolate, melt the "baking" and "bittersweet" in the same proportions.
- Place the finished cookies on waxed paper and peel them off the paper when the chocolate has hardened. Store in a tightly-covered tin for several days to facilitate flavor-devlopment and be sure not to invade this classified container until permission is given by the Cookie Mom.

Those Symphony excursions took place as I said on Friday afternoons — we traveled to the Opera House on a succession of clattery streetcars, the Nos. 22 Fillmore and 5 McAllister. Monday mornings we were back at the grind at Town School for Boys, Mr. Rich, our nerd/jock of a headmaster/super-grammarian standing at the blackboard with his left hand tucked in a rear pants pocket (brown pinstripe, usually) while the right with devilish chalk filled the wide-screen slate with one long paragraph of conversational English totally devoid of punctuation. Not a stream of consciousness. We, like so many pre-pubescent code-cracking Sir Alec Guinnesses, were supposed to write in our notebooks said conversation decked out with all the relevant so-far phantom commas-periods-colons-quotation marks-etc.-etc. An enigma supreme, with just one proper way to solve it. And lunch, perhaps, approaching, not that that held much gustatory promise. Our school catered to the sons of affluent parents, some of whom owned a county or two in the vicinity and could have underwritten for the student body a midday chef from Jack's downtown. But alas, Mr. Rich seems not to have been a gourmet (at the summer camp he administered in Napa Valley, long before Kendall met Jackson, beef stew was mated with chilled watermelon!) and he had in his, or the board of directors', service a mere flunky de cuisine, who turned out hamburger grenades and soggy pies from his basement laboratory . . . I mean kitchen.

But those phantom commas of Mr. Rich, even if I no longer use them very much — the difference between "restrictive" and "non-restrictive" clauses has been upstaged in my life by art and love — were absolutely three-star.

SWEET RAVIOLI OLD NORTH BEACH

(6 to 8 servings)

The bustling old Vanessi's in theatrical San Francisco's especially theatrical North Beach was heaven on earth, garlic in the air, a cimbalon player twanging in the bar, tall-toqued chefs cooking everything from omelettes to Chicken Valdostana before your eyes, maitre d' Modesto in his big bow tie sending mellifluous commands across the crowded room, such as: *Due tagliatelle burro dolci!*

And it was a fourteen-hour heaven: we'd go to Vanessi's for minestrone lunches, Caesar salad late lunches, Valdostana dinners, post-opera banana fritter festas after Valhalla burned, Samson demolished some expensive real estate or Gilda sang her last, virtually post-mortem, from Sparafucile's sack.

. . . And was that Jack Kerouac at the next table, thinking about his "rhythmic yawps of expostulation"? And Lawrence Ferlinghetti would have been dropping in, the same poet who, in 2001, was lunching up the street at the U.S. Restaurant not many feet from a San Francisco/Sicilian mural conspicuously including *himself*, in a dining position, I think . . .

At whatever hour, you found yourself swept along by Vanessi's tailwind of exhilaration: I don't mean you ate fast, you just felt good. It was art, life, pleasure, gossip, beauty, conviviality. And oh, that chicken.

Modesto recently revived his heady brasserie at Broadway and Kearny (at least for a while), complete with the most delicate cannelloni of my life plus this puffy dessert which we've simplified a bit, thanks in part to that faithful servant the won ton wrapper. Alas, the new incarnation lacked magic, or good p.r., and failed. Modesto was even so naughty as to die. But lately, thanks to a quirky transference of soul, I guess, the old Vanessi vibes live again across the street at Reed Hearon's spirited and nostalgic Black Cat.

Oh how I wish Modesto would turn up front-of-the-house!

- Make a filling by mixing together 1/2 pound of **ricotta**, 1/2 cup of **sugar**, 1 teaspoon of **cocoa**, a tablespoon of **orange liqueur**, 1/4 teaspoon of **cinnamon**, 1/2 teaspoon of **grated lemon peel** and 2 drops of **vanilla**.
- Then open a package of **square won ton wrappers**. Spread 2 teaspoons of the above goop onto wrapper no. 1, leaving a little space at the sides, run a watery finger around its edge and place wrapper no. 2 on top of the first one, carefully pressing the two together at their edges to make a pillow. Repeat the process until you have as many units — three, say, to a customer — as you need for one sitting. This much can be done in advance, in which case the "ravioli" should be covered until cooking time.

A little before dessert time, heat 1/4 inch of **canola or vegetable oil** in a large flat pan. When it's hot but not smoking, slide in several of the stuffed ravioli, one at a time. Don't crowd! Fry them until they're puffed and golden on one side, then turn them to achieve the same effect on side 2. After frying a batch drain it on paper towels and keep your puffy pillows warm while you fry the next set. Sprinkle them with **powdered sugar** before serving — which sould be as soon after frying as possible. Note well that these ravioli may be eaten with your fingers. Another interesting option is to plant them like pennants in a wavy crater of ice cream.

OUR FRUIT CRISP

(4 to 6 servings)

This classic makes for easy appeasement of sweet teeth.

And meanwhile I'm thinking of the clues that were thrown in my path to help with the construction of this book: a newspaper article about old Berlin that reminded me of uncle Moriz (the actor not the pianist), a monoplane that flew over our deck as if to ignite memories of sixty years ago, a sudden olfactory sensation awakening a delightful sniff of yesteryear . . . and everyday, it seems, I hear that waiter at Pop Ernt's chewing the consonants in his piscatorial spiel, c. 1939.

In a 9" by 14" by 2" pan combine 10 tart **apples**, peeled and sliced (or cherries, rhubarb, any fruit or combination of fruits you desire) with **lemon** juice, **sugar** and **cinnamon** to taste; flatten the top.

Next, combine 1 cup each of **flour** and packed **brown sugar** and 1/2 cup of **butter**, then stir in 1 cup of **oatmeal** and sprinkle the mixture over the top of the seasoned fruit and bake all at 350° for 45 or 50 minutes, until the top is "golden brown" and maybe even a tiny bit black here and there.

CECILY'S VERITABLE KOUIGN-AMANN

An aristocratic coffee cake, souvenir of a run through Brittany in 1985. Every bakery had it in the window, temptation was our constant companion.

Our premiere gastronomic experience in France's scrubby but enfolding West was a dinner in the pre-Laura Ashley precincts of Chez Melanie near Pont-Aven, where the great *bec fin* Curnonsky holed up during the '39 war. Like gung-ho philatelists eager to fill their album blanks, we had to eat here, amidst the faience and ferns. And a success it was, a soothing retro meal served by kindly coiffed Bretonnes adept at greasing the wheels of hospitality for such pilgrim foodies as Cecily and me. Suave local ham, mussels and rice, roast duck in brandied juices, ripe cheeses, flan with custard sauce, well, it was Mr. Liebling's heaven.

Combine 2/3 cup of water, 1 package of **dry yeast**, 1/2 teaspoon of **salt** and 2 cups of **flour,** mixing all together nicely with clean hands which will become very sticky in short order. Let the mixture rest for half an hour.

Then on a floured board with a floured rolling pin roll out the dough in a very long rectangle with a short side in front of you, after which you spread the bottom, or closer, two thirds with 6 tablespoons of quite soft **butter** and 6 tablespoons of **sugar**.

Now fold the top third down and the bottom third up over that (Who's on Third, interrupts Costello here), place your dough on wax paper, put it on a plate and and chill it for an hour. Repeat the rolling-folding-chilling procedure three times, without adding butter and sugar.

Finally, flatten the pastry in a 6 or 7" buttered pie pan and bake it at 425° for about 20 minutes, with a good prayer along the way, until it's quite golden. Cool, unmold and sprinkle with sugar.

SUMMER DESSERT IN OLD VERONA
—Gorgonzola and Peaches—

On leave from the Army in summertime Verona, the living was easy. At least it was after a pair of GI's looking for a hotel were found scratching their heads in a labyrinth of piazzas by Luigi Cozzi. Luigi was a roving concierge in black-and-braid who in his streetwise inventiveness must have been a graduate of some DeSican school of wartime hard knocks. "All this you want I have found," he announced, and off we trailed behind this piper to the Albergo Gabbia D'Oro.

Then we were ready for Quality Time.

There was breakfast with pin-cushion rolls and good marmalade next to the bead curtain and a warm outdoors, picnic lunch on the ramparts, opera in the arena by moonlight. I can hear the announcer barking across the piazza, "Sabato cinque Agosto, terzo di *Turandot* con Gertruda Groba-Prandl, Magda Olivero . . ." And the hawkers in the stadium intoning lustily like Parpignol in act 2 of *Bohème* the Italian equivalents of "beer, orangeade, ice creams."

At 9:15 the audience in the arena lights a sea of candles, then the conductor enters the giant orchestra pit (notice six harps!) and the opera duly commences — with, one night, a shirt-sleeved lions' roar when the well-meaning tenor momentarily cracked.

(By the way, our trip had been interesting so far: I especially remember the radio chromily embedded in the wall of our Geneva hotel's up-to-the-minute room, something unheard of in the antique France of 1954; the clawp-clawp-clawp of the horse-drawn milk wagon beneath the window of the Mozart Hotel in Vienna, this noticed after driving off the edge of the world through Austria's verdant, muddy Russian Zone, a kind of outdoors equivalent of those mysterious corridors in *Last Days at Marienbad*; then the sight-and-sound on pioneer Italian freeways of Lancias and Maseratis piloted by imitation Juan Fangios tooling along, if that's the word, at 180 kilometers an hour.)

In Verona's *Aida* there was lots of good singing, Fausto Cleva conducted authoritatively and the Ethiopian prisoners tumbled over the top of the arena, careening like spilled furniture onto the well-populated stage. But not before our dinner! . . . Invariably it was a pleasant scallopini with good pan juices followed by baseball-sized peaches and slabs of perfect gorgonzola. This combination was so satisfying the first night out there was no alternative but an encore *domani sera* — and another the evening after that . . .

You don't need a recipe here. Simply splurge on some nice gorgonzola cheese and the largest, juiciest peaches you can find and place slab and sphere on a rather large plate. Proceed with knife and fork and feel on top of the world.

ENVOI:

And now, as the gastronomical tourist folds his tent for the moment, I'm in the great hall of a French train station, the Austerlitz, say, in Paris, and over the P.A. comes the characteristically muffled admonition of that generic announcer so fondly remembered from the chaotic opening scene of *Mr. Hulot's Holiday*, proclaiming — and I translate as best I can — "Attention, attention, track 5, track 5, the express for Orléans, Vierzon, Châteauroux, Limoges, Brive, Cahors, Montauban . . . first class at the head of the train, All Aboard if you please, Last Call before departure . . . "

ABOUT THE AUTHOR

A music critic turned food writer, ARTHUR BLOOMFIELD has been an enthusiastic home chef for forty years and a frequent client of French and Italian country inns and bistros. He's the author of two books of restaurant criticism, one a best-selling guide to San Francisco restaurants, the other a far-ranging journal/memoir, as well as a history of the San Francisco Opera. Recently he conceived and wrote the program notes for a box of CDs titled *Sunday Evenings with Pierre Monteux*, a nominee in the first historical recordings awards of the *International Classical Record Collector*.